MONTAIGNE'S ESSAYS

MOMENTS OF VISION

MOMENTS OF VISION
The Poetry of Thomas Hardy

PAUL ZIETLOW

HARVARD UNIVERSITY PRESS
CAMBRIDGE, MASSACHUSETTS
1974

© 1974 by the President and Fellows of Harvard College
All rights reserved
Publication of this book has been aided by a grant
from the Andrew W. Mellon Foundation.
Library of Congress Catalog Card Number 73-8518-4
SBN 674 58215-2
Printed in the United States of America

FOR CHARLOTTE

PREFACE

Although Thomas Hardy had written poetry from early youth, his first collection did not appear until 1898, when he was fifty-eight years old, and most of his poems date from the remaining thirty years of his long life. The reader of his verse often senses the presence of an ancient man, in the winter of his lifetime, brooding over the past. Yet a mood of retrospective reflection is not the only effect in Hardy's poetry, for his performance as a poet is remarkably diverse. Moreover, every volume that he published, including his last, *Winter Words in Various Moods and Metres*, has poems dating from early in his life. Characteristically, words from spring and summer are intermingled with the musings of old age.

In his poetry, Hardy presents himself in a variety of guises, many of them contradictory. He is earnest and playful, bold and diffident, experimental and traditional. He is a skilled, conscious craftsman whose verse often seems clumsy and awkward. His poems reveal a sensitivity to meaning in apparently trivial moments; they express a perplexity over the irreconcilable contradictions in the nature of things; they record a respectful awe for the mysteries of the cosmos. Hardy was outraged at suffering and indignant with victimization; yet he was aware of his own guilt for opportunities missed and for damage inflicted on others. In his poetry, Hardy sometimes pictures himself as a devitalized remnant of a man, wrung dry of feeling, yet he also presents himself as a keen-eyed observer, compassionately alert to life in all of its manifestations. Although he was struck by a sense of the futility of vision and aspiration, he nevertheless continued to dream and hope in the face of thwarting circumstance and destructive time.

Hardy's ordering of poems in the original volumes, which is reflected in the arrangement of the *Collected Poems*, emphasizes the variousness of his poetry. Although certain groups are coherent and integral—such as "Poems of Pilgrimage" from *Poems of the Past and the Present*, "A Set of Country Songs" from *Time's Laughingstocks*, and "Satires of Circumstance" from *Satires of Circumstance, Lyrics and Reveries*—the poems appear in a random, haphazard order, under such headings as "Miscellaneous Poems" and "Pieces Occasional and Various." Mixed together are poignant lyrics, ungainly ballad tragedies, brief poems of contrived ironic incident, and poems that realistically describe incidental everyday experience. Melodramatic posturing appears next to humble meditation, anguished involvement next to chilling objectivity. Over one hundred poems express directly or indirectly Hardy's feelings about his first wife, and these could have been organized into a coherent sequence of love lyrics, yet with the exception of the twenty-one that he grouped under the title "Poems of 1912-13," they are scattered at random throughout the collection. Individual poems are similarly woven of disparate strands of feeling and technique. In the ballads, for example, Hardy exploits a traditional form that was popular in the nineteenth century to convey an idiosyncratic, curiously modern blend of stark pessimism and compassionate humanity, melodrama and historical realism, moral complexity and simple, earnest vision. The quasi-mythological poems mix philosophy and drama, bitter outrage, mocking jest, and sympathetic loving-kindness.

The diversity and complexity of Hardy's achievement as a poet must be stressed, for he has been charged with having a severely limited range of tone and ideas, and his poetry has been likened to a single musical note continuously repeated. Critics have focused on isolated aspects of his performance —on Hardy the lyricist, the ironist, the regionalist or the love poet—while other important areas of his work have received little attention. With few exceptions, the quasi-mythological poems have been dismissed, the ballads and narratives ignored, the contrived ironic vignettes and melodramas under-rated. In order to achieve a comprehensive view of Hardy, all of the kinds of poems he wrote must be taken into account.

A number of studies have shown an awareness of the diversity of Hardy's poetry, most notably the essays by Lytton Strachey, Edmund Gosse, G. M. Young, C. Day Lewis, John Crowe Ransom, Albert Guerard, and Irving Howe. Yet these essays are brief and general. Their sympathetic insights deserve application and illustration on a broader scale, by means of detailed analysis of numerous, diverse, and representative poems. The present study attempts to fill the need for a thorough explication of a large body of Hardy's verse within the context of a comprehensive and systematic view of his total achievement as a poet.

The method of the study is descriptive rather than evaluative. Hardy's poems reflect a strong experimental impulse, which often places a heavy demand on the reader's initial willingness to meet them halfway. Hardy himself was conscious of their assertively idiosyncratic character, which must be appreciated if the poems are to be understood and assessed. Hardy's poetry is both curious and bold—bold sometimes even in its extreme humility. In making poetry of "the homeliest of heartstirrings," Hardy took the risk that his subtle effects might seem to be no effects at all. A temporary suspension of ordinary critical standards and expectations, and an involvement in the work according to its own terms, are therefore necessary to an understanding of his poetry.

The focus of this study is on the *Collected Poems*. It does not consider the verse drama *The Queen of Cornwall* nor *The Dynasts*, with its experimental mixture of epic and drama, prose and poetry, narrative, theatrical, and even cinematic technique. Rather, the aim here is to describe Hardy's achievement as a poet, and that achievement is most evident in his more than nine hundred brief poems. The work does not place Hardy historically, nor, with few exceptions, does it trace the relationship between the poetry and fiction. It compares and contrasts only specific poems and Hardy's different poetic styles.

Two works of scholarship and criticism are of special relevance. J. O. Bailey's *The Poetry of Thomas Hardy: A Handbook and*

Commentary (Chapel Hill: University of North Carolina Press, 1970) gathers together all available bibliographical and biographical information and other source material for each of Hardy's poems. J. Hillis Miller's *Thomas Hardy: Distance and Desire* (Cambridge: Harvard University Press, 1970) examines the full Hardy canon and traces a consistent pattern throughout. Although Miller is less detailed in his treatment of the poetry and his thesis varies significantly from the general view presented here, his work is vital to understanding any area of Hardy's work.

My study opens with a survey of Hardy's first collection of verse, *Wessex Poems.* The originality and variety of these poems are related to Hardy's reasons for writing poetry and to his understanding of the poetic art, subjects closely influenced by the tension within himself between an impulse to withdraw and to participate. The rest of the poems are reviewed according to type: poems of ironic circumstance, ballads and narratives, philosophical fantasies, poems of the personal and historical past, love poems, and moments of vision or brief poems of the present moment. Although these categories overlap, they provide a useful system of distinctions, and together they comprehend all of Hardy's poetry. In general, the progression is from poems in which Hardy establishes a distance between himself and his subjects, to those in which he makes a direct, personal revelation. The power of Hardy's poetry as a whole lies in its variety of form, tone, and idea, in its boldness of style and dramatic conception, in the artistic cunning and complexity underlying its sometimes crude, sometimes graceful, surface simplicity, and in its direct or indirect revelation of a compassionate, humane vision.

I wish to thank several teachers and colleagues for their help and support. Arthur J. Carr first led me to recognize Hardy's stature as a poet and from the beginning encouraged and criticized my work. Howard P. Anderson and Robert J. Dunn read portions of this study and made useful suggestions. Donald J. Gray read the manuscript with sympathetic attention and, as chairman of the English Department at Indiana University, helped to promote and sustain a favorable atmosphere for the pursuit of scholarly interests. Robert E. Gross was unfailingly generous in spending the time to discuss general ideas and specific interpretations as the study progressed, and he read the manuscript with meticulous care.

I acknowledge with gratitude the assistance of Indiana University, which provided a grant for research in England in connection with this study.

For permission to quote from the *Collected Poems of Thomas Hardy* (copyright 1925; renewed 1953 by Lloyds Bank, Ltd., Executors), grateful acknowledgment is made to the Trustees of the Hardy Estate; Macmillan London and Basingstoke; The Macmillan Company of Canada, Ltd.; and Macmillan Publishing Company, Inc., New York. Acknowledgment for quoting from Florence Emily Hardy's *The Life of Thomas Hardy, 1840–1928* is also made to the Trustees of the Hardy Estate; Macmillan London and Basingstoke; and The Macmillan Company of Canada, Ltd. Permission to quote from the manuscript of Thomas Hardy's *Wessex Poems* and to reproduce two pictures from that volume was kindly given by the City Museum and Art Gallery of Birmingham.

CONTENTS

ILLUSTRATIONS

MOMENTS OF VISION

WESSEX POEMS

1

In December 1898, when Thomas Hardy was fifty-eight years old, he launched what was to become a thirty-year career as a poet by presenting the world with *Wessex Poems and Other Verses*. Later he would add substance and dimension to the kind of bold, original vision found in this first collection, while broadening his range of subject and undertaking new modes and forms. But in *Wessex Poems*, Hardy's nature as a poet was already fully present, for its strange and diverse features are characteristic of all of his poetry. These features perplexed his contemporaries, and they have remained perplexing. Early readers found the fifty-one poems printed extravagantly over 210 pages and illustrated with a number of idiosyncratic drawings executed by the poet himself. In the original edition, *Wessex Poems* is thus an integral work of art, uniting poetic and pictorial effects to create a unique impression.

The poems as a group are characterized by a bleak, pessimistic tone, with intermittent touches of the macabre, and by a curious variety of style, ranging from prosaic simplicity to a harsh complexity of syntax and diction. These were hardly the qualities commonly associated with poetic appeal in 1898. Hardy's subjects, unlike traditional materials of lyric verse, are the grotesqueries of fate, commonplace disillusionment, and the ironies of time and circumstance. Despite these overall similarities, the individual poems seem randomly various. In his Preface, Hardy calls the book, almost deprecatingly, a "miscellaneous collection of verse." There are love poems, nature poems, poems describing improbable, melodramatic situations, and even a stage epilogue in heroic couplets, in which an actress thanks the audience for attending a benefit performance *"on behalf of Lady Jeune's Holiday Fund for City Children"* (CP, p. 71).[1] There are personal meditations, historical narratives, songs, and sonnets. Roughly half of the poems are dated, but for no apparent reason, the rest are not. Some of the dated poems are of the 1870s and 1890s, but most are of the 1860s, from Hardy's youth. The arrangement of poems in the collection, like the arbitrary dating, seems haphazard. An apparent sequence of eight military poems (some of which have nothing to do with Wessex—indeed, there seem to be more "Other Verses" than "Wessex Poems" in the collection) is interrupted by a lyric, "The Stranger's Song," and two narratives, "The Burghers" and "Her Death and After," none of which have anything to do with war. At the end of the volume appears a section titled "Additions," which includes five disparate poems. Inexplicably, Hardy dates four of them, and two, "Heiress and Architect" and " 'I Look into My Glass,' " are among the most admired of the volume. Why the additions should not have been integrated into the collection remains a mystery; they seem to have been added as an afterthought. All in all, many features of *Wessex Poems* tend to justify the impression that Hardy had gathered together the sporadic poetic efforts of a lifetime and cast them casually in the face of the public.

Certainly many reviewers experienced this impression. "It is inevitable that when a man who has gained great distinction in one order of letters publishes a book in another, he should be told that his effort is creditable, but to be taken merely as a curiosity," wrote one. "Mr. Hardy must have expected such a verdict, and, to be frank, we think it might have been plausibly passed even if his verses had been better than they are." Another went so far as to deplore the effect of the book's publication on Hardy's reputation as a novelist: "Mr. Hardy has, by his own deliberate act, discredited that judgment and presentation of life on which his reputation rested." The reviewer lamented that Hardy did not burn the poetry in order to prevent its falling "into the hands of the indiscreet literary executor, and mar his fame when he was dead."[2] Along with other reviewers, these two writers seemed predisposed to regard *Wessex Poems* as something of a vanity effort, the work

2

of an old man using his reputation in a different field to gain publication of the poems he had written in idle hours. Their condescension was in part justified. Hardy's offer to underwrite the expense of publishing the book, although it was not accepted, suggests his own uncertainty about the venture. In 1898 he was known only as a novelist, whose books had stirred controversy because of their inconoclasm and pessimism. Although many of his contemporaries thought of his novels as having poetic qualities, these were primarily qualities of mood, atmosphere, temperament, and situation rather than qualities of form and style.[3] Before reading the Preface of *Wessex Poems*, few people knew that Hardy had been writing verse since his early youth.

Yet there was also a favorable response to *Wessex Poems*, and the disparities in judgment among the early commentators raise questions that are relevant to Hardy's total performance as a poet. Establishing lines of controversy that have characterized the criticism of Hardy's poetry up to the present day, the reviewers saw like features in different ways.[4] What appeared to some to be earnestness and sincerity, to others seemed to be naive, unpoetic discursiveness. Some saw the prevailing darkness of vision as an honest acknowledgement of the harshness of reality; others, as heavy-handed, pessimistic overstatement. The anguished voice crying out against victimization sounded like Hardy's own to most ears, but some commentators accepted Hardy's claim that the poems were, on the whole, dramatic in character, which suggested a distance between author and speaker. The grating acerbities of rhythm and diction seemed to the majority to be evidence of untutored clumsiness, but to a few they appeared to represent efforts at creating vivid stylistic textures. The reviewers all seemed to ask the same question, even though they gave different answers: Is *Wessex Poems* the work of a stumbling amateur or of a conscious poetic craftsman?

The Pictures

The thirty-one pen sketches done by Hardy himself, which play an integral part in setting the tone of the book, certainly suggest the hand of an amateur. Hardy mentions these illustrations in the final paragraph of his Preface (*CP*, p. 3), explaining that they were "recently made" and were "inserted for personal and local reasons rather than for their intrinsic qualities." His statement, characteristically defensive, is a reminder that his successful career as a novelist gave him the power to impose his whims on his publisher. The pictures, with their frequent lack of perspective, their wavering, uncertain lines, their macabre conceptions, and their lack of proportion and balance, seem at first glance to be the work of a child. The illustration for the poem "To Outer Nature," for example, representing an urn with drooping flowers surrounded by fallen petals, seems weird, grotesque, unskillful. The flowers are disproportionately small and seem to cling to the side of the urn as they hang limply and damply from its mouth. The illustration for "In a Eweleaze Near Weatherbury" shows a landscape speckled with stiffly drawn sheep, with a pair of spectacle rims in the foreground. Enigmatically, the spectacles produce no distortion or magnification in that part of the scene which is viewed through them. There are pictures of graveyards and corpses, and of desolate stretches of countryside, sometimes occupied by lone figures who are dwarfed by the indifferent landscape. The illustrations are disparate both in style and in their way of relating to the poems. Their ability to evoke morbid fascination and to produce bleakly moving effects might be called beauty, but it is the beauty of primitivism, embodied in surface simplicity, naiveté, and unpretentious seriousness. The pictures raise the same question as the poems: Are they the naive gropings of an amateur, or does Hardy exploit amateurish primitivism for deliberate effect?

Despite the pictures' undeniable amateurishness, Hardy had a highly developed, though idiosyncratic, visual imagination, and as an architect, he had learned to draw very well. The city square illustrating the poem "Leipzig" shows how competently he could execute a standard piece. More interesting, the drawing for "Heiress and Architect" (see figure) reveals his originality of visual conception. The picture shows a coffin being "haled" down a broad stairway. The lines are clear and simple, the point of view curiously narrow and exclusive. The focus is on the arms and legs of the pallbearers, straining and

4

bending to support the coffin, only the lower part of which can be seen at the top of the drawing. It is as if Hardy had taken a photograph askew from too close up, missing most of the coffin, and getting only the trunks and limbs of its bearers. The figures are drawn in line silhouette, leaving their bodies a blank white; no heads show. They have a kind of spectral anonymity, as if they were unfeeling, characterless, ghostly technicians, an impression consistent with the mood of the poem (*CP*, pp. 67-68), which ends with the line "'For you will die,'" spoken by a man of "cold, clear voice, and cold, clear view."

To turn from the firm skill of this picture to the illustration for the poem "Her Dilemma" (see figure) is to enter a different world. "Her Dilemma" (*CP*, pp. 10-11) deals with a woman who, being confronted in church by a dying man, takes pity on his hopeless condition and tells him, falsely, that she loves him. She risks this deliberate lie in a sanctified place because, " 'Twas worth her soul to be a moment kind." The illustration is a one-dimensional map of the setting of the poem, a cross section without perspective, including not only the interior of the church but also the ground underneath. Beneath the floor are two crypts, enclosing coffins and skeletons; the surrounding earth is mixed with skulls and bones. The characters of the poem, drawn in crude silhouette, stand above the crypts. The woman is a disfigured lump, her shoulders humped oddly over the trailing hem of her gown, and her gown at the front hanging straight down from her bosom to make her appear

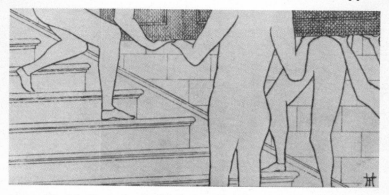

Hardy's Illustration for "Heiress and Architect" in *Wessex Poems*

unusually stout. The two figures are dwarfed by the architecture. What appears to be a row of choir stalls protrudes along the floor three-fifths of the way into the scene, looking like a line of oversized dominoes and overbalancing the four pews on the other side of the picture. Three columns support two-and-a-half arches overhead; the right side of the picture shaves off a third of one of the columns, and the left side slices one arch down the middle, as if Hardy had trimmed and framed it askew.

Hardy's Illustration for "Her Dilemma" in *Wessex Poems*

All in all this is a bizarre, macabre conception, executed apparently with the skill of a child, yet illustrating the poem significantly, even down to its primitivistic simplicity. Although nothing in "Her Dilemma" hints at the crypts, the skeletons, the skulls and bones, these pictorial features suggest mortality, which is the central fact of the poem, causing the dilemma. The drawing emphasizes the irony of the situation. While the lady holds the man's hand as if she were plighting her troth, the church itself is conceived of as a place of funerals and burials, not marriages or baptisms; the spiritual values it suggests offer no way out of the dilemma. The conception of the tiny figures with evidences of death beneath their feet and massive arches over their heads, trimmed and framed with dis-

6

regard for balance and proportion, "mocks humanity," as does the dilemma itself:

> And hence she lied, her heart persuaded throughly
> 'Twas worth her soul to be a moment kind.

> But the sad need thereof, his nearing death,
> So mocked humanity that she shamed to prize
> A world conditioned thus, or care for breath
> Where Nature such dilemmas could devise.

Both poem and picture show people, when facing the basic, primitive issues of love and death, to be awkward and helpless, living in a world askew. This and the other illustrations alert the reader to search for the artful intention underlying the surface grotesqueness and simplicity of the poems. As Hardy himself once wrote of Biblical narratives, "Their so-called simplicity is, in fact, the simplicity of the highest cunning."[5]

Pessimism

Like the pictures, the poems frequently deal in dull, bleak effects. The skulls and bones are beneath the characters' feet figuratively, if not literally, as in the graveyards of such poems as "She at His Funeral," "My Cicely," "Friends Beyond," and "Her Death and After." Throughout *Wessex Poems* the indifferent forces of nature assist the wary and unwary alike in their pilgrimages to disillusionment and death, and the "little chisel/ Of never-napping Time" does its remorseless work on the features and fortunes of men ("In a Eweleaze Near Weatherbury," *CP*, p. 63). Haunted voices speak weary messages from the grave, while living voices cry out in anguish and futile outrage. The sad note that dominates the collection, however, is not a single tone played in relentless repetition; counterpoint, harmony, and orchestration make it sound differently in different poems. The dark vision prevails, but continually modified and qualified. *Wessex Poems* illustrates how Hardy's idiosyncratic imagination, fully developed by 1898, transformed what is usually called pessimism into varied and complex drama.

In the first poem, "The Temporary the All" (*CP,* p. 5), the speaker enumerates the compromises with chance and change that have added up to his life of thwarted aims. In the second poem, "Amabel" (*CP,* p. 6), the speaker describes how time has disabused him of all illusions about the girl he once had loved. The third poem, "Hap" (*CP,* p. 7), introduces so distinctive a dramatic mode for expressing religious and philosophical pessimism as almost to comprise a unique subgenre for Hardy. Poems in this mode are distinguished by a tone of sincere, direct earnestness—the quality of many of the pictures. "Hap" is characteristic of the style in its headlong intensity, evident in the four stressed syllables commencing the first line, which is something of a metrical tour de force: "If but some vengeful god would call to me/ From up the sky, and laugh." Typical of the same mode is "A Sign-Seeker" (*CP,* pp. 43-44), in which the speaker passionately, insistently, searches for evidences of immortality, only to conclude that "When a man falls he lies." Likewise, the longing of "The Impercipient" (*CP,* pp. 59-60) for belief goes unfulfilled, and he laments that he must endure not only his failure to accept orthodoxy, but the accusation of willful agnosticism. These poems dramatize the anguish resulting from the recognition of God's absence from the world.

The lack of secure grounds for belief is not the only cause for anguish in *Wessex Poems.* Equally important is the painful vulnerability of the human heart, its subjection to change and chance, its inability to fulfill its own aspirations. Significantly, the intense earnestness of negative vision finds its way even into the love poems of the collection. "Ditty (E.L.G.)" (*CP,* pp. 13-14), a poem making reference to Hardy's first wife, describes the remote, isolated place where he had found her and expresses his pain at the realization that in other circumstances he might have "Loved as true" some other woman. Although he did find his true love, he offers this fact as proof of "What bond-servants of Chance/ We are all"; his gratuitous success is a sign of the precariousness of life. "Revulsion" (*CP,* p. 11) asserts that love renders the lover so vulnerable to suffering that the prize is hardly worth the game:

> For winning love we win the risk of losing,
> And losing love is as one's life were riven . . .

8

Let me then never feel the fateful thrilling
That devastates the love-worn wooer's frame.

The sonnet sequence "She, to Him, I-IV" (*CP,* pp. 11-13) presents a woman who, abandoned by her lover, remains "Numb as a vane that cankers on its point,/ True to the wind that kissed ere canker came." Her faithfulness is presented as a paralysis of the affections. As the word "canker" suggests, her love has become a kind of inner, cancerous corruption, destroying her emotional vitality and dehumanizing her: "This love puts all humanity from me," she cries at the beginning of the last sonnet. " 'In Vision I Roamed': To ——" (*CP,* p. 7) describes a grim, horrifying dream journey "through ghast heights of sky," but oddly, the apocalyptic description is the speaker's means of expressing his love for the unnamed addressee of the poem. Having traveled to fearful heights in his imagination, he finds "the sick grief that you were far away/ Grew pleasant thankfulness that you were near." He has the consolation that the cosmic distances he has imagined make earthly distances seem small; yet the two lovers nevertheless remain separated. These poems set love in the perspective of an indifferent cosmos and show its dependence on the chanceful workings of nature and the dangerous caprices of the lovers' own feelings. They dramatize the isolation and vulnerability of the sensitive heart.

A negative vision pervades the full range of *Wessex Poems,* from the religious and philosophical monologues to the love lyrics. The collection as a whole emphasizes the desperation of the human condition subject to the circumstances of nature and the failure of human compassion. Yet there are important qualifications. In subdued ways, Hardy in these poems evokes and affirms positive values and dramatizes viable postures for outfacing the destructive effects of time and circumstance. This sense of muted hopefulness plays like a secondary melody, counterpointing the prevailing darker tones. Equally important, the dramatic texture of the poems often mitigates the force of pessimistic statement; with varying effects, Hardy often holds his speakers at a distance. In some poems, he unambiguously exposes the dangers of obsessive pessimism, occasionally with grimly comic results. In others, there is a contrived balance between exposure and statement, making for an ambivalent effect. Even in the straightforward pessimistic monologues the details often undercut the validity of the statement, raising doubts in the reader's mind as to whether or not the speaker represents the author.

The evocation of positive values occurs even in such dark poems as "A Sign-Seeker" in which the speaker's quest is motivated partially by his sensitivity to the sufferings of others, "Earth's Frail," who "lie bleeding of her Strong." "The Impercipient" names values explicitly. Of the scornful orthodox believers, the speaker laments:

> Since heart of mine knows not that ease
> Which they know; since it be
> That He who breathes All's Well to these
> Breathes no All's-Well to me,
> My lack might move their sympathies
> And Christian charity!

Clearly, he sees that the moral significance of the disappearance of God is a heightened necessity for human compassion.[6]

A small number of poems in the collection directly expose the creative possibilities, limited but real, of the heart and the imagination. Along with the willingness of the woman in "Her Dilemma" to risk her soul to be "a moment kind," there is a self-searching objectivity and creative sympathy in the speaker of "A Confession to a Friend in Trouble" (CP, p. 9). He is aware that distance and time have weakened his feelings for a suffering friend, and he has the honesty to face the possibility *"That I will not show zeal again to learn/ Your griefs, and, sharing them, renew my pain."* Although he attempts to banish the thought, the fact that he could entertain it in the first place is a grim lesson: "can bitterer knowledge be/ Than that, though banned, such instinct was in me!" The speaker, who is horrified by his own callousness rather than the persecution of a cruel world, finds a way to compensate for his real shortcoming: he confesses it to the very friend whom distance is making him forget, and thereby renews and refreshes his sympathetic heart. His conscious self-exposure is a mode of compassionate commitment.

"Middle-Age Enthusiasms" (CP, pp. 55-56) reveals the same quality of creative objectivity. The characters face the indiffer-

10

ent world by consciously making the best of things despite their awareness of approaching death. Their means of dealing with middle age is to will enthusiasm: "[we] laughed at life and care,/ Although we knew no laugh lay there." They have long ago given up the search for signs; they know that "When a man falls he lies," but with good nature they pretend otherwise:

> "So sweet the place," we said,
> "Its tacit tales so dear,
> Our thoughts, when breath has sped,
> Will meet and mingle here!" . . .
> "Words!" mused we. "Passed the mortal door,
> Our thoughts will reach this nook no more."

Their lives are willed dramas, in which they consciously play the roles of hopeful people, deliberately assuming such roles as a means of defying the threat of mortality. That the "M.H." referred to in the subtitle is Hardy's sister Mary, who was close to him throughout her life, leaves little doubt that here he speaks directly, of and for himself. Poems like "A Confession to a Friend in Trouble" and "Middle-Age Enthusiasms" are evidence of the part played in *Wessex Poems* by an awareness of the positive, if limited, human potential.[7]

This sense of muted hopefulness is fairly easy to isolate and identify in the collection. Less obvious are the ways in which the dramatic nature of the poems limits and undermines negative vision. Often melodramatic intensities of tone approach willful exaggeration, and the result is ironic exposure of the dangers of obsessive gloom. Sometimes Hardy seems almost to play with melodramatic techniques and conventions, and negative vision becomes merely an element in an ambivalent drama. "A Meeting with Despair" (*CP*, p. 51) illustrates a common pattern, in which an earnest hero confronts a sadistic villain. The speaker sees a landscape "like a tract in pain"—" 'like my own life,' I said." Raising his eyes, he finds solace in a beautiful sunset and reproaches himself for "misrepresenting Good" by imposing his gloomy interpretation on the scene. But then Despair, a form "strange of mould," intervenes to blight his hopefulness:

"'Tis a dead spot, where even the light lies spent
  To darkness!" croaked the Thing.
"Not if you look aloft!" said I, intent
  On my new reasoning.

"Yea—but await awhile!" he cried. "Ho-ho!—
  Now look aloft and see!"
I looked. There, too, sat night: Heaven's radiant show
  Had gone. Then chuckled he.[8]

Underlying the poem is a serious philosophic point that provides an indirect criticism of the speakers of such poems as "Hap," "The Impercipient," and "A Sign-Seeker." To expect from indifferent nature support for one's moods and feelings is to invite despair. But the poem is also notable for its dramatic texture—the pathetic earnestness of the speaker, his intentness and rationality, contrasted with Despair's villainy. Despair preempts the last piece of stage action—a laugh. The effect is bitterly comic.

For his *Collected Poems* Hardy revised the last line and significantly altered the poem's final effect: "Heaven's radiant show/ Had gone that heartened me." The final version, despite the almost comic intensity of the villain's sadistic croakings, ends on a note of unambiguous seriousness reinforced by the meter. The energy suggested by the initial reversed feet in the lines of the dialogue—"'Tís a dead spot," "Nót if you look," "Yéa—but await," "Nów look aloft"—is brought under control by the metrical regularity of the revised last line. The melodrama of earnest hero versus sadistic villain leads not to comedy but to the pathos of the hero's defeat. The original line, however, suggests Hardy's awareness of the potentialities in melodrama for grotesque comedy, an awareness further evidenced in another statement of Hardy's: "If you look beneath the surface of any farce you see a tragedy; and, on the contrary, if you blind yourself to the deeper issues of a tragedy you see a farce." To recognize the effects of mordant comedy is essential to Hardy's poetry. As his wife wrote, undoubtedly echoing his own sentiments: "Hardy had a born sense of humour, even a too keen sense occasionally: but his poetry was sometimes placed by editors in the hands of reviewers

12

deficient in that quality. Even if they were accustomed to Dickensian humour they were not to Swiftian. Hence it unfortunately happened that verses of a satirical, dry, caustic, or farcical cast were regarded by them with the deepest seriousness."9

The problem of gauging the effect of melodrama exists in some of Hardy's most admired poems, like the frequently anthologized "Heiress and Architect." It is a rigorously structured dialogue between a young woman, the inheritor of the means for life, and an architect, who advises her about the house she plans to build. Her goal is to make the house a place of vital activity, but the architect progressively argues her out of each of her hopeful conceptions and crushes her with his logic. She wants "open ogive-work" to let in the colors, sounds, and scents of nature; the architect advises her to build "the close and surly wall,/ For winters freeze." She requests large windows of crystal glass, to enable the world to see her gaiety and beauty; he advises her to "house for secrecy,/ For you will tire." She asks for a small room where she can meet her lover; he warns her of the bitterness that will result when her lover abandons her, "For you will fade." Her final wish, expressed faintly, is for "Some narrow winding turret, quite mine own,/ To reach a loft where I may grieve alone!"; he advises her instead to build a broad staircase:

> "Give space (since life ends unawares)
> To hale a coffined corpse adown the stairs;
> For you will die."

The poem considers two mutually contradictory views of life. The heiress wants to live, to participate in the world, to expose herself, to love; the architect points out that the effect of participation and exposure is disillusionment and suffering. He recommends the protection of thick walls and narrow windows. But his view results in a form of self-entombment, of death in life. To live is to suffer; to avoid suffering is to thwart life. At the center of the poem is this dilemma, which sums up a philosophical position that Hardy held from his youth to the end of his days (the poem is dated 1867). What makes the poem perplexing, however, is its melodramatic form, which exaggerates and intensifies the terms of the dilemma. The structure—two introductory stanzas followed by a dialogue with alternate stanzas devoted to each speaker—makes the poem as neat and pat as an old chestnut on the stage. The heiress, so naive, so full of ignorant hopefulness, so animated by the vitality of her idealistic illusions, is the ingenue, sweet-natured, feeling, but vulnerable. The architect is the villain, an "arch-designer" with "cold, clear voice, and cold, clear view," "the man of measuring eye" whom "nought could warm to gallantries," who "swayed her like a shade." Hardy's language has the effect of discrediting the architect's position. Instead of associating him with the wisdom of knowledge and age found, for example, in "Middle-Age Enthusiasms," or with the passion of youthful disappointment found in "Revulsion," he relates him to calculation, coldness, and death. The baneful-ness of his last words, which end the poem, suggest a note of malicious triumph: "For you will die." Yet the ingenue's naiveté and ignorance discredit her postion as well, and she has not the courage to resist the mastery of the man hired to be her servant. Paradoxically, both sides of the dilem-ma—commitment to life and self-protection—are discredited in the melodrama of the poem. Is the result an absurd, dark, nihilistic comedy? Or is the melodrama a means of intensifying and structuring a profound vision? Is it farce or tragedy? Clearly, the poem is ambivalent.

Although poems like "Hap," "The Impercipient," and "A Sign-Seeker" lack any hint of humor, and exaggeration would be an inappropriate term for characterizing their intensities of tone, even in them certain excesses seem to undercut the valid-ity of their statements. These poems raise an important prob-lem of interpretation in Hardy's poetry. It may be that the excesses in such poems are intended merely to heighten the speakers' anguish, and that readers unsympathetic to unrelent-ing pessimism are justified in noting a kind of sentimentality in reverse. Yet in view of Hardy's complex understanding of dramatic postures, evident in such poems as "A Meeting with Despair," "Heiress and Architect," and "Middle-Age Enthusiasms," there is reason to suspect a certain distance between author and speaker in many of the pessimistic monologues. The speakers of "Hap," "A Sign-Seeker," and "The Impercipient" are all self-centered, a condition that is emphasized by the frequency of first-person pronouns, and they all feel a sense of persecution—by the "purblind Doomsters," by those "who, rapt to heights of trancelike trust,/ These tokens claim to feel and see," and by the "bright believing band" of the orthodox. By allowing their tone to approach self-righteousness and self-pity, Hardy may be implying criticism; their self-dramatization may be a form of self-exposure. Certainly they seem to derive gratification from their plights.

"A Sign-Seeker" is a case in point. The seeker suffers from a real affliction. His cry is like Job's: "O that one would hear me! Behold, my desire is that the Almighty would answer me, and that my adversary had written a book" (Job 32:36). But unlike Job, the sign-seeker hears no voice from the whirlwind. Yet his reaction is obsessive. He longs so urgently to believe that he literally pants, and he devotes his life to the fruitless search for immortality. Echoing Biblical language, he describes his futile survey of "All the vast various moils that mean a world alive"—the cycles of day and night, of the seasons, the sun, the rain, the mists, the surgings and strivings of men. His language indicates a painful, mortuary awareness of the finality of death and decay. He would be satisfied if only:

> a dead Love's lips, whom dreams reveal
>   When midnight imps of King Decay
>   Delve sly to solve me back to clay,
> Should leave some print to prove her spirit-kisses real.

He frequents graveyards and even sleeps in the beds of the dead, hoping to hear a voice saying that death is "Not the end!":

> I have lain in dead men's beds, have walked
>   The tombs of those with whom I had talked,
> Called many a gone and goodly one to shape a sign,
>
> And panted for response. But none replies;
>   No warnings loom, nor whisperings
>   To open out my limitings,
> And Nescience mutely muses: When a man falls he lies.

15

There is a certain irony in his plight. Although he has devoted his entire mortal life to seeking proof of immortality, the sumtotal of his knowledge consists of the bleak negatives of the final stanza. The only hope would seem to lie in ignoring the uncertainties of death and performing acts of mercy in the "world alive" on behalf of "Earth's Frail." "Canst thou by searching find out God?" is the question put to Job by Zophar the Naamathite, and the answer, he implies, is a negative (Job 11: 7). Perhaps "A Sign-Seeker" is designed to show that the destiny of the obsessive searcher is an endless, futile quest. That is, even this poem may contain an element of ironic exposure qualifying its negative statement.

There are poems in the collection without any distancing features and the contrast between them and "A Sign-Seeker" or "The Impercipient" is instructive. "'I Look into My Glass,'" (CP, p. 72), for example, the terminal piece in Wessex Poems, has every appearance of being a direct statement by Hardy himself, an aging man, lamenting his physical deterioration and saying a last word about his own condition. The poem is a brief, simple, comparatively unpretentious monologue, describing a commonplace human situation. Observing his "wasting skin" in a mirror, the speaker cries in characteristic anguish, "Would God it came to pass/ My heart had shrunk as thin!" His last lines also convey typically intense feelings of persecution:

> But Time, to make me grieve,
> Part steals, lets part abide;
> And shakes this fragile frame at eve
> With throbbings of noontide.

He feels himself to be the victim of time, that capricious thief whose intent is to cause him suffering, and he has real justification for his anguish, contrary to Hardy's other speakers, who could be accused of seeking out disquietude when expressing their aggressive sense of cosmic injustice. There is an element of absurdity in the sign-seeker's obsessive quest, and of disingenuous self-righteousness in the impercipient's expectation of Christian charity from his persecutors, for it is possible to withdraw from jeering accusers, and life offers more interesting alternatives than listening for voices from the dead. But whether or not God exists, or the soul is immortal, the swell of emotion in a wasting frame is a fact. There is no escape from the reality of the throbbing heart.

The Craft

The negative vision of *Wessex Poems* is thus qualified by the dramatic nature of the poems and by their testimony to the existence of more promising human possibilities. Hardy's range of response is not limited to reductive pessimism, and he shows an understanding of the complexities of tone and posture. His sense of complexity, however, is evident not merely in the dramatic and intellectual qualifications of statement. A bizarre imagination is at work in the poems, responding with careful craft to the perplexing disparities of existence, consciously exploiting the resources of language and poetic technique. It is this creative imagination that provides the most eloquent antidote to Hardy's negative vision. The throbbing heart in "'I Look into My Glass'" prompts Hardy to speak out almost in spite of himself, and each of the poems itself manifests the possibility of human accomplishment. Although the world is confusing, and making sense of it is a difficult task, the effort is valid. Again and again Hardy says what he can, and each statement, regardless of its prevailing tone, is somehow worth preserving. Whatever the ultimate facts of the human condition may be, the imagination is there, prompted by the heart, to shape something out of experience.

One of the most bizarre of the pessimistic monologues, "Nature's Questioning" (*CP*, pp. 58-59), illustrates Hardy's complex craftsmanship. As in all of the monologues, the organizing rhetorical pattern creates a sense of order, proportion, and climax. In this case the rhetorical pattern is a series of parallel unanswered and unanswerable questions. Supporting this structure is a secondary progression of shifting metaphors, which illustrates both the idiosyncrasies of Hardy's imagination and his ability indirectly to evoke positive values. The speaker in the poem regards a gloomy landscape, which he surprisingly compares to the faces of school children:

When I look forth at dawning, pool,
   Field, flock, and lonely tree,
   All seem to gaze at me
Like chastened children sitting silent in a school;

   Their faces dulled, constrained, and worn,
   As though the master's ways
   Through the long teaching days
Had cowed them till their early zest was overborne.

This image shows how men, in their attempts to educate and sharpen the "early zest" of their children, dull and suppress it instead; appropriately and honestly, the metaphor refers to men's partial responsibility for their own sorry condition. The area of overlap between the two terms of the comparison is the feeling of melancholy and disillusionment attendant on the speaker's awareness of the thwarted enthusiasm of children, and his similar feelings at regarding a gloomy landscape; in both cases nature, "natural" and human, appears suppressed and devitalized, as if by some superior power. But the visual difference between "dawning, pool,/ Field, flock, and lonely tree" and "chastened children sitting silent in a school" is so great that the comparison can only seem bizarre.

Later in the poem the metaphor becomes odder and even more complex, when it is the school children, not the speaker, who ask the unanswerable questions. In "lippings mere" they "wonder, ever wonder, why we find us here!":

"Has some Vast Imbecility,
   Mighty to build and blend,
   But impotent to tend,
Framed us in jest, and left us now to hazardry?

"Or come we of an Automaton
   Unconscious of our pains? . . .
   Or are we live remains
Of Godhead dying downwards, brain and eye now gone?"

The metaphorical structure of the poem approaches the grotesque. The elements of nature become the dulled, questioning school children, who, in a tentative moment, metamorphose themselves into the lower parts of a dying god. The

18

dull landscape remains the central subject of the poem; but the meaphor, the classroom, acquires a life of its own. This apparent indictment of nature calls attention to the part men play in blighting human life. In terms of the children's plight, the unconscious automaton and the Godhead dying downwards can only be man's corrupt and decaying social institutions. The poem ends characteristically on a quiet note of realistic vision:

> No answerer I . . .
> Meanwhile the winds, and rains,
> And Earth's old glooms and pains
> Are still the same, and Life and Death are neighbours
>   nigh.

"The Ivy-Wife" (*CP*, p. 50), an even stranger, more subtle poem, combines metaphor, melodrama, and a slightly comic tone to produce a deeply serious effect. It is a dramatic monologue of an ivy vine who "longed to love." She speaks like a stage villainness, the fatal seductress. After being twice repulsed by other trees, she gleefully describes her sadistic pleasure in destroying by her embrace her one trusting lover:

> In new affection next I strove
>   To coll an ash I saw,
> And he in trust received my love;
>   Till with my soft green claw
> I cramped and bound him as I wove . . .
>   Such was my love: ha-ha!

There is no balancing note to contrast with the ivy's villainy, like the earnestness of the speaker in "A Meeting with Despair." Her exaggerated tone goes unrelieved, becoming so grotesquely intense as almost to be a parody. Certainly the conclusion of the poem has an almost parodic effect. Neatly, symetrically, the villainess is hoisted by her own petard. Like a classical heroine, she is too pridefully intent on her triumph to see its inevitable consequences. The means of her rise is the cause of her fall, as she points out with near-comic abruptness:

> By this I gained his strength and height
>   Without his rivalry.
> But in my triumph I lost sight

Of afterhaps. Soon he,
Being bark-bound, flagged, snapped, fell outright,
And in his fall felled me!

The effect is ambiguous. One recognizes the exaggeration of tone and the contrived use of the conventional tragic pattern. This is a stage villain to be hooted and hissed, a grotesque, warped, demented creature, a playful figment of the imagination, bigger than life or smaller than life, but not life itself. But then one realizes that the theme of the poem is the self-destructiveness of possessive, competitive love. Hardy examines a certain psychological type, the wife who clings and clutches and grips, choking out her lover's life, as if she were an ivy vine destroying a tree. The poem is purely metaphorical. Hardy focuses on the vehicle, which conveys a lesson in nature's mutual destructiveness, and he names the tenor only in the title, "The Ivy-*Wife*." The effect of the play of tenor against vehicle is to heighten one's awareness of the predatory potentialities of the human psyche. In addition to the familiar nature "red in tooth and claw," there is also a "soft green claw," the destructive power in that self-centered possessiveness which sometimes masquerades as the most valuable of feelings, love. The ivy's voice becomes Hardy's realistic translation into words of emotions few people recognise, and even fewer confess. It is no exaggeration to say that every clinging vine, every parasitic lover, has the heart of a sadistic stage villain.

In this poem Hardy fuses a wide variety of poetic and intellectual traditions to convey a deep psychological insight. He deals in conventions of tragedy, melodramatic intensities of tone, and sexual sadism, all in the confession of an ivy vine who loved too well. In a compact dramatic metaphor, he exploits the Tennysonian vision of nature's mutual antagonisms, which by the late nineteenth century had become a cliché, in order to expose the masked hostilities of the human psyche. "The Ivy-Wife" is a profound human statement expressed with complex wit. It reveals a mind aware of the dimension of human responsibility for human suffering, and an imagination more than adequate to the disparate materials available to it.

Probably the poems that least appeal to modern tastes are the ten long ballads and narratives. In these poems, narrating unlikely stories of the Wessex countryside in galloping rhythms and obtrusive rhymes, Hardy's imagination works simply and crudely. He presents himself in the traditional role of the ballad singer, something of a historian, telling of the typical struggles, sufferings, and triumphs of people half real, half legendary—a role that must have seemed only slightly less archaic and improbable in 1898 than it does today. And yet, while Hardy writes with rough-and-ready strength, the ballads touch on subtle complexities of psychology and morality, and create curiously modern effects of uncertainty and quandary. Exploiting jolting infelicities of language and contrivances of plot, they evoke varieties of sympathetic response for their suffering heroes and heroines. Hardy shapes the poems with broad, crude strokes, but the rough surfaces and jagged edges often contribute to poignant effects.

One of the ballads, "San Sebastian (*August* 1813): With Thoughts of Sergeant M —— (Pensioner) Who Died 185—" is among the most strangely moving poems in the collection (*CP*, pp. 17–19). Like several other of the narratives, its inspiration was the Napoleonic wars, and it has a basis in fact. In "San Sebastian," Hardy characteristically exposes ironic moral complexities by recording the long-term destructive consequences of war in the life of a hero who helped save a continent from the tyranny of Napoleon. The hero of the ballad is a man obsessed with guilt, and its form is a confession spoken in answer to a sympathetic questioner:

> "Why, Sergeant, stray on the Ivel Way,
> As though at home there were spectres rife?
> From first to last 'twas a proud career!
> And your sunny years with a gracious wife
>   Have brought you a daughter dear."

What provokes the question is the contrast between the gaiety of the Sergeant's daughter, dancing in Arcadian innocence "Round a Hintock maypole," and the melancholy wanderings of the Sergeant himself. Yet it is precisely the vision of the daughter that has caused the old soldier's pensiveness. She is just the age of a girl he violated after the storming of San Sebastian, at his apparent moment of heroism; as he grows older, his sense of heroism fades and his guilt increases. What he remembers is the look of the wronged girl as she "raised her beseeching eyes" and said words of prayer "In her own soft language." Ironically, his daughter seems to have the same eyes:

> "Fatefully
> I copied those eyes for my punishment
> In begetting the girl you see!"

Despite all his reasons to be happy, he lives as a self-condemned moral outcast. Like Michael Henchard in *The Mayor of Casterbridge,* he compares himself to Cain:

> "So, to-day I stand with a God-set brand
> Like Cain's, when he wandered from kindred's ken . . .
> I served through the war that made Europe free;
> I wived me in peace-year. But, hid from men,
> I bear that mark on me."

The liberating war has ironically enslaved one of its heroic "chosen few," and the fruits of victory turn bitter in his mouth. In the last stanza the Sergeant neatly reverses the meanings of the terms used by the questioner at the beginning of the poem:

> "I delight me not in my proud career;
> And 'tis coals of fire that a gracious wife
> Should have brought me a daughter dear!"

Hardy exploits the contrast between benign pastoral values, suggested in part by the ballad form of this poem, and the real quandaries of human life. The poem, written in primitive dogtrot rhythms and heavily-accented internal rhymes, describes a countryside where maidens still dance around maypoles and old people still quote scripture—a fitting place for an aging hero of almost legendary wars to retire in pastoral comfort, surrounded by family and friends. But instead of a tale of honors reaped and enjoyed, instead of a memory pre-

22

served from Britain's heroic past, it presents the story of an essentially kindly, sensitive man, straying like Cain across the landscape, haunted by a vision of past violation in a foreign land, which the present blessings of home ironically keep alive for him. There is no mitigation—not in religion, not in philosophy, not in the old values of the countryside—for the intensity of his guilty suffering.

Like "San Sebastian," all of the narratives are idiosyncratic mixtures of primitivistic simplicity and moral complexity, of rural fatalism and nineteenth-century intellectual pessimism, of melodramatic oversimplification and realistic psychology. As "The Dance at the Phoenix" (*CP*, pp. 38-42) illustrates, the more melodramatic and bizarre the tale, the more curious and touching is the point of moral physiology at its heart. The poem works out the consequences in the life of the heroine, Jenny, of two conflicting impulses: her love for pleasure and her desire for domestic stability, which suggests another form of contrast between the mode of the heiress and the mode of the architect. After an immodest, promiscuous life, Jenny marries an innocent young man and bears him two sons. In her life with her husband, she redeems her past indiscretions:

> Her husband's trust
> In Jenny knew no bound,
> And Jenny kept her pure and just,
> Till even malice found
> No sin or sign of ill to be
> In one who walked so decently
> The duteous helpmate's round.

When she is fifty-nine, however, the King's-Own Cavalry, the regiment of her former lovers, returns to Casterbridge, and on Christmas, the day of new birth, she cannot resist the lure of music from the nearby Phoenix Inn, where a regimental dance is taking place. The ambivalent power of music and the paradoxical image of the phoenix control the central drama of the poem. To the strains of country dances, the egg hatches and the miraculous bird takes flight. Thus, Jenny leaves her husband's bed, hides her grey hair in a cap, and joins the party. The poem presents a weird picture of the "Gay

Granny," arisen with renewed youth, doing "Reels, jigs, poussettes, and flings" while the soldiers "cheered her as she soared and swooped." While she stands musing alone by the dying fire after her return home, "A something arrowed through her heart/ In shoots of agony." She slips back into bed and dies next to her sleeping husband. The well-meaning man never learns of her escapade nor suspects her unfaithfulness.

In outline the story is simple, pathetic, barely credible; yet Jenny's crisis is psychologically valid and morally complex. She devoted herself to husband and family until her sons grew up "And roamed, and were as not:/ Alone was Jenny left again." The King's-Own becomes a melodramatic image for whatever it is that disrupts the life of a middle-aged woman once her role as mother has ended, and fires her with a longing for the pleasures of youth that have been sacrificed to domestic stability. And yet Jenny cannot fully liberate herself into the world of energy and pleasure imaged by the dance. The ballad-singer, at the end of the poem, seems to side with the action and music and color associated with the cavalry regiment and the Phoenix Inn:

> Well! times are not as times were then,
>   Nor fair ones half so free;
> And truly they were martial men,
>   The King's-Own Cavalry.
> And when they went from Casterbridge
> And vanished over Mellstock Ridge,
>   'Twas saddest morn to see.

But from Jenny's point of view the music was a trap. Illustrating the poem in the original volume are elaborate scrolls of musical notation looking like an unfurled net, the net that entangles Jenny and causes her moral crisis. Tragically, she feels guilty for submitting to the lure of the music. Just before her death, she looks at her husband:

> A tear sprang as she turned and viewed
>   His features free from guile;
> She kissed him long, as when, just wooed,
>   She chose his domicile.
> She felt she would give more than life
> To be the single-hearted wife
>   That she had been erstwhile.

24

Ironically, pathetically, the faithfulness of her devoted domestic life is in her eyes belied by her last gay act. Like the Sergeant, she finds herself trapped by what she takes to be a crime; she can never atone for it, never return to her pristine state before the fall. From the ashes of her last fire there is no resurrection. In "The Dance at the Phoenix" and "San Sebastian," the reader can forgive the characters their sins, but the characters cannot forgive themselves. Hardy has created dramas of human beings pathetically enslaved by the scrupulosity of their own consciences.

Hardy's use of the phoenix image illustrates the craftsmanship of *Wessex Poems*. Throughout the collection, he draws imaginatively on a variety of poetic forms and techniques, besides creating new ones of his own. He ranges widely in the realm of experience, selecting and shaping with crudeness or delicacy, so that his poems have the substance, texture, and dimension of reality as well as the idiosyncratic mold of a personal vision. Oddness and versatility appear on the verbal level as well. Shifts in levels of diction, for example, frequently mirror rhetorical structures. The common rhetorical pattern in the monologues is a gradual building by means of parallel structures to a moment of anguished intensity, followed by a quiet, sincere statement of a realistic vision. The last four lines of "The Impercipient" illustrate Hardy's characteristic use of the abruptness of anticlimax, reinforced here in the shift from the metaphorical language of the cry to the staccato prosiness of the ending:

> O, doth a bird deprived of wings
> Go earth-bound wilfully!
>
> Enough. As yet disquiet clings
> About us. Rest shall we.

A bolder verbal effect appears in the last lines of "The Ivy-Wife." The ringing of syntactic changes on a single root word ("*fell* outright,/ And in his *fall felled* me!") shows that Hardy knew Greek and Latin figures of speech and could use them for his own effects. This figure, called a polyptoton, is found, for example, in Tennyson's line from *Maud*, "My own Heart's heart, my ownest own, farewell," and in Hardy's "Revulsion": "To fail obtaining whom one fails to miss./ For winning love

25

we win the risk of losing." In "The Ivy-Wife" there is special wit in having the prideful woman confess her ironic fall in a classical trope. Yet no feature of *Wessex Poems* evoked less favorable response than did the language.

The Language

What most bothered Hardy's contemporaries was the harsh, grating style of *Wessex Poems,* the diction and prosody. With feelings ranging from hostility to tolerance, reviewers referred to "the flaws and nodosities," the "little sense of rhythm . . . and little sense of music," the "rough hacking and involution of phrases to make them fit [the] metres," the deficiences "in form and technique" and the "difficulties with rhyme," and the "lines . . . clumsy with . . . almost inconceivable clumsiness."[10] The very first poem in the collection, "The Temporary the All," illustrates Hardy's boldness in confronting his readers with stylistic idiosyncrasies. He publicly launched his poetic career with this stanza, here quoted from the original edition of *Wessex Poems:*

> Change and chancefulness in my flowering youthtime,
> Set me sun by sun near to one unchosen;
> Wrought us fellowly, and despite divergence,
>   Friends interblent us.

The style seems awkward and uncontrolled. Considerations of meter would seem to have dictated the choice of the word "chancefulness" instead of "chance." "Sun by sun" seems an affected way of saying "day by day," and the alliteration and assonance appear forced and heavy-handed. "Wrought us fellowly" is an unusually contorted phrase for "made us friends," and the syntax of the line, employing the peculiar adverb "fellowly" instead of an adjective or noun, seems excessively mannered. The subject of the verb "interblent" appears at first to be "Friends," and it requires a moment to realize that the subject is actually "Change and chancefulness" of the first line. The difficulties multiply as the poem goes on:

> "Cherish him can I while the true one forthcome—
> Come the rich fulfiller of my prevision;
> Life is roomy yet, and the odds unbounded."
>   So self-communed I.

26

Thwart my wistful way did a damsel saunter,
Fair not fairest, good not best of her feather;
"Maiden meet," held I, "till arise my forefelt
    Wonder of women."

The tortured grammatical inversions ("Cherish him can I,"
"self-communed I"), the mixture of kinds of diction (the
archaic "damsel" and "Maiden meet," as opposed to the more
colloquial "roomy" and "odds unbounded"), the awkward
coinages ("forthcome," "self-communed," "forefelt"), and the
heavy alliteration ("Wonder of women") produce an effect of
unruliness, held clumsily in check only by the complex meter.
And the idea of the poem, when unraveled from the tangle
of language, is not altogether palatable. The speaker confesses
that a barely suitable acquaintance became his one friend, a
barely suitable woman became his mistress, a barely suitable
habitation became his dwelling, and so on; the sum total of
his life consists of a series of compromises he made with
chance and change. Even a reader as sympathetic to Hardy as
the late Carl J. Weber deplored "The Temporary the All": "If
Hardy had taken Robert Browning's advice as given in the last
line of 'Respectability'—'Put forward your best foot!'—he would
never have begun *Wessex Poems* as he did. For Hardy put forward his worst foot."[11]

If Hardy put his "worst foot" forward with "The Temporary
the All," he followed it with another worst foot, "Amabel,"
which continues the harsh, idiosyncratic style:

    I marked her ruined hues,
    Her custom-straitened views,
    And asked, "Can there indwell
        My Amabel?"

It is difficult to untangle the meaning: the speaker, regarding
Amabel's commonplace opinions and the effects of time on her
physical appearance, is wondering if the woman he once loved
could possibly "dwell" in her aged frame. In later stanzas
marked by awkward coinages, diction drawn from local dialect,
and contorted syntax, the speaker expresses his painful awareness, forced on him by chance and change, that disillusionment is a universal effect of time:

27

Knowing that, though Love cease,
Love's race shows undecrease;
All find in dorp or dell
    An Amabel.

—I felt that I could creep
To some housetop, and weep
That Time the tyrant fell
    Ruled Amabel!

"Undecrease" appears in the original edition of *Wessex Poems*. Hardy changed the word in *Collected Poems* to "no decrease," but the initial choice, in the context of the diction and syntax of the rest of the poem, suggests an intention at that time deliberately to create the effect of awkwardness.

Ungainly diction appears repeatedly in *Wessex Poems*. There are uncommon Latinate words, like "ostent," "subtrude," "indign," "aureate nimb," and "hodiernal." There are dialect words, and words drawn from the vocabulary of the Celtic and Anglo-Saxon past: "thirtover," "therence," "blee," "cromlech," "eyne." There are awkward negative coinages, such as "unknows," "unbe," "unblooms," "disennoble," as well as "undecrease." As William Archer remarked, "There are times when Mr. Hardy seems to lose all sense of local and historical perspective in language, seeing all words in the dictionary on one plane, so to speak, and regarding them all as equally available and appropriate for any and every literary purpose."[12] This same forthright refusal to discriminate is evident in the construction of lines as well as in the diction. There are many tongue-twisting phrases, often peppered with a high ratio of consonants to vowels: "vast various moils" and "that I fain would wot of shuns my sense" from "A Sign-Seeker"; "My sombre image, warped by insidious heave/ Of those less forthright, must lose place in thee" and "yield their space to shine of smugger things" from "To a Lady" (*CP*, pp. 57-58); "By the bough the firstling browses" from "Ditty"; "A shell was slent to shards anighst my ears" from "Valenciënnes" (*CP*, pp. 15-17); and the familiar lines from "Hap":

And why unblooms the best hope ever sown?
—Crass Casualty obstructs the sun and rain,
And dicing Time for gladness casts a moan. . . .
These purblind Doomsters had as readily strown
Blisses about my pilgrimage as pain.

The revisions found in the manuscript and in later printings of the poems show how carefully Hardy worked to get his lines the way he wanted them and provide evidence that the harsh effects were deliberately contrived.[13] The many cancellations and revisions in the fair copy that went to the printer suggest that Hardy worked on the poems right up to the end, and a comparison of the manuscript with the text indicates that he probably made changes even when the volume was in proof. Furthermore, the fair copies of the earliest poems bear much subsequent revision, so that even though these poems were conceived in Hardy's youth, the final phrasing was that of a mature man, choosing to write as he did. Two lines from the third stanza of "Postponement" (*CP*, p. 8), a poem dated 1866, illustrate the case. The manuscript, with cancellations indicated by brackets, reads:

> "Stricken, I stayed till
> ["I stayed me, & hoped at] the summer-tide
>
>   lewth of   house
> In [shielding] leaves to [throne] her bride."

Hardy apparently revised the lines in proof, for in *Wessex Poems* they appear:

> "Fear-filled, I stayed me till summer-tide,
> In lewth of leaves to throne her bride."

Hardy seems to be moving toward a more dramatic emphasis at the head of the first line, preferring an initial stressed to an unstressed syllable, and finally choosing a phrase that requires an increased stress on the second syllable as well: "I stáyed," "Strícken," "Féar-fílled." He makes these changes at the expense of clarity—in the revised lines "hoped" must be understood—but not at the expense of alliteration—"till summer-tide" echoes the sounds in "stayed," while "Fear-filled" contributes a new alliterative pattern. Hardy also moves toward more archaic and heroic language. He prefers "I stayed me till" to "I stayed till the," and "In lewth of leaves" to "In shielding leaves"—although the desire for alliteration also probably played a part in the latter choice. And after wavering between "house" and "throne," he settles for the more grandiose "throne." The heavy emphasis, bold alliteration, heroic bravado, and archaic diction contribute to the effect of crudeness, which the revisions show must have been intended.

The more complex changes in the last stanza of "The Casterbridge Captains" (*CP*, pp. 42-43) also illustrate the movement toward boldness of language as well as richness of meaning. The manuscript reads:

> Transcendent triumph in return
>
> No longer lit his brain
> [His heart no longer knew]
>
> lonely
> Transcendence rayed the [distant] urn
>
> Where slept the distant twain.
> [Above the other two.]

In *Wessex Poems* the last two lines are revised:

> Transcendence rayed the distant urn
> Where slept the fallen twain.

The revisions make for a cruder, tougher diction and syntax. The rejected lines, "His heart no longer knew" and "Above the other two," are clear in meaning and metrically graceful, but they lack the bite of the word "brain" and of the inversion "Where slept." The revisions also make for more consistent, denser meaning. If transcendence rays the dead, it also illuminates the living, as Hardy shows when he firms up the metaphor. The revisions of the last two lines enforce the meaning more consistently: the two fallen captains, although in a distant place, share the companionship of the grave, rayed by transcendence; it is the survivor of the battle who is benighted and lonely. Whether it was the flabbiness of his metaphor or the insipidity of the second and fourth lines that led Hardy to revise the stanza totally, his changes solved both problems.

Hardy's struggle with a single brief line from the last stanza of "The Impercipient" illustrates his apparent desire to make the meaning clear with unusual language. The manuscript reads:

30

to unbe
I'd rather [not have be]

"Not have be" must have seemed insipid, while "to unbe" contributes a thrust of originality. For *Wessex Poems*, Hardy made a further revision, replacing "rather" with an archaism: "I'd liefer have unbe." Yet he ultimately must have felt that the negative coinage was too difficult, for he restored his first ending of the line in *Collected Poems*: "I'd liefer not have be." Here is the history of his struggle with the line:

I'd rather not have be (manuscript)
I'd rather to unbe (manuscript)
I'd liefer have unbe (*Wessex Poems*)
I'd liefer not have be (*Collected Poems*)

He finally relied on the archaism alone to give the line the desired bite of strangeness. Unlike many other late-nineteenth-century poets, Hardy characteristically employed archaisms to toughen his language rather than to evoke a sense of languid, nostalgic medievalism. This must have been one of the features of his poetry that attracted Ezra Pound, John Crowe Ransom, and W. H. Auden, all of whom mix diction in similar ways. E. K. Chambers' speculation in his review of *Wessex Poems* turned out to be an accurate prophecy: "the note struck is strenuous, austere, forcible; it is writing that should help to give backbone to a literature which certainly errs on the side of flabbiness. And this applies to diction as well as sentiment."[14]

The evidence of the revisions, then, suggests that Hardy was a careful craftsman, working toward a highly idiosyncratic, personal style. His wife made his intentions explicit when she wrote: "In the reception of this [*Wessex Poems*] and later volumes of Hardy's poems there was, he said, as regards form, the inevitable ascription to ignorance of what was really choice after full knowledge. That the author loved the art of concealing art was undiscerned." She noted the use of "cunning irregularity" in architecture and asserted that Hardy carried into his verse this "Gothic art-principle": "the principle of spontaneity, found in mouldings, tracery, and such

31

like—resulting in the 'unforeseen' . . . character of his metres and stanzas, that of stress rather than of syllable, poetic texture rather than poetic veneer; the latter kind of thing, under the name of 'constructed ornament,' being what he, in common with every Gothic student, had been taught to avoid as the plague. He shaped his poetry accordingly."[15]

Hardy's adherence to the "Gothic art-principle," to "cunning irregularity," and to "poetic texture" as opposed to "poetic veneer," helps explain his choice of "The Temporary the All" for the first poem in the collection. The revisions of the poem show Hardy moving toward precision of meaning in a boldly experimental style.[16] In changing "fellowly" to "fellowlike" for his *Selected Poems* of 1916 he made the meaning clearer and increased the weight of stress carried by the three syllables in accordance with his meter. His revision of "Fair not fairest, good not best of her feather" in the first edition to "Fair, albeit unformed to be all-eclipsing" in *Selected Poems* avoids an absurd metaphor and approximates more closely the chosen meter, but the result is an increased warping of the meaning; this may be a line he never managed to get right. Other revisions are more successful and indicate an intentional pattern. On the manuscript, the fourth line, "Friends interknit us," shows a canceled alternative: "interwove." In *Wessex Poems*, Hardy chose "interblent." He seems to have been satisfied with the syntax of the line, but not with metaphors presenting friends as separate people whose lives are knit or woven together. Rather, he seems to think of friendship as the blending of personalities into a new whole, in which the separate natures, now merged, are no longer identifiable, like strands of thread in a piece of fabric. Hence, his choice of "interblent," the more unusual of the three possibilities, seems dictated by meaning. Hardy later changed the line to "Fused us in friendship," with the effect of preserving the sense of blending and merging, and also of making clearer the syntactic relationship of the phrase to the rest of the stanza. "Fused" at the head of the line is unambiguously parallel to "Set" and "Wrought" as part of the predicate of "Change and chancefulness." While reducing the syntactic confusion, the new line adds to the number of heavily accented alliterative phrases that play such an important part in the laden rhythm and stately pace of the poem.

Hardy also changed "Tenement uncouth did I fain abide in" on the manuscript to "Tenements uncouth I was fain to house in" for *Wessex Poems*. The crux of the change lies in the difference between "abide" and "house," with Hardy preferring the Anglo-Saxon word in its archaic use as a verb to the ordinary Latinate word. The key words in the revised line are now the Latinate "Tenements," the archaic "uncouth" and "fain," and the common Germanic "house" employed verbally; the result is a richer texture, as opposed to a veneer. In other revisions, when the choice is between Germanic and Latinate diction, Hardy chooses Germanic. Hence, "Then achievement large" on the manuscript becomes "Then high handiwork" in *Wessex Poems*. Indeed, his revision of the penultimate line of the poem seems to echo the prosody of Germanic four-stress alliterative verse; he changes "They as tokens sole of my sorry earth-way" on the manuscript to "Sole the showance those of my onward earth-track" in *Wessex Poems*. The line breaks into two parts, each with two heavy accents reinforced by similarities in sound, a pattern found frequently in this poem, the only unrhymed one in the collection:

Change and chancefulness in my flowering youthtime . . .
Wrought us fellowlike, and despite divergence,
   Fused us in friendship . . .

 "Let such lodging be for a breath-while," thought I,
   "Soon a more seemly."

"Youthtime," "forthcome," "odds unbounded," "forefelt/ Wonder of women," "breath-while," "life-deed," "onward earth-track"—these words and phrases resound with the toughness and dignity of Anglo-Saxon alliterative verse. And yet, as Hardy informs his readers in *Selected Poems* (having characteristically refrained from exposing his intentions in *Wessex Poems* itself), the meter is intended to be Sapphic. Like Swinburne, he makes a conscious effort to write modern English poetry in a complex, classic prosodic form. Carl J. Weber pointed out Hardy's knowledge of Swinburne's *Poems and Ballads* in the 1860s.[17] In that volume Hardy must have read "Sapphics," which very likely may have inspired his experiment in "The Temporary the All." To put the first stanzas of

33

the two poems side by side is to ratify Hardy's success. The prosodic markings above the lines indicate the standard Sapphic meter:

All the night sleep came not upon my eyelids,
Shed not dew, nor shook nor unclosed a feather,
Yet with lips shut close and with eyes of iron
Stood and beheld me.

Change and chancefulness in my flowering youthtime,
Set me sun by sun near to one unchosen;
Wrought us fellowlike, and despite divergence,
Fused us in friendship.

This poem shows that Hardy could rise to Swinburne's standard and, indeed, exceed it. The final stanza is a masterpiece of prosodic adaptation:

Mistress, friend, place, aims to be bettered straightway,
Bettered not has Fate or my hand's achievement;
Sole the showance those of my onward earth-track—
Never transcended!

The stresses should be read almost exactly according to the abstract prosodic pattern.

In "The Temporary the All" Hardy presents his credentials as a rigorous poet, a master of prosody, and an inheritor of the classic traditions. Yet the poem echoes Anglo-Saxon traditions as well, with its accented alliterative groups, its Germanic compound words, and its reference to the "Fate" that governs man's progress down his "onward earth-track." The manuscript of the poem bears the words "(To be thrown out)" in light pencil in Hardy's handwriting. Later, however, he came to regard the poem so highly that he chose to open his first collection with it and then revised it for republication in the *Selected Poems,* a volume that included only a third of the verse he had printed up to 1916. In "The Temporary the All" he was displaying the achievement of a learned experimenter in poetic form and technique.

The Preface

One of the puzzles of *Wessex Poems* is the contrast between the diffidence of the Preface, which is a major novelist's introduction of his first volume of poetry to the reading public, and the boldness of the poetry itself. The Preface gives barely a hint of the cunning, the wit, the experimentation, and the seriousness of the volume that follows. In five ungainly sentences Hardy manages to be stiff, laconic, bewilderingly casual, and surprisingly naive. In the first paragraph, for example, he claims that in "some few cases the verses were turned into prose and printed as such"—as if the author of "Heiress and Architect" and "The Ivy-Wife" believed that verse could be turned into prose and prose into verse without seriously changing the effect. It is true that some of the poems echo identifiable passages in the novels, like "She, to Him, II," which was "Prosed in 'Desperate Remedies,' " according to Hardy's own words on the manuscript. And it is true that other of Hardy's statements and practices convey this same rather naive view of poetry, such as his avowed method of starting with metrical "verse skeletons" and then filling in the words, which may be a reference to "The Temporary the All." But as a thinker about the nature of literature, Hardy could be complex, apt, and sophisticated. For example, he once defined literary realism in a brilliantly succinct metaphor as "artificiality distilled from the fruits of closest observation." It is difficult to reconcile his claim of turning poetry into prose with his interest in organic form, expressed in an essay published ten years before *Wessex Poems,* or with his definition in the same essay of style as "treatment"—"something more than literary finish"—which "depends upon the mental attitude of the novelist" and therefore enters "into the very substance of a narrative."[18] In this definition Hardy recognizes the interdependence of form and content, but in the Preface he implies

35

the less sophisticated notion that poetry is merely the versifica-
tion of thoughts and feelings, which could be expressed
equally well in other ways. In the Preface he chooses to be
casual and amateurish.

The second paragraph of the Preface refers to the diction
used in the poems: "Whenever an ancient and legitimate word
of the district, for which there was no equivalent in received
English, suggested itself as the most natural, nearest, and often
only expression of thought, it has been made use of, on what
seemed good grounds." This statement, so humble and
restrained, has the effect of concealing the boldness of Hardy's
language in the poetry instead of justifying it. The awkward
passive voice, the complicated syntax, the ungainly paralleling
of "most natural, nearest, and often only" hardly lead the
reader to expect a felicitous use of language in the poems.
More important, the statement is a truism for if a word is the
"most natural" conveyance of a particular thought, the
grounds for its use are by definition "good." And the word
"seemed" is open to several interpretations. It could mean that
the grounds for Hardy's word choices once seemed good to
him but do no longer. Or it could mean that Hardy made his
choices merely because of their apparent rather than their
actual worth. The evidence of the revisions indicates the pains-
taking care with which he worked toward precision of statement, whereas the Preface conceals the magnitude of this effort.
Curiously, the vulnerable phrase, "on what seemed good
grounds," which so seriously undercuts the force of the sentence, does not appear in the manuscript; Hardy must have
added it shortly before publication as a final hedge in what
was already a bland, timid assertion. The statement can easily
be taken as that of an insecure amateur defending himself in
advance against anticipated objections to his work.

The third paragraph of the Preface is equally defensive and
awkward, and even more cryptic: "The pieces are in a large
degree dramatic or personative in conception; and this even
where they are not obviously so." Hardy seems to be absolving
himself of the views expressed in the poems, as he attempts
to do, in one form or another, in the prefaces to *Poems of the
Past and the Present* (1902), *Time's Laughingstocks* (1909), *Late
Lyrics and Earlier* (1922), and *Winter Words* (1928). One is asked
to see the poems as "dramatic," or, should there be any dis-

36

content with the familiar word, Hardy adds the awkward, idiosyncratic, ambiguous synonym "personative." The views presented in the poems are those of created characters, not the beliefs of the author, even when "not obviously so." However, this is so only "in a large degree." Apparently in some small degree the poems are not dramatic but do express the convictions of Hardy himself. "Hap," for example, might very well reveal the state of Hardy's personal feelings in 1866, and many scholars have read the poem in this way; by dating the poem in the collection, Hardy provided some sanction, if not provocation, for this reading. But then again "Hap" may be one of the "personative" pieces. Those who take Hardy at his word will be disarmed in advance, at least "in a large degree." Uncharitable readers might accuse Hardy of imprecision or insecurity. Or there is the possibility that he intended the impression of amateurishness given by the passage. Certainly the last paragraph of the Preface, which ascribes the inclusion of the pictures to "personal and local reasons rather than . . . their intrinsic qualities," is the statement of an amateur.

The Preface, then—so vulnerable to misinterpretation, so modest and self-deprecatory in tone, so graceless, amateurish, and defensive—contrasts strikingly with the bold idiosyncracies of the poetry. Indeed, the Preface might well dispose one to see as failure the assertive, complex crudeness of the verse instead of viewing it as the cunning of a highly original artist. This ambiguity has led to difficulties in deciding what to make of *Wessex Poems*. It is almost as if Hardy were two people: in his poetry he is the "heiress" to a multiplicity of traditions, his imagination confident of vision, his intelligence fired with wit, his heart throbbing with compassion; whereas in the Preface he is the "architect" building thick walls for self-protection by minimizing the boldness of his commitment in the poetry. Throughout his life Hardy felt this tension between the desire to commit himself and the desire to remain invulnerable. It is one of the prevailing themes of his poems, as it is of the novels. An examination of how the dilemma manifested itself in his life, and of how he attempted to achieve its resolution, can lead both to an explanation of why he abandoned fiction for poetry at the height of a successful career, and to an understanding of what he took to be the nature of poetic art.

ON POETIC ART
2

Hardy wrote in 1918, "The reviewer so often supposes that where Art is not visible it is unknown to the poet under criticism. Why does he not think of the art of concealing art?"[1] The poetry and drawings of *Wessex Poems* illustrate some of the complexities of concealment and revelation of the art in Hardy's work, just as his Preface shows an attempt to conceal himself. The extreme tension between the desire to conceal and the desire to reveal, to which Hardy was subject throughout his life, is directly related to his understanding of the nature of art and to his decision to abandon fiction in favor of poetry. His goal was to find a method of exposing himself without making himself vulnerable—of reconciling the way of the heiress and the way of the architect. He came to regard the dramatic form of literature as a means of achieving such a reconciliation, and when the hostility to his novels emanating from certain elements of the public became too great, he determined to withdraw to a safer mode than fiction, which he saw as being poetry. But his decision to write poetry did not constitute mere withdrawal. Poetry, for Hardy, permitted freer revelations in the guise of greater concealment; his withdrawal was a form of liberation. Writing poetry was a means for discovering and exposing what was most uniquely and idiosyncratically himself.

Poetry and Fiction

The best material for studying Hardy's shift of career is in the biography attributed to his second wife, Florence Emily, a book that in itself illustrates a strategic reconciliation between

38

concealment and revelation. The last of Hardy's artful, self-deprecatory comments about his own life—"He said that if he had his life over again he would prefer to be a small architect in a country town"—occurs in a curious appendage to the biography, "Notes by F. E. H." These notes, written by the alleged author of the whole book, stand as internal evidence of a fact also established on the basis of external sources: that Hardy either wrote or dictated most of his own "biography." Hardy's pose of personal uninvolvement is maintained consistently throughout the work. "His memoranda get more and more meagre as the years go on," writes the puppet biographer, "until we are almost entirely dependent on letter-references, reviews, and casual remarks of his taken down by the present writer. It is a curious reversal of what is usually found in lives, where notes and diaries grow more elaborate with maturity of years. But it accords with Hardy's frequent saying that he took little interest in himself as a person, and his absolute refusal at all times to write his reminiscences."[2] With amusing irony, his "absolute refusal" to write his reminiscences is recorded in those very reminiscences; the "casual remarks" could hardly have been casual; the "curious reversal" is no reversal at all. Hardy did take enough "interest in himself" to make his own version of his life public, but without acknowledging his responsibility for doing so. He reveals, but only under conditions that conceal the source of the revelation.

According to this biography, Hardy's first serious literary efforts were poems written in the 1860s. Unable to get them published, he turned to fiction at the end of the decade, and through subsequent years built up a reputation and earned a fairly prosperous livelihood as a novelist. This career he pursued until the mid 1890s, when he abandoned fiction altogether in favor of writing poetry, an activity in which he had been engaged off and on throughout his life. This history is indisputable; the biographer's explanation of the motives underlying the facts, however, must be called into question. The biographer contends that poetry was Hardy's first love, and that it was, in his mind, a form of art superior to fiction. In all likelihood Hardy did hold the conventional view of poetry's supremacy as literary art. He had read the classical poets and knew enough literary history to understand the novel's place as a popular new genre. "The scarcity of perfect novels in any language," he once wrote, "is because the art of writing them is as yet in its youth, if not in its infancy." But that he was haunted by a gnawing sense of fiction's inferiority and regarded the writing of novels merely as a means of livelihood is difficult to prove. The puppet biographer is nevertheless insistent in his attempts to substantiate this interpretation. Hardy, the claim goes, wrote novels mainly to earn money, and writing them became for him mere mechanical drudgery: "Hardy by this time [1886—the period of *The Mayor of Caster-bridge* and *The Woodlanders*] had quite resigned himself to novel-writing as a trade, which he had never wanted to carry on as such. He now went about the business mechanically."[3] Poetry, by contrast, he practiced as a faithful artist, free of all care and worldly ambition:

He would tell that it used to be said to him at Sir Arthur Blomfield's [an architect who was one of Hardy's London employers in the 1860s]: "Hardy, there can hardly have been anybody in the world with less ambition than you." At this time the real state of his mind was, in his own words, that "A sense of the truth of poetry, of its supreme place in literature, had awakened itself in me. At the risk of ruining all my worldly prospects I dabbled in it . . . was forced out of it . . . It came back upon me . . . All was of the nature of being led by a mood, without foresight, or regard to whither it led."[4]

This view of the difference between fiction and poetry seems retrospective in that it is always presented through the voice of the biographer; not one of the many quotations from Hardy's notebooks and letters written before his decision to abandon prose asserts that poetry was his first love because of its superiority to fiction. The note referred to (but not quoted) for 1880—"at the end of November he makes a note of an intention to resume poetry as soon as possible"—and his own note dated Christmas Day, 1890—"While thinking of resuming 'the viewless wings of poesy' before dawn this morning, new horizons seemed to open, and worrying pettinesses to disappear"—merely anticipate the resumption of poetry and express consolation at the prospect; they do not indicate any abiding preference for poetry over prose because of its artistic superiority.[5] At one point the biographer, in an attempt to

40

establish Hardy's early commitment to poetry, flagrantly mis-
reads a letter of 1874. The result is unconvincing:

> However, that he did not care much for a reputation as a
> novelist in lieu of being able to follow the pursuit of poet-
> ry—now for ever hindered, as it seemed—becomes obvious
> from a remark written to Mr. Stephen about this time:
> "The truth is that I am willing, and indeed anxious, to give
> up any points which may be desirable in a story when read
> as a whole, for the sake of others which shall please those who
> read it in numbers. Perhaps I may have higher aims some day,
> and be a great stickler for the proper artistic balance of the
> completed work, but for the present circumstances lead me to
> wish merely to be considered a good hand at a serial."[6]

The biographer has taken the letter out of context and given
it a false interpretation. Although the "higher aims" that Hardy
is willing to postpone may be a reference to writing poetry,
this is highly unlikely. The letter appears to be a direct reply
to Leslie Stephen's letter of 17 February 1874, not referred to
in the biography, in which he recommends certain revisions
in *Far from the Madding Crowd* for the sake of serial publication;
"When the novel appears as a whole," he continues, "it may
very well come in in its present form."[7] Hardy replies, repeat-
ing Stephen's phrase "as a whole," that he is quite willing to
make the suggested changes for serialization. More important,
the letter actually contradicts the biographer's interpretation,
for it is evidence of Hardy's ambition. There would seem to
be not much difference between a "reputation as a novelist"
—for which, the biographer contends, Hardy cared little—and
being "considered a good hand at a serial," for which, as the
letter shows, Hardy was "willing, and indeed anxious" to sacrifice artistic principles. It is true that the tone is casually self-
deprecatory, almost hypocritically so: Hardy cares "merely" for
a reputation as a serialist and "perhaps" will have higher aims.
But this tone is not surprising in a letter from an obscure young
novelist to a distinguished editor of the *Cornhill Magazine* who
had praised his work.

As Carl J. Weber convincingly showed, Hardy took his career
as a novelist very seriously: "This picture [from the biography]
of a young Hardy, uninterested in prose fiction but forced

'under the stress of necessity,' by 'circumstances not under his own control,' to write novels, is a picture which soon fades when exposed to the bright sunlight of fact."[8] The biographer's contention that poetry was Hardy's first love, much more interesting to him than fiction because of its artistic superiority, is part of a myth of retrospective self-justification pervading the biography. It is Hardy's view in the 1920s of a decision he had made in the 1890s. His actual reasons for turning to poetry must lie elsewhere, for there is clear evidence that Hardy regarded fiction as having high artistic potential. Indeed, he seems to have seen fiction and poetry as a kind of continuum, as two interrelated manifestations of the same high art. His views on fiction provide an excellent starting place for examining his reasons for turning to poetry, because they illustrate his attempt to reconcile concealment and revelation by means of art.

Hardy was not given to writing self-explanations and manifestoes, but his literary principles can be induced from the prefaces to his novels and from the handful of theoretical articles that he wrote about fiction. His most explicit statement of the artistic possibilities of the novel, titled *The Profitable Reading of Fiction,* appeared in 1888, when he had arrived at full maturity and was developing his ideas for *Tess of the d'Urbervilles* and *Jude the Obscure*—but when, according to the biography, he was nevertheless writing novels mechanically for profit. He begins by describing some of the trivial and peripheral benefits to be derived from reading fiction. The uncritical reader can always gain pleasure, relaxation, and superficial enjoyment. On a higher plain, one can learn from "accidents and appendages of narrative," such as "excursions into various philosophies . . . didactic reflection . . . trifles of useful knowledge, statistics, queer historic fact . . . specimens of the manners of good or bad society," and even "quotations from ancient and other authors." But novels that abound in benefits of this type are usually inferior—"the product of cleverness rather than of intuition"—and are not what a novel should be, namely, "a picture of life in action." A fully artistic novel is an organic whole and an objective dramatization of life, from which one can derive the highest profit. "Aesthetic training" is gained from studying the relations between the whole and its parts, and from experiencing the beauty of the total structure and organization: "to a masterpiece in story there appertains a beauty of shape, no less than to a masterpiece in pictorial or plastic art . . . Briefly, a story should be an organism." A critic should "inquire whether the story forms a regular structure of incident, accompanied by an equally regular development of character—a composition based on faithful imagination, less the transcript than the similitude of material fact."[9]

Because of their self-contained artistic wholeness, stories are "representations of life," which have the quality of "self-proof or obviousness"; they are not views "*about* life." Statements "about" something are apprehended intellectually, not with a fullness of human response. The words "picture," "representation," "exhibition," and "similitude," which are Hardy's images for story or novel, refer to a kind of creation that is "less susceptible of error than a disquisition," for it depends "upon intuitive conviction, and not upon logical reasoning." For example, the narrator of the Joseph story in *Genesis,* unlike "moralizing chroniclers . . . brings out a dramatic sequence on ground prepared for assent, shows us the general principle in the particular case, and hence writes with a force beyond that of aphorism or argument. It is the force of an appeal to the emotional reason rather than to the logical reason; for by their emotions men are acted upon, and act upon others." The reader, having participated in the objective drama of the story, undergoes what Hardy calls a "humanizing education." The writer has "acted" upon his life, forcefully but indirectly, through drama rather than statement. The more the writer can be faithful to his imagination—that is, the more he can dramatize rather than state—the more influential he can be with others. Hardy's note of July 1883, quoted in the biography, illustrates this kind of effectiveness: "Poetry versus reason: *e.g.,* A band plays 'God save the Queen,' and being musical the uncompromising Republican joins in the harmony: a hymn rolls from a church-window, and the uncompromising No-God-ist or Unconscious God-ist takes up the refrain."[10] Imaginative art raises the observer out of the realm of intellectual conviction into the realm of felt experience. The result is paradoxical: the persuasive force of fiction emanates from the refusal to attempt persuasion. Art conceals art. As Hardy wrote:

It may seem something of a paradox to assert that the novels which most conduce to moral profit are likely to be among those written without a moral purpose . . . the didactic novel is so generally devoid of *vraisemblance* as to teach nothing but the impossibility of tampering with natural truth to advance dogmatic opinions. Those, on the other hand, which impress the reader with the inevitableness of character and environment in working out destiny, whether that destiny be just or unjust, enviable or cruel, must have a sound effect, if not what is called a good effect, upon a healthy mind.[11]

Curiously, Thomas Hardy, who is so often regarded as an aggressive pessimist, using his novels to berate the gods, celebrates fiction for its high artistic potential of form and drama. Instead of describing it primarily as a vehicle for moral instruction or "good effect," he defines its benefits in terms of the expanding awareness and sensibility or "sound effect." His criticism of the poet William Barnes for using "the dramatic form of peasant speakers as a pretext for the expression of his own mind and experiences" results from the implicit application to poetry of the principles he held for fiction, and his statement that the Wessex poems are generally "dramatic" or "personative" in nature evokes these same principles.[12] Clearly, Hardy wished as an artist to refine himself out of existence in his art, to conceal himself by submerging his personal vision in "dramatic form." He knew that the result would be revelation on a higher imaginative level. During the late 1880s, less than ten years before his decision to abandon fiction, he viewed the novel as having high potential for such form, and he understood that matters of balance, structure, and dramatization were not the exclusive province of poetry. One must therefore be skeptical of the biographer's contention that Hardy turned to poetry because of a life-long conviction of its "supreme place in literature."

Poetry As Withdrawal

Hardy's notion, presented in the biography, of the superiority of poetry to fiction appears, then, to be a retrospective

myth—a self-justification—rather than a consistently held conviction. Yet he did prefer poetry, and he did decide to devote
himself exclusively to it at a crucial moment in his career. His
motives were complex. Like his understanding of dramatic
form, they reflect both a desire to conceal and a desire to
reveal.

The character of the biography, as well as a number of defensive postures assumed and described in it, illustrates Hardy's
desire to withdraw and to hide himself. On the surface, the
biography tends to belittle the importance of Hardy's life. It
includes records of petty illnesses, of social gatherings
attended, of people met and invitations declined. The effect is
to reduce the poet's career to the commonplace. The scheme
of organization is a simple, straightforward chronology, so
that whole sections degenerate into mechanical month-by-
month records of disparate events and observations, often so
trivial as to appear meaningless:

In January of the next year (1916) a war ballad of some weird-
ness . . . was published in the *Sphere* and the *New York World,*
and later reprinted in *Moments of Vision.*
In February he was again confined to his room with a
cold . . .
A *Book of Homage* to Shakespeare was printed in April, for
which Hardy had written a piece . . .
In June he served again as Grand Juror at the Assizes, and
was at a rehearsal in Dorchester of *Wessex Scenes from the Dynasts* . . .
In the same month of June he paid a visit with his wife and
remaining sister to a house he had never entered for forty years
. . . it was possibly this visit which suggested the poems about
Sturminster that were published in *Moments of Vision.* [13]

Yet scattered among these records are passages of significant
revelation. Hardy tells of his painful sensitivity, of his moods
of despondency, and of his awareness of social inferiority:

He loved being alone, but often, to his concealed discomfort,
some of the other boys would volunteer to accompany him on
his homeward journey . . . He tried also to avoid being
touched by his playmates . . .
"November 28 [1878]. Woke before it was light. Felt that I had
not enough staying power to hold my own in the world . . .

45

"The decline and fall of the Hardys much in evidence here-about [around Woolcombe] . . . So we go down, down down."[14]

Besides these explicit revelations, the biography implicity reveals the poses and strategies that Hardy adopted to shield his sensitive nature, to protect himself from despair, and to assert his superiority despite his lower-class origins. One was the pose of a simple, sincere child. He explains that when he was forty-five, his aspect "was almost childlike in its sincerity and simplicity."[15] Later he describes how usefully this pose of "simplicity" functioned:

None of the society men who met him suspected from his sim-ple manner the potentialities of observation that were in him. This unassertive air, *unconsciously worn* [italics mine], served him as an invisible coat almost to uncanniness . . . [When] he encountered other writers and critics and world-practiced readers of character, whose bearing towards him was often as towards one who did not reach their altitudes, he was seeing through them as though they were glass. He set down some cutting and satirical notes on their qualities and compass, but destroyed all of them, not wishing to leave behind him any-thing which could be deemed a gratuitous belittling of others.[16]

The man who wrote this passage about himself, or at least dic-tated it to his wife, could hardly have been unconscious of the mask he was wearing, and of its strategic advantages. His pose of being simple and blind protected him from the hostile recep-tion that he imagined would otherwise be accorded his intel-lect. The double satisfaction came from his secret knowledge of the concealed destructive power of his superior perception. It almost appears that Hardy is making a confession in this passage, a confession he could make only by means of a pup-pet biographer. A reminiscence by Charles Morgan, who as an undergraduate met and entertained Hardy at Oxford, shows that the complexities of his personality were not always lost on those who encountered him: "He was not simple . . . there was something deliberately 'ordinary' in his demeanour which was a concealment of extraordinary fires—a method of self-protection common enough in my grandfather's generation, though rare now."[17] That the biography quotes this revealing passage is remarkable.

Another protective pose adopted by Hardy was that of the scientific observer of one's own life. In 1881 he recorded his inability "to reconcile a scientific view of life with the emotional and spiritual, so that they may not be interdestructive," which was another version of the conflict between the heiress and the architect. His only philosophical solution was to condemn the injustice of the situation: "The emotions have no place in a world of defect, and it is a cruel injustice that they should have developed in it." Yet this judgment was of no help to him in the practice of living. He needed to achieve a mode of life that would take into account both the "scientific" and the "emotional" view. In terms of Hardy's own career, the question was how he as an author could commit himself publicly to visions of life, on the one hand, but avoid public criticism, on the other. One solution was to discipline his emotions and regard himself scientifically: "Be rather curious than anxious about your own career; for whatever result may accrue to its intellectual and social value, it will make little difference to your personal well-being. A naturalist's interest in the hatching of a queer egg or germ is the utmost introspective consideration you should allow yourself." Thus, the biography asserts again and again that Hardy was not anxious about his own career, although the insistent tone has the effect of revealing his deepest anxieties: "lack of social ambition . . . followed him through life"; "He was not so keenly anxious to get into print as many young men are"; "He constitutionally shrank from the business of social advancement . . . in which respect he was quizzed by [Arthur Blomfield] for his lack of ambition"; "His personal ambition in a worldly sense, which had always been weak, dwindled to nothing, and . . . he requested that no record of his life should be made"; "Of course there was no 'grim determination', no thought of 'laurels' "; and so on.[18] In the Preface to *Wessex Poems* Hardy wears this same mask of simplicity and unpretentiousness.

Related to the pose of the disciplined scientific observer is that of the ghost in "The Dead Man Walking" (*CP*, pp. 202–203):

I have attempted many modes [of finding value]. For my part, if there is any way of getting a melancholy satisfaction out of life it lies in dying, so to speak, before one is out of the flesh; by which I mean putting on the manners of ghosts, wandering in their haunts, and taking their views of surrounding things. To think of life as passing away is a sadness; to think of it as past is at least tolerable. Hence even when I enter into a room to pay a simple morning call I have *unconsciously* [italics mine] the habit of regarding the scene as if I were a spectre not solid enough to influence my environment; only fit to behold and say, as another spectre said: "Peace be unto you!"[19]

To the sensitive individual, the transitoriness of life is a cause for barely tolerable "sadness." Those who attempt to "influence" their environment, who regard life as a present reality to be dealt with through action, can never fully succeed and will suffer commensurate disappointment. In order to find value in life—that is, to live free of the disappointment of thwarted aims and the sadness of passing time—one must "die" and become an observant ghost, regarding the changing present, even its most meaningful events, as immutable past, something that cannot be influenced. Avoid involvement, Hardy implies; be merely curious rather than committed; observe rather than act—that is the safe, sure way. Even Hardy's definition of pessimism can be seen as a protective strategy: "A Pessimist's apology. Pessimism . . . is, in brief, playing the sure game. You cannot lose at it; you may gain. It is the only view of life in which you can never be disappointed. Having reckoned what to do in the worst possible circumstances, when better arise, as they may, life becomes child's play."[20]

Hardy's decision to abandon prose in favor of verse was in part an act of protective withdrawal—an attempt to play the "sure game." His writings of the 1890s and after often imply that poets are somehow less vulnerable than novelists. In a note dated Good Friday, 1892, Hardy describes the writing of novels as a way of voluntarily making a target of himself—a dangerous game indeed: "Read review of *Tess* in *The Quarterly* . . . How strange that one may write a book without knowing what one puts into it—or rather, the reader reads into it. Well, if this sort of thing continues no more novel-writing for me.

A man must be a fool to deliberately stand up to be shot at."
In his essay from the same period, *Candour in English Fiction*
(1890), he shows how the novelist makes himself vulnerable
to hostile attack if he remains true to his vision. Tragedy
always involves the violation of conventional morality, but
according to prudish critical mandate, "the crash of broken
commandments shall not be heard." Readers of fiction tend
not only to shun moral realism but also to misunderstand the
dramatic nature of all good stories: "A question which should
be wholly a question of treatment is confusedly regarded as
a question of subject."[21] Anyone writing novels in the face of
this restrictive understanding of morality and literary naiveté
might as well offer himself for target practice.

The poet, in contrast, seems less vulnerable. People appear
to understand that the main question in poetry is treatment,
not subject:

> Poetry. Perhaps I can express more fully in verse ideas and
> emotions which run counter to the inert crystallized
> opinion—hard as a rock—which the vast body of men have
> vested interests in supporting. To cry out in a passionate poem
> that (for instance) the Supreme Mover or Movers, the Prime
> Force or Forces, must be either limited in power, unknowing,
> or cruel—which is obvious enough, and has been for cen-
> turies—will cause them merely a shake of the head; but to put
> it in argumentative prose will make them sneer, or foam, and
> set all the literary contortionists jumping upon me, a harmless
> agnostic, as if I were a clamorous atheist, which in their crass
> illiteracy they seem to think is the same thing . . . If Galileo
> had said in verse that the world moved, the Inquisition might
> have let him alone.[22]

Poetry is a safer game, for the audience is generally willing
to forgive a poet his advanced views—if indeed there is an
audience: "The poet is like one who enters and mounts a plat-
form to give an address as announced. He opens his page,
looks around, and finds the hall—*empty*." And even should
there be a contemporary audience for a poet, only posterity
can judge his work: "No man's poetry can be truly judged till
its last line is written. What is the last line? The death of the
poet. And hence there is this quaint consolation to any writer

of verse—that it may be imperishable for all that anybody can tell him to the contrary."[23] Hardy could have as easily claimed that fiction cannot be "truly judged" during the lifetime of the novelist, but he chooses to ascribe this "quaint consolation" to poetry. The reasons are clear: he is creating a safe mode for his own career, one in which he can reveal himself without making himself vulnerable. The poet can "cry out in a passionate poem" whatever he wants, but few will listen, and those who do will merely shake their heads. Secure in this assumed knowledge, Hardy can devote himself exclusively to poetry.

Poetry As Revelation

J. Hillis Miller emphasized Hardy's desire to withdraw to a distance and conceal himself in order to avoid the painful results of intense involvement and commitment. He interpreted all of Hardy's writing, the novels as well as the poems, as an attempt to participate in life while remaining invulnerable. For Miller, Hardy's art "holds things at a distance and imitates in another pattern the objective patterns in the outside world . . . Such an art is at once a reaction to the external world, and a protection against it. It is a transformation of the reaction into a shape which imitates it at a distance." In Miller's view, Hardy remains throughout his literary work a spectator. Spectatorship itself, however, is one "mode of involvement," according to Miller. This form of involvement consists of artistic description and imitation—"objective recording of the way things are"—but not emotional commitment, and certainly not self-revelation.[24]

Yet in his poetry (and to a great extent in his novels) Hardy is not merely a spectator but an active searcher, attempting to penetrate the surface of things in order to expose and understand the inner realities. And the active searcher also exposes himself, for where he looks and how he describes what he sees manifest his values, his aspirations, his passions. There is evidence that in Hardy's view the withdrawal into poetry expanded the possibilities for greater involvement, deeper penetration, and fuller personal revelation. Having in his own mind freed himself from the demands of an ignorant public and from the pain induced by hostile criticism, Hardy felt liberated to search for what he took to be the inner realities of life, and to expose to its fullest potential his unique imagination. Indeed, it was the function of poetry, he came to believe, to probe beneath the surface and to reveal the idiosyncrasies of the artist. Both fiction and poetry could be "poetic" in this sense, but the historical circumstances of the late nineteenth century were such that, in his view, only the writer of poems could be fully poetic. Poetry thus became his means of triumphing over the impulse to withdraw.

For Hardy, certain areas of human experience came to seem more appropriate to literary treatment than others. In *The Profitable Reading of Fiction* he attacks the notion that novels should "depict life in the upper walks of society." This notion "proceeds from the assumption that a novel is the thing, and not a view of the thing"; that is, it confuses subject and treatment. The subject is unimportant so long as the treatment penetrates the surface of behavior to the permanent impulses of human nature, for "education has as yet but little broken or modified the waves of human impulse on which deeds and words depend," and "social refinement" has made "the exteriors of men their screen rather than their index."[25] Hardy wants to reveal the interior consciousness of men beneath the exterior screen, and he conceives of this sort of penetrating treatment as being "poetic." Indeed, he asserts in the biography that he had not written "novels proper," by which he means "stories of modern artificial life and manners showing a certain smartness of treatment." Instead, he had "mostly aimed at keeping his narratives close to natural life and as near to poetry in their subject as the conditions would allow."[26] He had tried to write "poetic" novels, but the "conditions" did not allow him sufficient freedom.

Certain evidence in the biography suggests that Hardy gradually developed the idea of the inner, emotional life as being the universal poetic subject of all literature. A number of notes from late in the 1880s show that Hardy was thinking increasingly often of the distinction between external, mechanical behavior and real, conscious life. A revealing sequence of related items begins with the biographer's statement that Hardy in 1886 "now went about the business [of novel-writing] mechanically." On the next page is Hardy's own note dated

December 1886: "I often view society-gatherings, people in the street, in a room, or elsewhere, as if they were beings in a somnambulistic state, making their motions automatically—not realizing what they mean." On the following page is another note contrasting appearance and reality in painting:

I don't want to see landscapes, *i.e.,* scenic paintings of them, because I don't want to see the original realities—as optical effects, that is. I want to see the deeper reality underlying the scenic, the expression of what are sometimes called abstract imaginings.

The "simply natural" is interesting no longer. The much decried, mad, late-Turner rendering is now necessary to create my interest. The exact truth as to material fact ceases to be of importance in art—it is a student's style—the style of a period when the mind is serene and unawakened to the tragical mysteries of life.[27]

This note is dated January 1887; a comment by the biographer for August of the same year relates the idea of mystery to "the difference between children who grow up in solitary country places and those who grow up in towns—the former being imaginative, dreamy, and credulous of vague mysteries; [Hardy gives] as the reason that 'The Unknown comes within so short a radius from themselves by comparison with the city-bred.' " Hardy's note of March 28, 1888, refers to the "fiendish precision or mechanism of town-life."[28] Finally, a note for December 18, 1890, describes the habit of mind of the countryman as being poetic:

Mr. E. Clodd this morning gives an excellently neat answer to my question why the superstitions of a remote Asiatic and a Dorset labourer are the same: "The attitude of man," he says, "at corresponding levels of culture, before like phenomena, is pretty much the same, your Dorset peasants representing the persistence of the barbaric idea which confuses persons and things, and founds wide generalizations on the slenderest analogies."

(This "barbaric idea which confuses persons and things" is, by the way, also common to the highest imaginative genius—that of the poet.)[29]

It is no coincidence that immediately following this passage occurs Hardy's Christmas Day, 1890, statement: "While thinking of resuming 'the viewless wings of poesy' before dawn this morning, new horizons seemed to open, and worrying pettinesses to disappear." In the late 1880s Hardy seems to have felt that the mechanical, external realities of life and nature conceal and repress the important inner realities. These inner realities are tragic and mysterious, as great artists like the "mad late-Turner" reveal in their art by penetrating the "original reality" of the surface. Life in the city tends to be mechanical, while in the country people are more imaginative; they acknowledge the tragic mysteries and the "Unknown" by confusing persons and things and "found[ing] wide generalizations on the slenderest analogies"; they, too, are "mad." In this respect country people are like persons of "highest imaginative genius," that is, poets. This line of thought, recorded during the period shortly before Hardy's decision to abandon fiction, complements his notion that the poet is less vulnerable than the novelist. The poet's safer, more secure position allows him greater freedom to penetrate imaginatively the inner recesses and explore the tragic mysteries of life. With relative impunity he can be "mad" like the late Turner, he can confuse persons and things, he can make the widest generalizations on the slenderest analogies, he can deal more directly with the "waves of human impulse" that are glossed over by traditional education and social refinement. Free of public pressures, he can function more fully as the imaginative artist.

Crucial to the ability to penetrate to the mysterious, tragic heart of the human consciousness is a fidelity to the artist's unique and personal mode of regarding experience. Faithfulness to reality means selectivity according to one's own idiosyncrasies, so that a work of art becomes a vision resulting from the complex interplay of the self and the world, from imaginative involvement rather than mere spectatorship: "As, in looking at a carpet, by following one colour a certain pattern is suggested, by following another colour, another; so in life the seer should watch that pattern among general things which his idiosyncrasy moves him to observe, and describe that alone. This is, quite accurately, a going to Nature; yet the result is no mere photograph, but purely the product of the writer's own mind."

Indeed, style results from idiosyncrasy: "A writer who is not a mere imitator looks upon the world with his personal eyes, and in his peculiar moods; thence grows up his style, in the full sense of the term." The more one is in tune with internal mysteries, the more one's "mental attitude" will enter "into the very substance" of his art. Paradoxically, withdrawal into the self results in revelation. Hence, Hardy came to admire most the art that most reveals the peculiarities of the artist: "I prefer late Wagner, as I prefer late Turner, to early (which I suppose is all wrong in taste), the idiosyncrasies of each master being more strongly shown in these strains . . . To-day it was early Wagner for the most part: fine music, but not so particularly his—no spectacle of the inside of a brain at work like the inside of a hive."[30]

What the artist reveals is the play between his own mode of regard and reality, not reality itself. "Art is concerned with seemings only," writes Hardy in his notes: "the views in [my works] are *seemings*, provisional impressions only"; "I hold that the mission of poetry is to record impressions, not convictions." The provisional character of these impressions means that there can be no final solutions. Hardy felt strongly that mysteries can only be acknowledged, not solved, that there are "certain questions which are made unimportant by their very magnitude." Nevertheless, these impressions do make up a kind of philosophy, define a mode of regard, and reveal a valid personal way of approaching things. As Hardy explains in the Preface to *Poems of the Past and the Present*, "Unadjusted impressions have their value, and the road to a true philosophy of life seems to lie in humbly recording diverse readings of its phenomena as they are forced upon us by chance and change."[31] The role of the poet, in Hardy's view, gave him the freedom to create such "humble records," which conceal by their tentativeness and their humility the magnitude of their revelation.

The Identity of the Poet

Hardy's practice as a poet and his theoretical justification for writing poetry enabled him to overcome certain shortcomings as a novelist. His discussion of the necessity for organic coherence in a story, and his distinction between objective statements and "dramatic sequence," relate explicitly to problems that were difficult for him to solve in his fiction. Again and again in Hardy's novels there are tensions, if not direct disparities, between the dramatic sequence of the story and the narrator's explicit understanding of it. Robert Heilman gave a detailed account of some of these tensions and disparities in *The Mayor of Casterbridge*. Sometimes, he pointed out, Hardy fails in full dramatization, and sometimes his narrator fails in interpretation: "Hardy functions in two ways—as 'editor' and as 'reporter,' as man of opinion and as artist—and . . . the two sides may be overlapping, supplementary, or inconsistent. When they are inconsistent, it is the dramatic picture that is trustworthy." What makes the novel valid is the drama of the story itself, not the narrator's impression of the story's meaning. Bernard Paris exposed a similar flaw in *Tess of the d'Urbervilles*, where the narrator presents a number of "conflicting value systems" as intellectual means for understanding the drama of the novel, none of which is fully adequate: "The novel has no real thematic core." Paris also found "an overarching unity of feeling and . . . a confused, inadequate treatment of theme." It is the unity of feeling that validates the novel. Hardy himself seems to have been conscious of his difficulties in integrating interpretation and drama. In his Preface to the first edition of *Jude the Obscure*, for example, he writes: "Like former productions of this pen, *Jude the Obscure* is simply an endeavour to give shape and coherence to a series of seemings, or personal impressions, the question of their consistency or their discordance, of their permanence or their transitoriness, being regarded as not of the first moment."[32] In this passage Hardy seems to be not so much asserting the dramatic nature of literary art as apologizing for the internal inconsistencies and discordances of his narrative. He seems to be confessing an artistic flaw.

When Hardy insists, in similar language, that his poems are "feelings and fancies written down in widely different moods and circumstances," "dramatic monologues by different characters," or "fugitive impressions," he is not so much apologizing for artistic flaws as asserting a positive explanation of his philosophical inconsistency.[33] Such statements usually occur in the context of defending himself. To accusations of being a pessimist, Hardy replies that there is no systematic philosophy underlying his work but rather a consistent attitude as to the nature of poetry. Novels, because of their length, require an overarching coherence of interpretative vision, which Hardy found difficult to achieve and even unrealistic to attempt. Hence, the "endeavour to give shape and coherence" to his impressions in the novels may have failed. It is almost as if the novel as a form was uncongenial to Hardy's understanding of the nature of experience. Because of their brevity, however, poems enable the writer to surrender fully to the temporary mood of the moment and therefore allow greater potential for exploring the resources of his personality and imagination. Poetry emerges from the interplay of the fullest and most diverse—even contradictory—internal resources for responding to the immediacies of the ever-changing, external world. It records moments of awareness distilled from the fluid, transitory consciousness of the poet, whose commitment consists in opening his resources to whatever experience is available at any moment at whatever the cost. The poet is freed from the demands on the novelist for sustained consistency.

The diction that Hardy employs in describing poetry indicates his difficulties in defining it precisely. The states of the poetic consciousness, the kinds of experience that it apprehends and assimilates, and the nature of its response defy fixed categorization. Although the interaction between the world and the consciousness may be discussed in terms like "mood," "vision," "idea," "fancy," "whim," "impression," or "readings of phenomena," no term is fully adequate. Hardy never finds the perfect word. Indeed, his sense of the variety and uniqueness of his own poetry leads to apparent discontent with the word "poem" itself, and in the titles of his volumes or subsections he continually uses different kinds of generic terms to specify his poetical works, such as: "Pieces Occasional and Various"; *Satires of Circumstance, Lyrics and Reveries;* "Miscellaneous Pieces"; *Moments of Vision and Miscellaneous Verses;* "A Set of Country Songs"; *Human Shows, Far Phantasies, Songs, and Trifles; Winter Words in Various Moods and Metres.* The implication is that each poetic work of his has a uniqueness which would be belied if the too common, too restrictive, too imprecise word "poem" was applied to it.

The poet's commitment, then, is not to a sustained interpretation of life, but to moments of experience and to the accurate recording of them. He must surrender to these moments and their artistic possibilities regardless of consequences. He must ignore rational consistency from poem to poem, must defy poetic and intellectual traditions if the mood so moves him, and must offend readers with his views if those views are felt responses to realities accurately perceived. When he writes a poem, he speaks not as a person with an ongoing, consistent, historical identity—the identity, relatively speaking, of the narrator in a novel—but as one who has felt the full weight of a transitory impression. As the speaker in a poem, his identity is defined by the nature of the impression and its means of conveyance, and may bear little relationship to any "real," historical identity: he writes "dramatic monologues by different characters."

This theory justifies the more playful or fanciful flights of the imagination that often occur in Hardy's poetry. But the theory also sanctions deeply serious modes, because a full response to the unique moment brings the poet's self into temporary focus. For a moment, the poet achieves a clear, fixed identity, crystallized from the surging, contradictory being of his consciousness, just as the Immanent Will, in one of Hardy's favorite images, manifests itself in the workings of perceived history. Identity, then, can be realized only by yielding fully to the affective weight of a given moment. At such a moment one becomes a reality—not the totality of what one could be, but a single aspect of that potential, made concrete by means of a specific response to an objective experience. For example, in the poem "So Various" (CP, pp. 830–832), Hardy describes twelve different and contradictory identities: an old man and a young one, a faithful lover and a man changing in affections, a fool and a sage, a happy man and a sad one, a slow, unadventurous man, and a bold, enterprising one, a man without sympathy and a man of compassionate goodwill. All these men are, in reality, the poet himself:

> Now. . . . All these specimens of man,
> So various in their pith and plan,
>   Curious to say
>   Were *one* man. Yea,
>   I was all they.

57

Despite the simplicity of the poem, there is considerable sophistication in the vision it expresses. In reality, Hardy suggests, there is no such thing as a fixed identity. The human consciousness consists of the potential for assuming a multiplicity of contradictory identities as time goes on and as the circumstances of life change. A person is only what he or she seems to be at a given moment, and there is no certainty that the identity emerging from the relationship between the consciousness and the circumstances of life at any particular time will become fixed and endure. Indeed, to demand consistency would rob life of its richness of possibility. Paradoxically, to be most stable is to be most flexible, and to have the firmest sense of values is to be most responsive to the exigencies of time: "the road to a true philosophy of life seems to lie in humbly recording diverse readings of its phenomena as they are forced upon us by chance and change."

Different Voices

Any attempt to understand Hardy's poetry must therefore begin with an acknowledgement of the distinctiveness of each poem. A comparison of poems as similar as "Discouragement," "Hap," and "The Sleep-Worker" illustrates the variety of voices and identities in Hardy's poetry. All are sonnets; two of them, "Hap" and "Discouragement," were written in the same period, the mid 1860s; and all are pessimistic in outlook. Yet in each poem quite different voices and quite different shades of meaning can be identified.

"Discouragement" (*CP*, p. 789), published late in Hardy's career but written much earlier, reads like a straightforward statement of fact:

> To see the Mother, naturing Nature, stand
> All racked and wrung by her unfaithful lord,
> Her hopes dismayed by his defiling hand,
> Her passioned plans for bloom and beauty marred.
>
> Where she would mint a perfect mould, an ill;
> Where she would don divinest hues, a stain,
> Over her purposed genial hour a chill,
> Upon her charm of flawless flesh a blain:

58

Her loves dependent on a feature's trim,
A whole life's circumstance on hap of birth,
A soul's direction on a body's whim,
Eternal Heaven upon a day of Earth,
Is frost to flower of heroism and worth,
And fosterer of visions ghast and grim.

To the extent that the literary term "tone" refers to the emotional quality of the speaker's attitude toward his subject, his audience, and himself, this poem is technically almost without tone, for the speaker has no attitudes. It is true that emotional qualities are implied in the relation between tenor and vehicle of the metaphorical figures employed, and the details described should produce emotions in the reader. The personification of "naturing Nature" as a mother "racked and wrung by her unfaithful lord" evokes emotions like pity, dismay, and discouragement. But the poem does not call attention to the "as if" quality of the personification. The speaker does not assert that the flaws in the natural world make him think of a well-intentioned wife tortured by a cruel, unfaithful husband. Instead, the main assertion is framed as an objective, impersonal description of what happens when one sees nature in such terms: "To see . . . Is frost . . . And fosterer." This formulation holds the speaker at a distance. One assumes that for him too the flower of heroism and worth has been blighted, and that he has had ghast, grim visions, but only because of his allegation that to see what he describes (and has therefore probably seen himself) will have such effects. The rigid organization of the poem tends to enforce the sense of tonelessness and objectivity. The regularity of the meter, the consistent end-stopping after the first line, the lists of parallel antitheses and parallel syntactic structures with balancing elements and key phrases often heavily stressed by means of alliteration—all these features tend to produce a sense of mechanical declamation. The speaker describes how discouragement is produced, while the author submerges his own feelings in metaphors presented as fact.

There is a remarkable difference between the objectivity of the speaker in "Discouragement" and the self-dramatizing posturing of the speaker in "Hap" (CP, p.7), a poem of the same period:

If but some vengeful god would call to me
From up the sky, and laugh: "Thou suffering thing,
Know that thy sorrow is my ecstasy,
That thy love's loss is my hate's profiting!"

Then would I bear it, clench myself, and die,
Steeled by the sense of ire unmerited;
Half-eased in that a Powerfuller than I
Had willed and meted me the tears I shed.

But not so. How arrives it joy lies slain,
And why unblooms the best hope ever sown?
—Crass Casualty obstructs the sun and rain,
And dicing Time for gladness casts a moan. . . .
These purblind Doomsters had as readily strown
Blisses about my pilgrimage as pain.

The speaker begins by positing what appears to be the most desperate metaphysical possibility of all—not simply a malign god but a "vengeful" one, a god not merely ill-intentioned but who bears a grudge that can only be satisfied by the speaker's suffering. He imagines this god as speaking in words dripping hatred, bitterness, and contempt, expressing his pleasure in the speaker's pain. Yet he explains that he could accept such a deity, because then he could die "steeled," "half-eased." But he would not merely die; he would "bear it, clench [him]self, and die," like a hero, not merely having suffered but having borne the suffering and endured. He would die only after a final, defiant, self-defining gesture—a clenching of the fist, a hugging of the body, or a doubling up in self-enclosure.

The sestet describes the speaker's reality, which for him is even more desperate than what he had imagined: "Crass Casualty," "dicing Time," and the "purblind Doomsters" have blighted his life. The question arises as to why he could not still bear it, clench himself, and die. His fate is still unmerited; he is still the victim of a force more powerful than himself. The answer is that he craves to be the object of specific ire, the victim of special intention. He imagines God as speaking to himself alone, not to all mankind. He prefers to think of himself on center stage, as not merely the leading actor but the only actor in a drama of vengeful injustice meted out by the all-powerful on a hero who endures, chooses his own moment of death, and refuses to be broken. The speaker elevates his whole life to the condition of high drama. He has experienced sorrow, lost love and shed tears, felt joy, and harbored "the *best* hope ever sown"; the course of his life has been a "pilgrimage." His phrasing relies on contrasting extremes, antithetical absolutes: "sorrow"–"ecstasy," "love's loss"–"hate's profiting," "gladness"–"moan," "blisses"–"pain." The final lines, which are clogged with consonants, syntactically contorted, and punctuated with metrically stressed plosives, employ Hardy's harsh style to express intensities of bitterness, hatred, contempt, and self-pity: "These purblind Doomsters had as readily strown/Blisses about my pilgrimage as pain." This is one of those poems in which the distance between the speaker and the author is difficult to gauge. Yet in my judgment no irony is intended in the speaker's view of himself, despite the overt self-dramatization. The poem produces an effect of exaggeration without parody; the reader is aware of ego, not egomania. The speaker's mode resembles the posturing of romantic heroism, in the tradition of Heathcliff, Manfred, and Eustacia Vye.

In contrast, the tone of "The Sleep-Worker" (*CP*, pp. 110–111) is that of an earnest, impassioned questioning:

> When wilt thou wake, O Mother, wake and see—
> As one who, held in trance, has laboured long
> By vacant rote and prepossession strong—
> The coils that thou has wrought unwittingly;
>
> Wherein have place, unrealized by thee,
> Fair growths, foul cankers, right enmeshed with wrong,
> Strange orchestras of victim-shriek and song,
> And curious blends of ache and ecstasy?—
>
> Should that morn come, and show thy opened eyes
> All that Life's palpitating tissues feel,
> How wilt thou bear thyself in thy surprise?—
>
> Wilt thou destroy, in one wild shock of shame,
> Thy whole high heaving firmamental frame,
> Or patiently adjust, amend, and heal?

The speaker here directs his attention outward. His focus is not on his own plight but on the plight of the sleep-worker, and the possibilities foreseen for action are not his, but hers. He addresses her with fondness, reverence, sympathy. His earnest prayerfulness is already established in the first line by the Biblical second person singular and the rhetorical repetition: "When wilt thou wake, O Mother, wake and see." Life is envisioned by him not in the absolutist, extremest terms of hope unblooming, joy blighted, and love lost; instead, the antitheses he sets up define the paradoxical complexities of existence—its enmeshment, orchestration, blending of fair and foul, right and wrong, song and shriek, ache and ecstasy. Life, though blunderingly contrived and chance-directed, is not bitter but "strange," "curious," and it moves the speaker not to defiant posturing but to questioning: When will you wake? How will you bear your surprise? Will you destroy, or will you heal? Although the language bears marks of Hardy's harsh style ("Strange orchestras of victim-shriek and song," "Wilt thou destroy, in one wild shock of shame"), the note terminating both octave and sestet is one of gentle, graceful eloquence, metrically regulated: "And curious blends of ache and ecstasy"; "Or patiently adjust, amend, and heal." The speaker expresses no pity for himself but implies compassion for "Life's palpitating tissues." His treatment of his particular purblind Doomster is sympathetic, since he assumes that she has the moral awareness to experience surprise when she discovers the unintended faults in her creation. This gentle, compassionate, curious speaker has a voice quite different from that of the posturing hero of "Hap" or the objective declaimer of "Discouragement."

"The Temporary the All"

Consistent with Hardy's theories about poetry, the identities of his speakers vary from poem to poem in terms of their attitudes toward themselves and their subjects, their range of emotions, and the ways in which they perceive and structure reality. To a considerable extent, even in the apparently overt, philosophical poems like "Hap," "Discouragement," and "The Sleep-Worker," Hardy does write "dramatic monologues spoken by different characters." Yet all of the statements are Hardy's own; all of the characters are manifestations of himself, structured as a result of the interaction between his special

62

imagination and chance or change. The temporary crystalliza-
tion of the self is the most that one can hope for; indeed, the
temporary is the all.

   The complex interplay of traditions in "The Temporary the
All" (*CP*, p. 5) establishes Hardy's credentials as a confident,
learned poet and helps to explain its prominent place in *Wessex
Poems*. But there seems to be a personal biographical revelation
in it as well, for Hardy is apparently announcing the intention
to change his career. In the poem, the speaker acknowledges
the power of "Change and chancefulness," which have provided him with a friend, a woman, a home, and significantly,
a "lifedeed," all of which fall short of his high aims:

> Bettered not has Fate or my hand's achievement;
> Sole the showance those of my onward earth-track—
> Never transcended!

The poem, which is "in a large degree dramatic or personative," presents a character who learns the painful, commonplace lesson that his temporary compromises make up his all.

   This poem was deliberately chosen by Hardy to launch him
publicly as a full-time poet. That he decided to begin his first
volume with a poem he had earlier intended to discard suggests not only a new recognition of the quality of the poem
but also a new understanding of its meaning. Of the first nine-
teen *Wessex Poems*, Hardy identifies by date all except the first,
and all come from early in his career. That he does not date
"The Temporary the All" is evidence that he may have wanted
it to be seen as a contemporary statement, namely, that by 1898
he had decided no longer to compromise with "Change and
chancefulness" as he had in the past by writing novels for a
hostile public. To date the poem, which was probably written
much earlier than 1898, would reduce the possibility of recognizing this personal interpretation. "The Temporary the All"
thus seems to be a concealed revelation of Hardy's intention
to transcend his enslavement to "Intermissive aim" by embark-
ing on a new career.

   Related to the possible biographical relevance of "The Temporary the All" is its thematic importance to all of Hardy's
poetry. The speaker in it awakens to a tragic awareness that

his life has consisted of a series of petty compromises, and the effect on him is disheartening. For the poet, however, this kind of awareness can be the basis for a new sense of freedom. The day-by-day involvement of the consciousness in life defines one's self. The alternative to grudging compromise thus becomes immersion and commitment. One can stand mute and bewildered in the face of endless, chaotic change, or one can exert one's imagination to fashion a concrete response. It may seem inconsistent to declaim objectively in one poem, posture defiantly in another, and question passionately in yet a third. But all three of these poems are not compromises with chance and change, but discrete, integral statements—selective, structured, eloquent, made by conscious choice. Paradoxically, the way to conquer the temporary is to make of it the all, to commit oneself for a moment to the way things look now, to achieve a moment of vision. Through poetry, Hardy fulfills his highest aspirations by embodying in poetic form and drama his impressions of life's "phenomena as they are forced upon us by chance and change." Bold, structured visions of the meaning of the temporary transcend the temporary; an active, informing mode of regard is the all; and the accumulation of coherently realized, provisional impressions is "the road to a true philosophy."

These visions reveal the deepest personal self of the poet. The harsh, contorted, curiously mixed language of "The Temporary the All" manifests the poet's uniqueness; it orchestrates the "spectacle of the inside of a brain at work like the inside of a hive." As Hardy himself explained, "Art consists in so depicting the common events of life as to bring out the features which illustrate the author's idiosyncratic mode of regard."[34] All art is concealed revelation of the self. Poetry, for Hardy, was the mode of art that provided the greatest potentiality for such revelation.

POEMS OF IRONY
3

Hardy maintains the greatest distance from his poetic world in the poems of ironic circumstance, which expose disparities between expectation and fulfillment, appearance and reality, rewards earned and blows received. Several of the *Wessex Poems* illustrate this mode. In "She at His Funeral," social norms prevent a dead man's mistress from wearing mourning and standing with his family, while, ironically, his relatives gathered around the grave wear black as an expression of the grief they do not feel. Time in "Her Initials" has preserved the record of a man's passion for a woman as an ironic reminder of a love now faded. In "To a Motherless Child" (*CP*, p. 58), "niggard Nature's trick of birth" has blended in the infant's face the features of the despised father as well as the beloved mother. Central to all of these poems is the exposure of a basic disparity, a fundamental irony, a trick of circumstance. Writing in this mode, Hardy guards his sympathies and withholds his judgment. He presents and exposes from a detached position, the effects ranging from chilling hopelessness to mordant comedy. This is reality, the poems seem to be saying, and there is little one can do to change it. Yet there are dangers in distance. Mordant comedy borders on nihilistic cynicism, and the poet who describes life's destructive ironies runs the risk of becoming a heartless accomplice in producing a sense of hopelessness.

Distance and Its Dangers

"The Conversation at Dawn" and "The Dame of Athelhall" deal, typically, with love and infidelity. Both present dupes

65

and victims caught in traps laid by circumstances and by their own illusions. The one poem, however, presents the situation as a hopeless dilemma, the other as a cruel joke, and together they illustrate the two major tonal effects of Hardy's poems of ironic circumstance. In "A Conversation at Dawn" (*CP*, pp. 344–350), one of the longest of Hardy's poems, light dawns for a husband as he provokes his newly-married wife into a troubled conversation. Their dialogue progresses remorselessly through a series of brutal disclosures. The wife, who has been cold toward the husband, is asked by him to explain her feelings. In her response, she refers to his kindly patience during the period of courtship—"In that late long spell of delays undue!"—and assures him that she recognizes his probity and generosity. "But you flung my arms away from your side,/ And faced the wall," says the husband. Revealing a certain imaginative sympathy, he asks if there might be another man, and after a pause, she confesses that she passionately loves a man bound by law to a wife who had deserted him and was then imprisoned for committing a crime. Unable to marry her lover and urged by friends to accept her present husband's offer, she submitted, after a period of vacillation, to the pressures of circumstance. Now, ironically, she has learned of the death of her lover's wife.

At this news, the husband suffers his first phase of disillusionment, expressed in one of Hardy's most oddly awkward lines: "So you've lost a sprucer spouse than I!" The wife causes him still worse pain by contradicting him: she has not lost the man, for she has received a letter from him renewing his vow to marry her. She pleads with her husband to release her, appealing to his view of marriage as "a plain event/ Of black and white." "So my idyll ends,/ And a drama opens!" says the husband. He might have been able to endure his wife's love for a more attractive man, but he takes her request for freedom as a sign of depravity. In response, his wife goes a step further and makes an even more damaging revelation: she and her lover had enacted a mock wedding ceremony, "A contract vain/ To the world, but real to Him on High," and then slept together. Hearing this, the husband "stood as stiff as a caryatid," only to receive the final blow: his wife's real reason for accepting his proposal was her fear of pregnancy:

"And to cloak it by marriage I'm not the first,
Though, maybe, morally most accurst
   Through your unpeered
And strict uprightness."

The husband replies:

"So, my lady, you raise the veil by degrees. . . .
I own this last is enough to freeze
   The warmest wight!"

Stunned by his wife's revelation, he announces that he will abide by his rigid moral principles. Since no one knows the story, he will claim the child if there is one, and he will coerce his wife into obedience. He draws her out of bed and forces her to kneel on the floor and vow fidelity:

"I'm a practical man, and want no tears;
You've made a fool of me, it appears;
   That you don't again
Is a lesson I'll teach you in future years."

The poem presents an irreconcilable dilemma. The wife is prevented from marrying her lover by a tangle of circumstances beyond her control. The perfidy of the lover's wife releases him from her morally, but his legal marriage makes illicit his relationship with the woman he loves. Her fear of pregnancy, the urgings of her friends, and the importunities of her suitor in effect force her into marriage. The unforeseeable death of the lover's wife enables the disastrous revelation at dawn, which she makes reluctantly only after her husband's urgings. Undeniably, his reaction is harsh. Yet the pressures on the wife were perhaps not so great that she could not have resisted them more forcefully. Her character seems a shade too submissive: "I was not brave!" she says. She lacks the courage to rebel against her husband and flee to her lover in the face of her husband's vow to "damn/ Opinion" and "fetch her" if she does. There is a note of defiant sarcasm in her calling herself "maybe, morally most accurst," but her own deception of an innocent man, regardless of the circumstances, is not necessarily less reprehensible than the crime of her lover's wife.

Although her husband is responsible for bringing about her confession, there is an unwitting cruelty in the way she lifts the curtain by degrees, so that a series of increasingly painful revelations culminates in a profound shock to his pride. She has taken advantage of his generosity and fidelity, the brighter side of his moral strictness, which was well known to her before marriage and which makes his reaction to her story almost inevitable. In the final analysis, she has made a fool of him.

The result is an impasse. As the last stanza indicates, husband and wife are locked into a condition of tortured stasis, of death in life. The husband has asked for no tears, and the wife sheds none:

> She answered not, lying listlessly
> With her dark dry eyes on the coppery sea,
>   That now and then
> Flung its lazy flounce at the neighbouring quay.

The effect is deep despair at the spectacle of life's crushing disparities, a state beyond tears. The narrator stands at a distance, exposing life reduced to a level of hopeless desperation.

In "The Dame of Athelhall" (*CP*, pp. 141–143), the combination of exaggerated diction and contrived, ironic plot helps to create a sense of mocking manipulation, in contrast to realistic exposure. The poem, in which a married woman, the Dame of Athelhall, leaves her husband to elope with another man, establishes its melodramatic tone in the first stanza, when she speaks to her lover:

> "Dear! Shall I see thy face," she said,
>   "In one brief hour?
> And away with thee from a loveless bed
> To a far-off sun, to a vine-wrapt bower,
> And be thine own unseparated,
>   And challenge the world's white glower?"

The archaic second person, the absolutist contrast between "a loveless bed" and "a vine-wrapt bower," the idealistic expectation of eternal union, and the conception of true lovers facing a hostile world—all contribute, a little too neatly, a little too

68

consistently, to the romantic heightening. While the lovers are fleeing to the coast, seeming hardly to touch the ground as they "[cleave] the air/ Upon whirling wheels," the woman has second thoughts, occasioned by a glance at a cameo portrait of her husband. Her soul feels a "twinge of teen," and she decides to return "To hinder household wrack!" After watching her lover's ship sink beyond the horizon, she goes back to Athelhall, where she secludes herself and assumes a self-dramatizing posture of repentance and grief: "And she stole to her chamber, there to grieve/ Lone, kneeling, in the gloom." The poem ends, however, with a crushing, ironic blow. While kneeling in her room, the wife overhears her husband on the lawn below celebrating her departure. As he explains to a friend, now he is free to marry his mistress:

"A quick divorce; she will make him hers,
      And I wed mine.
So Time rights all things in long, long years—
Or rather she, by her bold design!
I admire a woman no balk deters:
      She has blessed my life, in fine."

The ironies are blunt, symmetrical: unknown to one another, the husband has had his mistress, the wife her lover. Her sinful elopement is in reality a liberation for all four characters, and her return to morality is a final enslavement. Her admired boldness is overcome by destructive timidity, and her conscience is her undoing. Time, instead of righting matters, has made them worse, and the husband and wife face many years of tortured memories of what might have been. And yet, because of the symmetry of the ironies, the melodramatic exaggeration of language and situation, and the almost comic surprise of the final reversal, a half-humorous grimace rather than sympathetic identification seems to be the appropriate response. To a certain extent the wife is vain and foolish—vain in her self-dramatization and sense of self-importance; foolish in her sentimentality, her blindness to her husband's infidelity, and her lack of courage to carry out her own design. She dupes herself. To ignore the mocking, distancing effect of the exaggeration and contrivance is to take the plight of the Dame of Athelhall too seriously.

It would be a mistake to see Hardy's mode in these poems to be mere exposure. Both the husband in "A Conversation at Dawn" and the Dame of Athelhall have brutal tricks played on them, and each could have been presented in a different manner. Hardy could have emphasized the husband's illusions and exposed the folly in his stubborn pursuit of a reluctant younger woman. Instead, he shows how circumstances transform an essentially kindly man into a self-righteous oppressor, and a submissive young lady into a mercenary conniver. Hardy could have dwelled on the Dame's good intentions in returning to husband and household, and concluded the poem by drawing attention to the pathos of her plight. Instead, he emphasizes the crushing ironies of the situation and ends with lines that make a mockery of the Dame's illusions. The effect of life's ironies depends on how they are viewed; one can laugh, or one can cry. The poet who describes reality as he sees it shares responsibility for its impact on the reader. Distance is not neutrality.

The story-teller's shaping hand is most evident in the comic effects found occasionally in the poems of ironic circumstance —effects of which Hardy himself was consciously aware. In his "Apology" to *Late Lyrics and Earlier* (1922), he goes so far as to blame some of the critical abuse he had suffered on the inability of reviewers to gauge properly his intended tone: "There is a contingency liable to miscellanies of verse that I have never seen mentioned . . . I mean the chance little shocks that may be caused . . . by the juxtaposition of unrelated, even discordant, effusions . . . An odd result of this has been that dramatic anecdotes of a satirical and humorous intention following verse in graver voice, have been read as misfires because they raise the smile that they were intended to raise, the journalist, deaf to the sudden change of key, being unconscious that he is laughing with the author and not at him."[1] Commentators have seldom emphasized the humor in Hardy's poetry, partly because many poems are plainly ambiguous in effect. But Hardy sometimes works out the ironies with such methodical contrivance that a strange sort of corrosive humor seems unambiguously intended. "The Church-Builder" (*CP*, pp. 156–158), for example, an ironic monologue of a man duped by his own illusions, ends in a weirdly comic punch line. Having devoted his wealth to building a church to "glorify the Lord," the man suffers a reversal of worldly circumstance:

> But, as it chanced me, then and there
> Did dire misfortunes burst;
> My home went waste for lack of care,
> My sons rebelled and curst;
> Till I confessed
> That aims the best
> Were looking like the worst.

Even more disillusioning to him is the fact that his church enkindles "No burning faith" and "The deeper thinkers sneer and smirk,/ And give my toil no mind." Crushed by his lesson in the rewards of pious generosity, he determines, as an expression of final outrage, to hang himself in the church, "Midway 'twixt Cross and truss." But at the last moment he has a grimly playful thought, which confirms that the mode of the poem is black humor:

> Well: Here at morn they'll light on one
> Dangling in mockery
> Of what he spent his substance on
> Blindly and uselessly! . . .
> "He might," they'll say,
> "Have built, some way,
> A cheaper gallows-tree!"

Here there can be no doubt that the intended effect is mocking, mordant comedy.

The notorious " 'Ah, Are You Digging on My Grave?' " (CP, pp. 310–311) creates a similar effect. One by one the hopeful expectations of a dead woman are methodically crushed as she carries on a dialogue with an unknown person who digs on her grave. Her lover is not digging to plant flowers, the voice bluntly tells her, for "yesterday he went to wed/ One of the brightest wealth has bred." Nor is the digger her enemy, for the voice claims that the dead woman is now "no more worth her hate." When the dead woman discovers that the voice belongs to her little dog, everything seems to become clear:

"What feeling do we ever find
To equal among human kind
A dog's fidelity!"

But even this final illusion is destroyed by the dog:

"Mistress, I dug upon your grave
To bury a bone, in case
I should be hungry near this spot
When passing on my daily trot.
I am sorry, but I quite forgot
It was your resting-place."

The obvious contrivance of these poems plays a large part in releasing in the reader modes of humorous response—a sarcastic grimace, a mordant smile, a sardonic laugh. The ironies appear with such brutal insistence, and the expectations are overturned with such crushing regularity, as to suggest a deliberate method of exaggeration, a process of selection and manipulation. The narrator of these poems does not expose irony in life so much as he creates grim jokes on the basis of life's potential for irony, and he exhibits a propensity to dupe his listener. One can go along with this joke-teller, smiling at destruction, because the story is patently contrived. Hardy's exaggerated use of certain literary modes and conventions adds to the sense of conscious manipulation. In " 'Ah, Are You Digging,' " for example, he uses the ballad convention of a voice from the grave, which allows a symmetrical pattern of question and answer and creates a fantasy situation. A. E. Housman employs the same convention in "Is My Team Ploughing," in which the protagonist learns in a gentle way that he has been forgotten: "She lies not down to weep:/ Your girl is well contented."[2] Hardy pushes the lesson to an absurd and painful extreme, which creates the effect of parody. He not only dramatizes the ironies of infidelity but also undercuts, by means of exaggeration, a literary convention for dramatizing such ironies. His play with artifice contributes to the reader's freedom to smile at an otherwise grim situation in the poem.

There is something discomfiting about the humor in these poems. It may be that, by mocking human illusions and weaknesses, they help to guide the reader toward a sustaining breadth of vision. From his broader perspective, the reader may see more than the deluded and entrapped characters can see. But there is the danger that readers may take the lessons learned by the characters as the ultimate messages of the poems. The church-builder decides that his life is futile, and he dies making a joke of his own self-inflicted death. The lady calling earnestly from the grave learns that fidelity is to be found nowhere, not even in the heart of man's best friend. One might legitimately conclude that these poems expose the folly of believing in anything and the vanity of all human wishes. They may in fact make a mockery of all life. Hardy's comic mode often approaches nihilistic cynicism, a dangerously dehumanizing way of looking at things, as Hardy himself was aware: "All tragedy is grotesque—if you allow yourself to see it as such," he wrote in a note in the biography. "A risky indulgence for any who have an aspiration towards a little goodness or greatness of heart!"[3]

Even in the ironic poems that are unambiguously serious in tone there is often such a straining to make the tricks of change and chance brutally clear that the poet seems to be a willing accomplice in the grim joke. The iron logic of circumstance in "A Conversation at Dawn" locks the characters into a condition of hopelessness, and the irrevocable disclosures of the dialogue allow for no way out; the effect is desperation without purgation, suffering without tears. There are bitter energies expressed in the poems of ironic circumstance, manifested in crudeness of language, a heavy-handed balance and antithesis, and the remorseless presentation of contrasting, mutually canceling values and perspectives. One example is "She at His Funeral" (CP, p. 10):

> They bear him to his resting-place—
> In slow procession sweeping by;
> I follow at a stranger's space;
> His kindred they, his sweetheart I.
> Unchanged my gown of garish dye,
> Though sable-sad is their attire;
> But they stand round with griefless eye,
> Whilst my regret consumes like fire!

Here the victim of social custom, consumed by regret, cries out in anguish. The whole poem seems colored in a "garish dye."

The writer who conceived the situation and shaped the poem is not merely describing things as they are but assists energetically in conveying an effect of passionate hopelessness. His creation both draws attention to the pain of victimization and, in its cutting symmetries, suggests a certain niggardly withholding of sympathy. Time and circumstance play a cruel trick, and the poet, in exerting himself to explain the joke, somehow becomes an accomplice.

"The Slow Nature" (CP, pp. 61–62) mixes together both tonal modes of Hardy's ironic poems, grim comedy and chilling desolation. The tragedy has its grotesque side, which leaves the detached observer torn between the impulse to laugh and the impulse to cry. In the poem, a woman is told of the accidental death of her husband. Because the messenger is Kit Twink, the town jester, she thinks the news is a joke and responds accordingly. Circumstances not only blight her life; they also trick her into outright laughter at her husband's death. After she has "gazed and gazed" at Kit, however, at that "face which had long deceived," she sees the truth. But even then her reaction is petty: "O my chamber's untidied, unmade my bed,/ Though the day has begun to wear!" She worries about what the neighbors will think when they visit to express their sympathy. When she bustles off to clean up her house, Kit remains behind, depressed by his neighbor's death and by the wife's trivial reaction. As the last stanza indicates, the wife soon experiences the full impact of her loss:

> But a fortnight thence she could take no food,
> And she pined in a slow decay;
> While Kit soon lost his mournful mood
> And laughed in his ancient way.

The poem ends by focusing on a man who regards life as a laughing matter, a view that is in part justified by the situation. Yet the desolation of the woman's plight makes laughter inappropriate. The narrator remains at a distance, leaving the reader uncertain as to how to respond. This puzzling effect is achieved again and again in Hardy's poems, but most notably in the "Satires of Circumstance."

74

Satires of Circumstance

Hardy developed the mode of reductive irony into a compressed, pointed form. It is best illustrated by his "Satires of Circumstance," a coherent group of fifteen poems, none longer than twenty-two lines, appearing in the 1914 volume of the same title. In these poems ironies jar, perspectives clash, humor blends with pathos, and the reader remains puzzled as to the proper final response. The poems portray characters ironically caught in hopeless traps: the husband in "At Tea" (CP, p. 391) married to a woman not of his choice and tormented by a visit from his first love; the newlyweds of "In the Nuptial Chamber" (CP, p. 395–396) trapped by their shared knowledge that the wife prefers another man—"And it's he I embrace while embracing you"; the speaker of "In the Moonlight" (CP, p. 398) haunted by his love for a woman now dead, "Whom during her life I thought nothing of."

"In the Room of the Bride-Elect" (CP, pp. 392–393) illustrates the curious humor found in many of the "Satires." Ironically, the bride-elect, who is about to marry the man of her choice, berates her parents for having allowed her to go her own way. She accuses them bitterly of not having been forceful enough in imposing their will on her:

> "But Father and you should have stood out strong!
> Since then, to my cost, I have lived to find
> That you were right and that I was wrong;
> This man is a dolt to the one declined. . . .
> Ah!—here he comes with his button-hole rose.
> Good God—I must marry him I suppose!"

The humorous detail of the button-hole rose characterizes the groom's doltishness, a trait now seen too late by the angry bride. Although she has superior insight into the situation, she resigns herself to the fate of her own choosing.

In contrast, "At the Altar Rail" (CP, p. 395) presents a man who is freed amusingly from the jaws of the trap before they close. An ignorant farmer, he is jilted at the last minute by the loose town woman he is about to marry. The telegram that the selfish woman sends to the man has the effect of humiliating him by exposing his naiveté:

" 'It's sweet of you, dear, to prepare me a nest,
But a swift, short, gay life suits me best.
What I really am you have never gleaned;
I had eaten the apple ere you were weaned.' "

Although this is the kind of message that the recipient ought to keep to himself, Hardy further reveals the simplicity of the duped farmer by having him read it to a friend. Thus, he is freed from the trap, but the last laugh is on him.

Hardy's mode of reductive satire characterizing most of these poems dominates "In the Cemetery" (*CP*, pp. 393–394). Its effect is to undermine all the value systems invoked. The situation is morbid, the tone mordant:

"You see those mothers squabbling there?"
Remarks the man of the cemetery.
"One says in tears, ' 'Tis mine lies here!'
Another, 'Nay, mine, you Pharisee!'
Another, 'How dare you move my flowers
And put your own on this grave of ours!'
But all their children were laid therein
At different times, like sprats in a tin.

"And then the main drain had to cross,
And we moved the lot some nights ago,
And packed them away in the general foss
With hundreds more. But their folks don't know,
And as well cry over a new-laid drain
As anything else, to ease your pain!"

Mothers of dead children are reduced to trivial squabblers. Their loyalty and love take the form of petty bickering over a plot of ground. The word "Pharisee," hurled in violent insult, evokes a context of Biblical values which, by contrast, further reduces and trivializes the actors in the poem. That requirements for a sewer line take precedence over the sanctity of the grave exposes the callousness of social values and the modern abandonment of traditional belief. Yet the cemetery man's moral, spoken in the last two lines, contains an element of wisdom running counter to traditional belief. Pain at bereavement is an ineradicable fact, and it is outlandish to think that tears wept over a dead body can make any difference. The cemetery man himself, however, is also undercut. His comic disrespect for the dead evidenced in the phrase "like sprats in a tin" is not admirable, and his final statement exposes a lack of human sympathy. To be wise in the way of the detached mocker is to fail in humanity. The poem thus portrays human callousness and pettiness, reduces profound feelings to trivial possessiveness, undermines the validity of traditional social customs, and shows the inhumanity of objective wisdom. In a skewed way, the mode is satirical.

The "Satires" as a whole exhibit this twisted character and illustrate what the biographer seems to be referring to when describing Hardy's humor as "Swiftian."[4] The "Satires" expose human folly and vanity, the petty vices and trivial pretentions of man, his blindness to reality, and the short-sightedness of his self-centered aims. These are among the traditional materials of satire, but what sets Hardy's mode apart is the absence of any clear moral perspective enabling the satirist, secure in his own belief, to manifest a confident attitude toward what he exposes. There is no moral outrage at human failings, no prevailing sense of ridicule, no sane laughter at a world gone mad. As a result, Hardy's dramas of trapped humans entangle the reader in disturbing quandaries. If one could merely laugh at the absurdities or feel outrage at the moral weakness and short-sightedness, one would himself be free; but laughter and pity intermingle in the reader, dividing his sympathies. To participate in the perplexities is to involve oneself in the world being exposed and to become oneself a victim of its ironies.

"In Church" (CP, pp. 391–392), for example, exposes the vanity of a preacher, a common satiric theme, by describing his enactment before a mirror, after delivering his sermon, of "Each pulpit gesture in deft dumb-show/ That had moved the congregation so." The ridicule potential in the scene is complicated by the point of view of the poem, for a young girl—"a pupil of his in the Bible class,/ Who adores him as one without gloss or guile"—sees, through a half-opened door, the preacher's reenactment of his successful gestures. The vanity of the preacher is ridiculous, yet it causes the disillusionment of a child. To laugh at the preacher is to be callous toward his pupil, for from the child's point of view, the vanity is no laughing matter. Yet to refrain from laughter is to deny oneself the appropriate response to vanity. Moral outrage, one possible reaction, would seem to be excessive, for the speaker's failing is pettiness, "gloss or guile," not malice. Pathos and ridicule are a jarring combination, which seems to deny any adequate, comprehensive perspective on the situation.

This destructive conflict of perspectives is evident in most of the "Satires." "In the Study" (*CP*, pp. 394–395) exposes the pathetic attempts of a genteel spinster, the daughter of a poor, deceased clergyman, to conceal her poverty. On a mission to sell some of her father's books, she makes light of the task:

> And lightly still she laughs to him,
> As if to sell were a mere gay whim,
> And that, to be frank, Life were indeed
> To her not vinegar and gall.

The pathetic old lady demands sympathy, yet Hardy exposes the vanity of her desire to preserve appearances, as well as the futility of her attempt. It is hard to know how to react to such a woman. Significantly, the poem ends before the lady's host either speaks or acts.

In "At a Watering-Place" (*CP*, p. 393) a man tells his friend, as they watch a newly married couple on the esplanade, of his former intimacies with the bride. He concludes, "Well, bliss is in ignorance: what's the harm!" The reader sees not only the deceptions of the wife and the naiveté of the husband, but also the callousness of the speaker, who exposes his own lack of humanity by telling the story and bringing down ridicule on the unknowing husband. Yet the speaker's point has some validity, for if the newlyweds love each other in the present, the past does not matter.

It is difficult, then, to gauge the effect as a whole of the "Satires of Circumstance." Hardy's mode in them seems to be to establish a distant place from which human beings appear as benighted, vain, and petty, tangled foolishly in a web of laughable circumstance; yet the characterizations of the cemetery man and the speaker in "At a Watering-Place" show that detached wisdom is also a form of inhumanity. Hardy's guilt at the publication of the group, described by the biographer, indicates explicitly his awareness of the moral dangers inherent in a detached, ironic stance: "These ["Satires of Circumstance"] were caustically humorous productions which had been issued with a light heart before the war. So much shadow, domestic and public, had passed over his head since he had written the satires that he was in no mood now to publish humour or irony, and hence he would readily have suppressed them if they had not already gained such currency from magazine publication."[5] But the group cannot be taken merely as the series of bold, grim jokes that Hardy seems to have thought it was. Characters like the disillusioned child, the poor spinster selling her dead father's books, and the workman realizing too late his love for a dead woman are pathetic figures, demanding sympathy despite their failings. Significantly, Hardy does not sustain a consistently detached, satiric stance, but to the extent that he thinks he does, he feels guilty. His more usual attitude toward the characters in his poetry is one of sympathetic involvement, which often produces ironies that are benign and instructive in their effects.

Instructive Ironies

One of the oddest and most contrived of Hardy's extended satires of circumstance is "The Satin Shoes" (*CP*, pp. 387–389), which appears a few poems before the "Satires of Circumstance" group at the end of the 1914 collection. It tells the story of a country girl with one desire in life:

> "If ever I walk to church to wed,
>   As other maidens use,
> And face the gathered eyes," she said,
>   "I'll go in satin shoes!"

Unfortunately, on her wedding day it rains. " 'A coach would be required!' " to carry her down the muddy lanes to church, she exclaims, and in the absence of such luxury, "For thickest boots the shoes were doffed." Thereafter she gradually declines into madness, obsessed with disappointment, and eventually a coach does come, one to carry her off to the madhouse. She refuses, however, to enter it, until the madhouse man ingeniously allows her to wear her satin shoes. In a moment of grotesque irony, the "madhouse man smiled pleasantly/ To see the wile succeed." The poem does not explore the causes of the girl's wishes, nor is there any hint of the folly of vanity or the perniciousness of fashion. Rather, it portrays the odd pathos of obsession and the mystery of a wasted life.

Other poems about country girls illuminate the ironies of "The Satin Shoes." In "From Her in the Country" (*CP*, p. 217) for example, a "rural maid" makes an amusing confession:

> I thought and thought of thy crass clanging town
> To folly, till convinced such dreams were ill,
> I held my heart in bond, and tethered down
> Fancy to where I was, by force of will.
>
> I said: How beautiful are these flowers, this wood,
> One little bud is far more sweet to me
> Than all man's urban shows; and then I stood
> Urging new zest for bird, and bush, and tree;
>
> And strove to feel my nature brought it forth
> Of instinct, or no rural maid was I;
> But it was vain; for I could not see worth
> Enough around to charm a midge or fly,
>
> And mused again on city din and sin,
> Longing to madness I might move therein!

In "The Ruined Maid" (*CP*, pp. 145–146), another girl, more blissfully naive than the speaker in "From Her in the Country," meets a former friend in town, who is dressed, as the girl points out, in " 'fair garments . . . gay bracelets and bright feathers.' " The friend speaks in newly polished language and exhibits a new-found liveliness of temperament. Her explanation for her change in life is simple: " 'O didn't you know I'd been ruined?' said she." The poem concludes:

> —"I wish I had feathers, a fine sweeping gown,
> And a delicate face, and could strut about Town!"—
> "My dear—a raw country girl, such as you be,
> Cannot quite expect that. You ain't ruined," said she.

In contrast to the caustic ironies of Hardy's satires, the humor in "From Her in the Country" and "The Ruined Maid" seems benign. The speakers display a certain constructive naiveté, an endearing hopefulness based on limited vision. One is amused by the rural maid's conscientious efforts to arouse in herself an "instinct" for nature, and by the reversal of the Wordsworthian ideal. There is also poignancy in her impassioned desire to escape to the town in view of the part played by wretched slums, faulty sewers, crime, drunkenness, and prostitution in the urban "din and sin" of Victorian England for which she longs. The ingenuous pride of the "ruined" maid shows a level of sophistication only slightly advanced over that of her ignorant and surprised friend; clearly, she has not yet suffered actual ruination. Both poems assume on the part of the reader a fuller knowledge than that possessed by any of the speakers, a higher state of sophistication, a broader perspective. The author stands at a distance, confidently assessing the meaning of what he sees and smiling benignly. Significantly, both poems were written in 1866, during the period of Hardy's youthful residence in London, and for both of them Hardy identifies the place of composition, Westbourne Park Villas. He writes confidently and sympathetically of the contrast between country and town life from the broader perspective of his London address.

Although "The Ruined Maid" is on the whole fantastical, there is an important note of instructive realism in it, for the girl has really improved her status. "You left us in tatters, without shoes or socks,/ Tired of digging potatoes, and spudding up docks," her friend says, pointing out that her hands had been "like paws" and her face "blue and bleak." In this context, one might ask what charm a rural maid could be expected to find in the life of peasants struggling in an environment of subsistence wages and uncertain harvests, who were increasingly uprooted by a changing tenancy system, scientific agriculture, and the gradual industrialization of the hinterlands—the kind of life imaged in *Tess of the d'Urbervilles* by Marlott and Flintcomb Ash as opposed to the idyllic Valley of the Great Dairies. It is less easy for the sophisticated city-dweller to smile at the naive longings of rural maidens once he comes to understand what life in the country is really like. The desire for greater freedom and economic security—a realistic element in the longing for the city—was in Hardy's mind a valid urge, despite its destructive consequences for the old order. "That seclusion and immutability, which was so bad for their [the peasants'] pockets, was an unrivalled fosterer of their personal charm in the eyes of those whose experiences had been less limited," writes Hardy in his essay *The Dorsetshire Labourer* (1883). "But the artistic merit of their old condition is scarcely a reason why they should have continued in it when other communities were marching on so vigourously towards uniformity and mental equality . . . They are losing their individuality, but they are widening the range of their ideas, and gaining in freedom. It is too much to expect them to remain stagnant and old-fashioned for the pleasure of romantic spectators."[6]

This line of reasoning helps to justify the intense disappointment of the peasant girl in "The Satin Shoes." Her wedding day was to be the one occasion in her life when she would transcend her benighted rural condition and set herself off from "other maidens." When the rain forces her to wear the "thickest boots" of the peasantry, it drives home once again the lesson that people in her station cannot afford coaches even when they get married; she is able to ride in style only when a social institution sends to have her incarcerated. Seen in this light, "The Satin Shoes" rests in part on a sense of injustice and includes a submerged element of social protest. It seems not only to dwell on the pathetic irony of one particular blighted life, but also to convey instruction in the general condition of rural maidens.

There is further evidence for this point. The irony in Hardy's poems of the countryside frequently results from the contrast between an unrealistic, limited view of rural life—romantic or pastoral idealism, or an Olympian condescension—and a broader, more realistic view. Sometimes the effect is explicit. "The Milkmaid" (*CP*, pp. 143–144), for example, begins with a harmonious picture of a gentle maid milking her cow "Under a daisied bank" and invokes the romantic viewpoint of pilgrims who come into the country for contact with pastoral nature: "Few pilgrims but would choose/ The peace of such a life in

such a vale." The peace, however, is broken by an exclamation
from the girl:

> The maid breathes words—to vent,
> It seems, her sense of Nature's scenery,
>   Of whose life, sentiment,
> And essence, very part itself is she.

But expectations are reversed when she "lets escape a tear,"
showing that she is not happy. A cause for her unhappiness
immediately suggests itself: "Is it that passing train,/ Whose
alien whirr offends her country ear?" Again, expectations
prove false:

> Nay! Phyllis does not dwell
> On visual and familiar things like these;
>   What moves her is the spell
> Of inner themes and inner poetries:

> Could but by Sunday morn
> Her gay new gown come, meads might dry to dun,
>   Trains shriek till ears were torn,
> If Fred would not prefer that Other One.

The humorous irony implicit in the use of the pastoral name
Phyllis is obvious. She would be happy with the railroad if
it only meant that her gown would be delivered on time.
Involved as she is in sexual competition, she is indeed a "very
part" of nature, but not in the sense intended by the pilgrims
to the countryside. From their point of view, her "inner themes
and inner poetries" are quite unpoetic. Here Hardy explicitly
contrasts, with ironic effect, the romantic, pastoral view of the
milkmaid with the actualities, thereby broadening one's understanding of nature and poetry. The ironies instruct the reader.

A similar contrast between pastoral and realistic conceptions
of the country is implicit in "The Satin Shoes." Hardy provides
an idyllic description of the girl in the second stanza, which
he repeats almost word for word in the last, where it resonates
ironically:

> Yet she was fair as early day
>   Shining on meads unmown,
> And her sweet syllables seemed to play
>   Like flute-notes softly blown.

To look closely at the Arcadian countryside is to find fair, sweet-voiced shepherdesses who are profoundly discontented with the thick boots, muddy lanes, potato digging, calloused hands, and weatherbeaten skin associated with their real life close to nature. It is to see them occasionally driven mad when their innocent aspirations for a more elegant, graceful status are thwarted by their reduced social and economic situations or the elements of nature. The ironies in these poems, emanating as much from a sense of injustice as from a sense of absurdity, have the effect of dispelling romantic illusions, focusing on realities, and arousing compassion. In that they define an area of reality worth contemplating and reveal its significant aspects, they instruct rather than destroy. One may occasionally smile at the ingenuous country maidens, but the corrosive laugh is unwarranted.

A more elaborate picture of the countryside is presented in *The Dorsetshire Labourer*, which begins with a direct attack on the pessimistic view of the rural scene. Its initial rhetorical tactic is to posit a sophisticated Londoner on a visit to Dorsetshire who expects to find a community of "Hodges"—dull-witted, oppressed drudges. What he discovers is that there is no Hodge, but instead a diverse group of individual people: "He [Hodge] has become disintegrated into a number of dissimilar fellow-creatures, men of many minds, infinite in difference; some happy, many serene, a few depressed; some clever, even to genius, some stupid, some wanton, some austere; some mutely Miltonic, some Cromwellian." That is, the countryside is as diverse as life itself. For the educated man of wide perspective who goes to it to find differences from the great world he knows, the differences turn out to be merely superficial. In its essential diverseness and complexity, life is everywhere the same. The fault in Hardy's Londoner, in contrast to the pilgrims of "The Milkmaid," is not his romanticism but his pessimism. Hardy characterizes his expectations: "Misery and fever lurk in [Hodge's] cottage, while, to paraphrase the words of a recent writer on the labouring classes, in his future there are only the workhouse and the grave. He hardly dares to think at all. He has few thoughts of joy, and little hope of rest." But this view is false. Those who look down "from the Olympian heights of society" can "rarely" estimate the happiness of a class to which they condescend. In reality there may be poverty, ignorance, and misery, as there are in Dorsetshire, but "wherever a mode of supporting life is neither noxious nor absolutely inadequate, there springs up happiness, and will spring up happiness, of some sort or other."[7]

The instructive progression moves from illusion to reality. Life is tougher and more complex than the idealistic visionary imagines it to be. Equally important, it is never so bad as the aloof, sophisticated pessimist expects. The final irony is that in the countryside, as well as everywhere else, one finds in the midst of misery and suffering an element of irrepressible joy:

> Sing; how 'a would sing!
> How 'a would raise the tune
> When we rode in the waggon from harvesting
>   By the light o' the moon!
>
> Dance; how 'a would dance!
> If a fiddlestring did but sound
> She would hold out her coats, give a slanting glance,
>   And go round and round.
>
> Laugh; how 'a would laugh!
> Her peony lips would part
> As if none such a place for a lover to quaff
>   At the deeps of a heart.
>
> Julie, O girl of joy.

This poem, "Julie-Jane" (*CP*, pp. 229–230) appears in "A Set of Country Songs" from *Time's Laughingstocks* (1909), Hardy's fullest lyric presentation of the countryside. The set consists of an introductory poem, "Let Me Enjoy," seven poems grouped under the heading "At the Fair," and ten additional poems about country people. Although all are written in song stanzas and regular song meters, they are, with few exceptions, monologues in which a character, usually a woman, describes her particular situation, usually an ironic one. That is, like the "Satires of Circumstance," "Country Songs" is a group of brief dramas. Yet in range of vision and variety of ironic effect, it provides a fitting contrast to the "Satires." The effect of the "Country Songs" is usually sympathetic rather than satirical, and the ironies result from the fundamental complexities of the human condition rather than from circumstances. The narrower and more caustic "Satires" generally do not have a specific regional location. They could take place in country or city, town or village. The broader, more sympathetic "Country Songs" locate their action in the Wessex countryside—"Down Wessex way," as one of them begins. This poem, "The Spring Call" (*CP*, pp. 228–229), explains that while the blackbird sings "prattie deerh" in Scotland, "pehty de-aw" in Middlesex, and "purrity dare" in Ireland, it sings "pret-ty de-urr" in Wessex. By examining the southwest countryside, therefore, one can find particular manifestations of general realities, the particular translation of the universal song. Whereas the "Satires" present a number of grim, isolated ironic moments, poems from "Country Songs"—such as "A Spring Call," "Let Me Enjoy," and "After the Fair"—illustrate an instructive mode by inviting the reader to see the general condition in the particular instance. They affirm the meaningful continuity of human experience.

"News for Her Mother" (*CP*, pp. 230–231), which presents the musings of a girl walking the last mile home after saying yes to her suitor, is typical. She bounds "Like a ball or leaf or lamb along the ground," through a landscape rich with the autumn harvest. Yet she trembles with subdued fear at what her mother will say:

> I said "Yes,"—that
> His I'd be,
> Ere I thought she might not see him as I see!

She apprehends the human reality that union with a man usually means division from one's mother, and with her last words she attempts pathetically to resist it:

> O my mother,
> Can another
> Ever bar
> Mine from thy heart, make thy nearness seem afar?

The girl's eagerness to relate the news turns into reluctance, for she has come face to face with unexpected complexities: her new-found joy has raised the possibility for new sorrow as well. The structure of the situation is ironic, although not in the caustic manner of "In the Room of the Bride-Elect" from the "Satires," which deals with a similar conflict. There Hardy works out the grim, circumstantial possibilities that might emerge from a disagreement between parents and daughter over the choice of a husband. In "News," circumstance plays very little part. There is no angry reproach, no doltish groom with a button-hole rose, no sigh of life-defining resignation; one learns nothing about the suitor or the mother, and very little about the specific personality of the daughter. Instead, one observes a general human quandary. Hardy portrays the divided state of mind of an ordinary person, a simple country girl in a rural lane, as she recognizes the implications of choosing someone to marry. Her condition is general, and it demands sympathy.

"After the Club-Dance" (*CP*, p. 224) presents another country girl walking home after a definitive moment in her life:

> Black'on frowns east on Maidon,
>   And westward to the sea,
> But on neither is his frown laden
>   With scorn, as his frown on me!
>
> At dawn my heart grew heavy,
>   I could not sip the wine,
> I left the jocund bevy
>   And that young man o' mine.
>
> The roadside elms pass by me,—
>   Why do I sink with shame
> When the birds a-perch there eye me?
>   They, too, have done the same!

The specific case is here conveyed in general terms. The girl is any girl after the fall, walking not down a particular country lane but through a vast, generalized landscape of high hills, elms, and birds, a landscape that almost seems to include the sea toward which the hills frown. She departs not from a

87

specific group of people but from a "jocund bevy," and not from a specifically identified lover but from "that young man o' mine." Her personal problem merges with the general, universal human conflict between the logic of natural impulse and the demands of social norms. Her response to her situation is complex. Her "shame" leads her to personify the landscape, yet she turns back on her own imaginative projection and questions the logic of her guilt. The poem is not a satire of circumstance but the exposure of a fundamental, general human conflict, and the questioning, suffering country maid evokes sympathy.

"The Husband's View" (CP, pp. 232–233) works out the circumstantial consequences of a maiden's waywardness and, like many of the "Satires," ends with a half-comic flip. Yet the contrast with the "Satires" is striking, for the final effect is the establishment of ironic reconciliation and solution, rather than grim quandary. A girl, obsessed with her guilt, confesses her plight to an older woman. Arrived at a new place "to flee my sin," she falls in love and accepts a proposal made "In gentle voice and true." She knows, however, that "ere the days are long/ Untimely fruit will show":

> "Discovery borders near,
> And then! . . . But something stirred?—
> My husband—he is here!
> Heaven—has he overheard?"

He has, but his attitude is quite different from what the young woman expected:

> "Yes; I have heard, sweet Nan;
> I have known it all the time.
> I am not a particular man;
> Misfortunes are no crime:
>
> "And what with our serious need
> Of sons for soldiering,
> That accident, indeed,
> To maids, is a useful thing!"

Ironically, there is a way out of the wayward girl's plight, for contrary to expectation, her husband is even more gentle and true than he appeared; he views the bright side of the accidents of chance and change, forgives her her deception, and makes a gentle joke of it all. The irony is benign.

In general, the "Country Songs" dwell, with tender irony, on ordinary human beings whose typical situations demand sympathy. There are the middle-aged women of "Former Beauties" (CP, p. 223), "with lips thin-drawn,/ And tissues sere," who once were "the muslined pink young things to whom/ We vowed and swore." There is "The Market-Girl" (CP, p. 224), shy, unnoticed, the "prize" of the more confident man who finally noticed her and bought her wares. There is Patty Beech of "The Inquiry" (CP, pp. 224–225), whose lover was prevented by time and chance from marrying her, and who, grown old, laments, "And Time, that dooms man's love to die,/ Preserves a maid's alive." There is the forlorn woman of "A Wife Waits" (CP, p. 225), who stands in the cold outside the clubroom while her husband dances with someone else. There is the fearful bride of "The Homecoming" (CP, pp. 234–235), who, alone with her husband for the first time, wishes she were "at home again with dear daddee!" And there is "The Orphaned Old Maid" (CP, p. 228), who, to her deep regret, rejected her sweetheart in order to care for her aging father:

But now father's gone, and I feel growing old,
And I'm lonely and poor in this house on the wold,
And my sweetheart that was found a partner elsewhere,
And nobody flings me a thought or a care.

This last stanza illustrates Hardy's effort to dramatize realistic, domestic situations in song form, with heavy, regular rhythms and a high correlation between line and syntactic structure evidenced by frequent end-stopping. Although specific ironies are at work within the individual poems, there is a more important irony prevailing in the group as a whole, hinted at in the title "Country Songs," and evident in the tension between the lyric lilt of the song form and the prosaic realities described. Although "The Ballad-Singer" (CP, p. 223), the first poem in the subgroup "At the Fair," associates singing with joyful forgetfulness, it rather emphasizes the sorrows to be forgotten than the possibilities for forgetting:

Sing, Ballad-singer, raise a hearty tune;
Make me forget that there was ever a one
I walked with in the meek light of the moon
   When the day's work was done.

Rhyme, Ballad-rhymer, start a country song;
Make me forget that she whom I loved well
Swore she would love me dearly, love me long,
   Then—what I cannot tell!

Sing, Ballad-singer, from your little book;
Make me forget those heart-breaks, achings, fears;
Make me forget her name, her sweet sweet look—
   Make me forget her tears.

Hardy's songs, emerging from a realistic vision of the country, are filled with "heart-breaks, achings, fears," and the unforgettable tears of "sweet sweet" maidens; they stimulate memory rather than forgetfulness. Music itself is shown to be ambivalent, for it lures one with a rush of emotion into entanglement and suffering, as expressed by the country musician in "The Fiddler" (*CP,* pp. 231–232):

He twangs: "Music hails from the devil,
   Though vaunted to come from heaven,
For it makes people do at a revel
   What multiplies sins by seven.

"There's many a heart now mangled,
   And waiting its time to go,
Whose tendrils were first entangled
   By my sweet viol and bow!"

Yet Hardy does not dwell exclusively on inevitable suffering, for he portrays women whose joyful passion, remembered, outweighs guilt and pain. Significantly, "The Fiddler" is followed by "The Husband's View," with its portrait of the gentle, forgiving husband. The woman seduced in "The Dark-Eyed Gentleman" (*CP,* p. 227) has her "fine lissom lad":

No sorrow brings he,
And thankful I be
That his daddy once tied up my garter for me!

90

Preeminent among such poems is "Julie-Jane," about a "girl of joy" who sang and danced and laughed, then died in child-birth:

> "I suppose," with a laugh, she said,
> "I should blush that I'm not a wife;
> But how can it matter, so soon to be dead,
> What one does in life!"

Her common-sense wisdom appears sane and benign in contrast to the observation about death from the speaker of "In the Cemetery": "And as well cry over a new-laid drain/ As anything else, to ease your pain"; or to the comment: "Well, bliss is in ignorance: what's the harm!" from "At a Watering-Place." Her view emerges from her love of movement, laughter, and of love itself, from her irrepressible gaiety. As her friends sit by her deathbed, she wonders, "Dears, how can you keep from your lovers, adorning/ In honour of me!" Her last request is that her illicit lovers should bear her coffin to the grave:

> Bubbling and brightsome eyed!
> But now—O never again.
> She chose her bearers before she died
> From her fancy-men.

With this arch, defiant act, she affirms joy in the midst of sorrow.

Julie-Jane's mode of life is the one recommended in the first poem of the group, "Let Me Enjoy" (*CP*, p. 222):

> Let me enjoy the earth no less
> Because the all-enacting Might
> That fashioned forth its loveliness
> Had other aims than my delight.

To recognize the "heart-breaks, achings, fears" and yet to focus on remembered joys is a difficult mode, but it is not altogether impossible, and success in it results in miraculous effects. In "Former Beauties," the poet gazes at middle-aged women in the marketplace and wonders:

Do they remember those gay tunes we trod
  Clasped on the green;
Aye; trod till moonlight set on the beaten sod
  A satin sheen?

They must forget, forget! They cannot know
  What once they were,
Or memory would transfigure them, and show
  Them always fair.

This is a bold, positive statement: to keep the memory of joy alive is to remain beautiful.

While the "Satires of Circumstance" has the general effect of revealing the petty ugliness in human beings, "A Set of Country Songs" attempts to show maidens of the countryside as "always fair." The final instructive irony is that in the painful struggles and aspirations of ordinary people in a provincial place lies a primitive beauty, to be exposed and celebrated in the hearty tunes and rhymes of the ballad-singer. The "all-enacting Might" may have other aims than human pleasure, but "Let me enjoy the earth no less." This capacity for happiness is available everywhere and always has been, as Hardy points out in the last stanza of "After the Fair" (*CP*, p. 226):

And midnight clears High Street of all but the ghosts
  Of its buried burghees,
From the latest far back to those old Roman hosts
  Whose remains one yet sees,
Who loved, laughed, and fought, hailed their friends,
    drank their toasts
  At their meeting-times here, just as these!

Hardy's poems of the countryside affirm the meaningful continuity of human experience.

BALLADS AND NARRATIVES

4

In his country songs Hardy presents, with redeeming sympathy, ordinary people caught in the common, fundamental complexities of life. To the extent that these characters are worth studying as exemplars of the human condition, and that their lives occasionally achieve joyful fulfillment, the poems in which they appear sound a strong, positive note. To see Hardy's country people at their most particular and complex, however, one must turn to his narratives and ballads, where he achieves the fullest realization of his vision of country life.

Old Illusions and New

Hardy's ballad "The Dead Quire" (*CP*, pp. 240–243) begins:

> Beside the Mead of Memories,
> Where Church-way mounts to Moaning Hill
> The sad man sighed his phantasies:
> He seems to sigh them still.

The sad man describes a Christmas Eve past, when youths of Mellstock, carousing at an inn, proposed blasphemous toasts:

> "Now 'tis Christmas morn;
> Here's to our women old and young,
> And to John Barleycorn!"

They collapsed into a drunken sleep, in which their ancestors from the "Mellstock quire of former years" seemed to them to rise from their graves, singing, as the sad man continued, "words of prayer and praise/ As they had used to sing." The youths awakened and went home chastened: " 'Twas said that of them all, not one/ Sat in a tavern more." The poem ends with the sad man drifting away to the "Mead of Memories." Three degrees of religious perspective are presented here: the piety of the ancient Mellstock choir, the repentance of the fallen youths who experience the miracle, and the wistful melancholy of the tale-teller, who presumably is sad because the conditions for piety and repentance no longer exist ("Church-way mounts to Moaning Hill"). In effect, Hardy depicts the stages in the religious history of a culture. He himself occupies a fourth degree of perspective, for the denizen of the "Mead of Memories" is not Hardy, but the old man. Hardy himself stands in a neutral, distant position, from which the story, told by another, appears to be an interesting "phantasy," worth preserving in a more skeptical age.

"The Dead Quire" is typical of Hardy's ballads and story poems in that the narrator usually appears as a distant observer, either retelling a traditional tale that is current in the society, or recording a factually based story associated with real places and people in the rural Wessex of the past. He seems to be the objective preserver and guardian of the memory of a folk. Hardy's titles reflect this stance. The frequent use of the words "Tale" or "Ballad" suggests a debt to tradition; the time of the action is often the distant or not-so-distant past; and often a Wessex setting is clearly specified: "The Sacrilege: A Ballad-Tragedy (Circa 182–)," "The Supplanter: A Tale," "A Sound in the Night (Woodsford Castle: 17—)," "No Bell-Ringing: A Ballad of Durnover," "At Shag's Heath, 1685 (Traditional)." As a story-teller, Hardy thus remains morally and philosophically neutral. Purportedly the events were shaped by history and tradition, not him. He merely records them in these poems, without comment on their meaning and without using them as occasions for meditation; he experiences no flashes of personal insight. Taken as a group, the narratives imply that any story with a clear shape, an interesting twist, a tantalizing element of mystery, or an instructive lesson is worth the telling. Because it actually happened, or because it represents an imagined response to realities, any story not invented by the author helps to preserve and clarify the history of the society

94

in which it occurred, to sanctify the place where it happened, and to exemplify significant qualities of life.

The logic of his role as historian explains in part why Hardy, the agnostic and iconoclast, wrote narratives describing the intervention of the supernatural in human life. He preserves the memory of a time when the old illusions of truth were current, when, if miracles did not actually occur, at least people believed they did. "The Paphian Ball" and "No Bell-Ringing" describe Christmas and New Year's Eve miracles. "The Lost Pyx: A Mediaeval Legend" (*CP*, pp. 158–160) offers a tale explaining the meaning of a Wessex landmark, the Cross-and-Hand, a mysterious and ancient pillar standing, Hardy reveals in a footnote to the poem, "on a lonely table-land above the Vale of Blackmore." In the first stanza, Hardy characteristically establishes his role as the recorder of a tale originated by others in the past:

> Some say the spot is banned: that the pillar
> Cross-and-Hand
> Attests to a deed of hell;
> But of else than of bale is the mystic tale
> That ancient Vale-folk tell.

According to the story, a priest, aroused from sleep in a violent storm, refused to make a difficult journey to administer last rites to a dying man. After he fell back to sleep, "a Visage seemed/ To frown from Heaven at him." He awakened in a fright and set off "through the dark immense," only to discover that the Pyx containing the consecrated wafer of the Eucharist had disappeared: "I've lost . . . the Body of Christ Himself!" He started back toward home, groping in the darkness until a ray of light from heaven guided him to the Pyx:

> unharmed 'mid the circling rows
> Of Blackmore's hairy throng,
> Whereof were oxen, sheep, and does,
> And hares from the brakes among;
>
> And badgers grey, and conies keen,
> And squirrels of the tree,
> And many a member seldom seen
> Of Nature's family.

The priest marked the scene of the miracle with a pillar. This poem preserves an old illusion of truth in a style approaching the mannered delicacy of Pre-Raphaelite medievalism. The inversions ("badgers grey, and conies keen") and the archaic syntax ("Whereof were oxen," "brakes among") support the effect of remote quaintness. In his footnote Hardy points out that *Tess of the d'Urbervilles* records a different tradition as to the origin of the pillar—the tradition alluded to in the poem that it "Attests to a deed of hell." Faithful to his role as tale-teller, Hardy tells both of these disparate stories to enrich and embellish the meaning of the landscape.

In a larger sense, however, Hardy as tale-teller is not at all neutral. The phrase "old illusion" echoes a term Hardy uses in his essay *The Science of Fiction* (1891), in which he attacks Zola and the school of literary naturalism for falsely assuming that art can be "complete copyism." The essay expresses Hardy's conviction that all artists select and shape facts in ways which reveal their own values and peculiar visions; that no artist can be a neutral recorder; that art presents an illusion of truth, not truth itself. The literary naturalists, in Hardy's view, make the mistake of ignoring "the need for the exercise of the Daedalian faculty for selection and cunning manipulation." This faculty is affected not only by the personal values and idiosyncrasies of the writer, but also by the current ideas of the period in which he lives: "with our widened knowledge of the universe and its forces, and man's position therein, narrative, to be artistically convincing, must adjust itself to the new alignment . . . Nothing but the illusion of truth can permanently please, and when the old illusions begin to be penetrated, a more natural magic has to be supplied."[1]

Poems like "The Lost Pyx" present "old illusions" of the truth. Their reliance on supernatural events appeals merely to an antiquarian interest in the past and to a nostalgic longing for the certainty of old forms of belief. The magic they depend on has been discredited by the "widened knowledge" of a skeptical age. In contrast, the majority of Hardy's ballads and narratives employ the "more natural magic" of intuitive deduction. He creates illusions, but they seem to be true because he imagines them in terms of relationships that the modern age accepts as real, based, for example, on psychological motivation or on naturalistic cause and effect. The more deeply and

96

fully he imagines, however, the more complex and disturbing become his illusions of truth. Often motivations are obscure, and cause and effect are disproportionate. Actuality, as he conceives it, is as mysterious as supernatural miracle. Hardy defines the new magic in *The Science of Fiction*, where he celebrates the writer's power to penetrate "the superficial" and to expose "the intrinsic." The writer's mode of imaginative inference is akin to the scientific method; his powers are natural and human: "What cannot be discerned by eye and ear, what may be apprehended only by the mental tactility that comes from a sympathetic appreciativeness of life in all of its manifestations, this is the gift which renders its possessor a more accurate delineator of human nature than many another with twice his powers and means of external observation, but without that sympathy. To see in half and quarter views the whole picture, to catch from a few bars the whole tune, is the intuitive power that supplies the would-be storywriter with the scientific bases for his pursuit."[2] In Hardy's finest ballads and narratives his "sympathetic appreciativeness of life in all of its manifestations" enables him to "see in half and quarter views the whole picture," and to conjure up the mysterious, bewildering complexity at the heart of things—a vision that has the illusion of truth.

The contrasts between "On Martock Moor" and "A Tramp-woman's Tragedy," two ballads similar in many ways, point up the idiosyncratic propensities of Hardy's narrative imagination and the modern twist he gave to the ballad. "On Martock Moor" (*CP*, pp. 777–778) shows his skill in imitating features of the traditional form:

I
My deep-dyed husband trusts me,
 He feels his mastery sure,
Although I leave his evening hearth
 To walk upon the moor.

II
—I had what wealth I needed,
 And of gay gowns a score,
And yet I left my husband's house
 To muse upon the moor.

97

III

O how I loved a dear one
Who, save in soul, was poor!
O how I loved the man who met
Me nightly on the moor.

IV

I'd feather-beds and couches,
And carpets for the floor,
Yet brighter to me was at eves,
The bareness of the moor.

V

There was a dogging figure,
There was a hiss of "Whore!"
There was a flounce at Weir-water
One night upon the moor. . . .

VI

Yet do I haunt there, knowing
By rote each rill's low pour,
But only a fitful phantom now
Meets me upon the moor.

The characters are common ballad figures: the prosperous husband, the poor lover, the unfaithful wife. The action is characterized by the simplicity and violence of traditional ballads: a tryst, discovery by the husband, the death of the lover. The morality of the poem is the primitive, masculine ethic of retribution: the wife's penalty for infidelity is to be called "Whore"; the lover pays with his life. As in many traditional ballads, the ethic reflects the inevitabilities of human emotion rather than an objective moral system. Love demands fulfillment, but with equal force, trust and generosity demand fidelity. The husband's humiliation at his wife's betrayal, on the one hand, and her love for another man, on the other, are both fully valid human facts, and to the extent that her love requires consummation, his humiliation requires revenge. The logic here is merciless, divisive, and tragic, but it goes unquestioned. The characters are victims neither of one another nor of schematized social and moral values, but of the realities of human action and emotion. Yet there is no wailing against the human condition. Nor is there any hint of either romanticism or puritanism, for the husband is no more presented as a villainous oppressor than the wife is pictured as a wayward sinner. Cause and effect are in proportion, and the characters are responsible for what they cause. There is an objective, tragic purity in the presentation of situation and action, a quality common to traditional ballads.

This quality is embodied in the stylistic features of the poem —in the controlled rhythms, the austerity of language, the balance and symmetry, the economy of exposition, and the stabilizing repetition of the word "moor" at the end of each stanza. The first four stanzas set up the dichotomy: the trust, comfort, prosperity, and security of husband, hearth, and home, as opposed to the wife's love, expressed in the outburst of stanza three, for the poor man on the barren moor. The fifth stanza, in a way typical of the traditional ballad, focuses on the key moment, describing it in terms of a few selected facts, things heard and seen rather than emotions felt: the "dogging figure," the "hiss of 'Whore,' " the "flounce at Weir-water." This is the moment of terrifying discovery and violent death, yet the method of description, by leaving the terror and violence to the imagination of the reader, makes an important contribution to the effect of objective, tragic purity created by the poem as a whole. Likewise the last stanza conveys the wife's passion and longing only indirectly. The word "haunt" turns her into a ghost; though living, she is no more alive in her emotional life than is the "phantom" lover, and the reference to her knowledge of the moor recalls the intensity and frequency of their meetings in life. Balance and symmetry also characterize the prosody and alliteration. Lines tend to be defined not only by syllable number, meter, end-stopping, and rhyme, but also by alliterative groupings:

> —I had *w*hat *w*ealth I needed,
>   And of *g*ay *g*owns a score,
> And yet I left my *h*usband's *h*ouse
>   To *m*use upon the *m*oor.

The variations in the position of the alliterating groups illustrate Hardy's control:

> I'd *f*eather-*b*eds and *c*ouches,
> And *c*arpets *f*or the *f*loor,
> Yet *b*righter to me was at eves,
> The *b*areness of the moor.

In this poem Hardy demonstrates his mastery of the techniques necessary to achieve in narrative verse the effects of control, economy, balance, distance, and objectivity.

Hardy dates "On Martock Moor" 1899, the general period of *Wessex Poems* and narratives like "San Sebastian" and "The Dance at the Phoenix," yet the poem did not first appear until 1925 in *Human Shows*. Both *Poems of the Past and the Present* (1902) and the next volume, *Time's Laughingstocks* (1909), include many narratives involving a wide variety of themes and techniques. It seems strange that Hardy withheld from publication a poem as skillful as "On Martock Moor" when he published other narratives and ballads from the same period. A comparison of "On Martock Moor" with the poems written at the same general time but which Hardy chose for immediate publication suggests a probable answer. Hardy's narratives seldom create the effect of objective, tragic purity produced by "On Martock Moor." Seldom does the logic of emotion and action go unquestioned. Rarely is the structure of situation characterized by simplicity, spareness, and inevitability. Nor does the use of language usually reflect control, restraint, and emotional distance. In his other narratives motives are obscure and ambiguous, situations complicated and ironic, the language diverse, mannered, tortured, highly textured. Instead of a clear vision of the elements leading inevitably to tragedy, Hardy usually reveals a complex, agonizing awareness that tragedy is not inevitable—a consciousness of the fragility of circumstance and motive. A characteristic ending is a leading figure's sense of guilt for his part in the tragedy, rather than the muted acceptance found at the end of "On Martock Moor." That is, in his narratives Hardy reveals an "idiosyncratic mode of regard" despite the neutrality of his narrators. Although he seems to have developed a full mastery over traditional ballad techniques and effects, he preferred to reveal a personal, untraditional vision. He may well have withheld "On Martock Moor" from publication because it fell short of what he wanted in his ballads.

"A Trampwoman's Tragedy" (*CP*, pp. 182–185) provides a fitting contrast, for it was a ballad that Hardy himself much admired. Referring to the year 1902, the biographer of the *Life* stated: "In April . . . he was writing 'A Trampwoman's Tragedy'—a ballad based on some local story of an event more or less resembling the incidents embodied, which took place between 1820 and 1830. Hardy considered this, upon the whole, his most successful poem."[3] In the poem the tramp-woman describes her life with an unnamed "fancy-man" and their two companions, Mother Lee and "jeering John." At the climax, the trampwoman flirts with John, her jealous lover kills him and is hanged for the murder, and the trampwoman bears a stillborn baby. At the conclusion she meets with the phantom of her fancy-man, professes her love for him, and lives out her career "Haunting the Western Moor." The similarities with "On Martock Moor" are obvious: the setting, the love triangle, the violent death, the bereft woman haunting the site of her love.

In contrast to the abstraction of "On Martock Moor," the trampwoman describes her wanderings with her fancy-man in terms of concrete physical toil:

> The sun-blaze burning on our backs,
> Our shoulders sticking to our packs,
> By fosseway, fields, and turnpike tracks
>   We skirted sad Sedge-Moor.

What unites the two lovers is their shared struggle, their move-ment together across the landscape despite obstacles and hard-ships. The poetry particularizes their efforts by naming places and employing action verbs. The effect is a sense of energy, texture, physicality, and exuberant triumph.

> For months we had padded side by side,
>   Ay, side by side
> Through the Great Forest, Blackmoor wide,
>   And where the Parret ran.
> We'd faced the gusts on Mendip ridge,
> Had crossed the Yeo unhelped by bridge,
> Been stung by every Marshwood midge,
>   I and my fancy-man.

101

The next stanza names the "Lone inns we loved, my man and I": "King's Stag," "Windwhistle," "The Horse," and "The Hut." The description creates the impression of a concrete landscape, known and loved, harsh but beautiful, dotted with places of human refuge. The goal of the particular journey of the poem, attained at sundown, is a favorite inn near Poldon top, a place of unusual beauty: "I doubt if finer sight there be/ Within this royal realm." But it is here, in this longed-for place, that the tragedy occurs. For a second time the tramp-woman teases her lover, whereupon he commits the murder:

> Then up he sprung, and with his knife—
> And with his knife
> He let out jeering Johnny's life,
> Yes; there, at set of sun.
> The slant ray through the window nigh
> Gilded John's blood and glazing eye,
> Ere scarcely Mother Lee and I
> Knew that the deed was done.

The violence is described with considerable immediacy: the speed of the killer's spring, the blood, the glazed eye, the irony of the sunlight. The events proceeding from the murder are also described forthrightly in blunt, even crude language: "at Ivel-chester jail/ My Love, my sweetheart swung," or "On his death-day I gave my groan/ And dropt his dead-born child." Absent is the refining, distancing tact of "On Martock Moor," the economy of exposition that leaves the violence and terror to the reader's imagination. "A Trampwoman's Tragedy" vividly depicts the moments of violence and terror, transforming the woman who had been touched by the beauty of a natural scene into the equivalent of a beast—she "drops" her dead offspring alone on the barren moor.

Despite superficial similarities in the endings, "A Trampwoman's Tragedy" concludes on a note quite different from that of "On Martock Moor." The wife in the latter poem is in a state of memory and desire, not guilt. She has fulfilled her passion and paid the consequences. The trampwoman, in contrast, meets the ghost of her lover not to commune with him, but to make amends. The ghost asks:

"Ah, tell me this!
Was the child mine, or was it his?
Speak, that I rest may find!"

O doubt not but I told him then,
   I told him then,
That I had kept me from all men
   Since we joined lips and swore.
Whereat he smiled, and thinned away.

She tells him when it is too late, then wanders "alone . . .
Haunting the Western Moor." She is isolated by her guilt, with
memories not of consummated passion but of what might have
been. The question arises as to whether she is guilty, and if
so, of what. In the answer lies the main difference between
"A Trampwoman's Tragedy" and "On Martock Moor."

The trampwoman is both guilty and not guilty. The poem
evokes two conflicting perspectives from which to judge its
action, and the final effect is ambivalence. From one point of
view there is a clear line of responsibility for the tragedy. The
brutality of the language is justified by the brutality of the
characters, particularly of the trampwoman, whose yielding to
a cruel impulse touches off a transformation of beauty into
ugliness; she brutalizes her own world. Tramps lead free,
unstable lives on the moors, remote from civilizing conventions
and humanizing responsibilities. They wander unfettered by
place or social structure. In a sense they are outlaws: theirs
is the world of "Blue Jimmy," who "stole right many a steed."
The fancy-man, who has also been a thief, carries a knife and
knows how to use it. Relations are shifting, the couple having
traveled together only for months, not years, and death is ever-
present. Mother Lee, for example, dies mysteriously before the
fancy-man hangs. In such an unstable world the trampwoman's and fancy-man's love is something of a triumph,
an instance of fidelity under circumstances where infidelity to
person, place, occupation, and conventional social structures
is the norm. But the trampwoman betrays the achievement.
She allows herself to become a wanderer at heart, a tramp in
the sense of "trollop," as well as being a wanderer across the
landscape: "I teased my fancy-man in play/ And wanton idleness." Although play and wanton idleness are hallmarks of the

103

behavior of irresponsible wanderers, up to this point the lives of the trampwoman and her lover had been characterized by serious struggle and "care" for one another. Almost as an act of will, the trampwoman ignores the effects of her playfulness: "I would not bend my glances on/ My lover's dark distress." At the inn she impulsively continues the game, despite the ominous tone in her lover's voice:

> Then in a voice I had never heard,
>   I had never heard,
> My only Love to me: "One word,
>   My lady, if you please!
> Whose is the child you are like to bear?—
> *His?* After all my months o' care?"
> God knows 'twas not! But, O despair!
>   I nodded—still to tease.

The tease is brutal beyond endurance, given their brief history of love and fidelity. In an unstable, lawless world, ever on the brink of death and violence, close to the harshness of nature as well as its beauty, the fancy-man's act of ultimate vengeance seems to follow an inevitable logic of cruelty, developing from the trampwoman's first idle wantonness. It is a logic leading to death, on the one hand, and to isolation and guilt on the other—the fates, respectively, of the fancy-man and the trampwoman.

From another point of view the trampwoman, though she causes the tragedy, is not responsible for it. The disparity between what she has actually done and its result is senselessly out of proportion. No matter how cruelly vain or possessive the impulse to which she surrendered, it does not warrant the consequences. A few thoughtless words and gestures result in three lost lives, and a fourth person condemned to a lonely, guilt-stricken death-in-life. The wife in "On Martock Moor" commits her acts of passion and pays the price without guilt or remorse. The trampwoman makes a heedless mistake, and the result is total catastrophe. She is guilty of a careless yielding to impulse and a failure of perception. She failed to understand that hers was not a situation for play, because of the depth of her lover's feelings and his capacity for jealousy. These are serious errors, meriting correction, but her object lesson is the destruction of her world. What she learns becomes for her no longer worth knowing. Ironically, the means of her instruction destroy the conditions under which her new knowledge could have any value. "A Young Man's Epigram on Existence" (*CP*, p. 281), the last poem in *Time's Laughingstocks*, where "A Trampwoman's Tragedy" also appears, makes explicit the same ironic point:

> A senseless school, where we must give
> Our lives that we may learn to live!
> A dolt is he who memorizes
> Lessons that leave no time for prizes.

The logic of "A Trampwoman's Tragedy" thus leads to a grotesque disparity between error and consequences. The poem calls into question the notions of guilt and responsibility and the relation between them in such a way as to make final judgment impossible. And whatever the solution to the moral ambiguities, the facts of death and suffering remain. By showing human beings to be unstable wanderers across a barren land, victims of the uncertainties of both the external world and their own psyches, Hardy infuses into the traditional form of the ballad the modern anguish of rootlessness, precariousness, and complexity. "The Trampwoman's Tragedy" is an excellent example of his attempt to devise a new kind of illusion of truth.

Moral Complications

In Hardy's narratives and ballads, therefore, despite his pose as the recorder and disseminator of known tales, he exercises the "Daedalian faculty for selection and cunning manipulation." This is not to say that he creates his stories out of whole cloth, for usually, as in the case of "A Trampwoman's Tragedy," there is some historical basis for them.[4] Generally they grow out of hints Hardy actually received from local traditions and the artifacts of the countryside. His imagination, stimulated by these half and quarter views, creates a whole picture, at the center of which is a moral conflict. The sorts of conflict involved tend to be reducible to balanced, simple terms, like love versus duty, husband versus lover, family ver-

105

sus country—the kinds of conflict found in traditional ballads. But there are always complications.

"The Mock Wife" (CP, pp. 723–725) is a useful poem for illustrating the way in which Hardy's poetic imagination worked with historical materials, for he also wrote a full prose account of the incident, based on careful research he had done. The differences between the prose and the poem are instructive. In Maumbury Ring (1908), an essay summarizing the history of the Roman earthworks on the outskirts of Dorchester, he describes in detail the case of Mary Channing, who was convicted of poisoning her husband, a grocer, and was executed in the Ring in 1705. Hardy focuses sympathetically on the girl, a "thoughtless, pleasure-loving creature" only eighteen years old, who had been compelled against her wishes to marry a man of her parents' choice. He leaves little doubt that he feels her to have been innocent of the charges brought against her. Having examined the record of the trial "more than once," he reports "no distinct evidence" that she committed the crime, but "much to suggest that she did not. Nor is any motive discoverable for such an act. She was allowed to have her former lover or lovers about her by her indulgent and weak-minded husband, who permitted her to go her own ways, give parties, and supplied her with plenty of money." Hardy shows little sympathy here for the husband. Mary Channing was nevertheless convicted and executed. Hardy describes her skill in conducting her own defense, emphasizes her pregnancy (the execution being delayed until she had given birth to her baby), and dwells on the wasting sickness from which she suffered after the birth. He goes into some detail in his account of the execution: "this girl not yet 19, now reduced to a skeleton by the long fever, and already more dead than alive" is taken by cart to Maumbury Ring, and, before "many thousands" of eager spectators, strangled, apparently not to death but to insensitivity, and then burned to ashes. Hardy concludes, "Was man ever 'slaughtered by his fellow man' during the Roman or barbarian use of this place of games or of sacrifice in circumstances of greater atrocity?"[5] Hardy's view of the historical event is clear: Channing was a fool; his wife, a lively, pleasure-loving girl, was most likely innocent of the crime; and the execution constituted a cruel atrocity.

"The Mock Wife," Hardy's poetic description of the same event, is spoken by a modern man looking back over two centuries to 1705. The poem begins, "It's a dark drama, this," but then continues on a different tack from the prose account: "and yet I know the house, and date;/ That is to say, the where and when John Channing met his fate." The setting of the central action of the poem is thus Channing's house. Hardy does not mention the Ring, let alone exploit the ironic potentialities of its pagan and Roman history. Although Mary Channing's possible innocence is referred to three times, and the brutality of the execution is noted, the issue at the center of the poem is the pathos of the husband, not the tragedy of the wife. It is as if Hardy, musing over the case and sympathetically imagining its wider implications, came to see something that "cannot be discerned by eye and ear" in the historical record—namely, that Channing's plight was a source of poetic interest.

The circumstances of Channing's death form the subject of the poem. He does not know that his wife has been accused of poisoning him, and because of his real affection for her, as shown by his earlier indulgence, he wants her to be at his bedside. When he asks to see his wife once again, it poses a problem to the friends gathered around the deathbed, who know that she is already in jail charged with the crime. It is this problem that is at the heart of the poem:

> "Guilty she may not be," they said; "so why should we
>   torture him
> In these his last few minutes of life? Yet how indulge
>   his whim?"
>
> And as he begged there piteously for what could not
>   be done,
> And the murder-charge had flown about the town
>   to every one,
> The friends around him in their trouble thought of a
>   hasty plan,
> And straightway set about it. Let denounce them all
>   who can.

The fact of Mary Channing's possible innocence is presented not as the moral crux of the poem but as an element in the

107

quandary of the bedside friends. Since she may, after all, be innocent, it would seem all the more reasonable not to disillusion her dying husband. The friends solve the problem by persuading a "buxom woman not unlike his prisoned wife" to impersonate her:

> Well, the friendly neighbour did it; and he kissed her;
>   held her fast;
> Kissed her again and yet again. "I—knew she'd—come
>   at last!—
> Where have you been?—Ah, kept away!—
> I'm sorry—overtried—
> God bless you!" And he loosed her, fell back tiredly,
>   and died.

With double irony his dying words are a blessing on the imposter of the wife accused of murdering him, in a situation that recalls the story of the deceived Isaac blessing Jacob instead of Esau. The poem goes on to describe Mary "strangled and burnt to dust" before ten thousand onlookers, "as was the verdict then/ On women truly judged, or false, of doing to death their men." Although the possibility of Mary's innocence and the harshness of her execution are here implied, no mention is made of her youth, her pregnancy, or her illness. The concluding stanza returns attention to the quandary of the friends:

> Some of them said as they watched her burn: "I am glad
>   he never knew,
> Since a few hold her as innocent—think such she could
>   not do!
> Glad, too, that (as they tell) he thought she kissed him
>   ere he died."
> And they seemed to make no question that the cheat
>   was justified.

In Hardy's prose description of the case he makes a clear moral judgment, which implicitly indicts the spectators at the execution. In the poem, the situation is more complicated. On one hand, Hardy is ironically exposing the callousness of the burghers who, as they watch a woman burn, attend to a matter of trivial moral scruples instead of the cruelty and possible

108

injustice of the woman's death. Yet the parallel with the Isaac and Jacob story makes their concern for Channing's plight seem more significant. There was a real moral issue at stake in the friends' quandary, which they dealt with sympathetically. The last line seems absolutely straight: in the complex moral situation surrounding Channing's death, all agree that Channing's happiness was worth what would otherwise have been a cruel deception, just as Esau's selling of his birthright justifies the cruel deception of Isaac. This poem is altogether typical of Hardy's ballads: he chooses what appears to be a clear-cut moral situation as his general subject—in this case the execution of a woman who is probably innocent—and then complicates the issue by imagining attendant circumstances—in this case the circumstances of the husband's death. The reader could condemn the friends for their indifference to Mary's brutal death, or praise them for their sympathetic, flexible response to John's plight. Hardy's treatment of the case in the poem leaves one with a perplexing sense of uncertainty.

Frequently in his ballads and narratives Hardy imagines historical events in terms of individual moral crises. He shows that history results from the particular actions of ordinary people faced with the necessity of making a choice under stress. The relationship between an ordinary husband and wife, for example, may play a crucial part in a grand historical drama. The effect is not to reduce history to trivialities; Hardy's intention is not to show that a kingdom was lost for want of a nail. Instead, Hardy views the past as a complex fabric woven of the interlocking destinies of individual human beings, each of whom merits attention. Indeed, it would be a simplistic view of history to remember only the grand significance of an event and to forget the human complexity of attendant circumstances. The betrayal and death of a duke are worth recording; but so is the tragedy of an ordinary life. Although such common tragedies seldom appear in the records, Hardy's poetry shows that a poet, working on the basis of fragmentary hints, can reconstruct the whole picture. He can serve the past as effectively as the historian by affirming imaginatively its human complexity.

In "At Shag's Heath: 1685 (Traditional)" (*CP*, pp. 712–714) the subject is the death of the Duke of Monmouth, but Hardy's focus is on the plight of the woman who betrayed him to his executioners. Newly married, she has been told by her husband that any man making friendly advances "means ill to thee." A handsome stranger, who comes to her door to inquire "but the way to go," seems to confirm the husband's warning by stealing a kiss; fleeing, he asks her to "keep faith!" When the pursuing soldiers tell her that the unknown man claimed to be "King Monmouth," she assumes that he is a deceiver and betrays his hiding place. His words to her before he is carried off to his death convince her that "he was no hind":

> "I wished all weal might thee attend,
> But this is what th'st done to me,
> O heartless woman, held my friend!"

The tale is complicated by the way that Hardy merges the wife's guilt and her disillusionment with her husband. She has betrayed her rightful ruler, a handsome man who meant her only good, because of her husband's jealousy: "he'd spoke lies in jealous-wise!" Monmouth admired her beauty and kissed her, but he had no intention to violate and betray her. The relation between appearance and reality is more complex, the wife learns, than her husband has taught her: "As truth I took what was not true." The poem ends with the wife, haunted by the bloody ghost of Monmouth, resolving to drown herself:

> When comes the waterman, he'll say,
> "Who's done her thuswise?"—'Twill be, yea,
> Sweet, slain King Monmouth—he!

Ironically, it is the husband's jealousy that makes Monmouth the destroyer of his wife. Hardy's sources for the poem were local legends, standard histories, and tales handed down through his mother's family, some of whose members, according to family tradition, had been involved in the Monmouth rebellion.[6] Characteristically Hardy chooses to work with the traditional theme of the guilty betrayer, developing it in this instance from a wife's disillusionment with her husband, to her introduction to the complexities of reality, her fatal, well-intentioned mistake, and finally her oppressive, destructive guilt. In Hardy's tale, however, the guilty betrayer is innocent.

Although the poem entitled "The Alarm (Traditional): In Memory of One of the Writer's Family Who Was a Volunteer During the War with Napoleon" (*CP*, pp. 30–34) has a happy ending, it also portrays a moment important in the historical traditions of Wessex in terms of the moral crisis of a specific individual. A young soldier on his way to the coast stops "In a ferny byway/ Near the great South-Wessex Highway" to reassure his pregnant wife that Napoleon is "not like to land!" Marching on alone, he sees the signal fires announcing the impending invasion—the notorious false alarm that plays a part in *The Trumpet Major* and *The Dynasts*. The soldier is caught in a moral dilemma: should he return to his wife, or should he join the battle? Besides his fear for his wife's safety, he is concerned about her confidence in him:

> "Else, my denying
> He'd come, she'll read as lying—
> Think the Barrow-Beacon must have met my eyes—
> That my words were not unwareness, but deceit of her,
> while vying
> In deeds that jeopardize."

He sees a bird tangled in undergrowth and decides, before releasing it, that he will take the direction of its flight as a divine sign. The bird flies toward the coast; the soldier marches on, discovers that the alarm was false, and returns home to sing a Te Deum with his wife and friends: "We praise Thee, Lord, discerning/ That Thou hast helped in this!" The Lord has helped save the young man as well as the nation. "At Shag's Heath" ends in tragedy; "The Alarm," in an affirmation of divine providence. Hardy's stance is neutral as to the religious and philosophical questions. His values, the shaping and selective processes of his imagination, are evident in what the poems share, their particularization of historical moments in terms of the moral crises in the lives of specific individuals. Both poems merge national history with issues of personal fidelity.

"The Inscription (A Tale)" (*CP*, pp. 641–644), a story allegedly passed down to the narrator by "talebearers," presents a curiously tainted and obscured conflict of fidelities. The object on which Hardy bases his narrative is one of the several tomb inscriptions known to him that included the names of both husband and wife, but the date of death of only the husband; in the poem he refers specifically to a real inscription in Yetminster Church (here called "Estminster") near Dorchester. As Hardy imagines it, the husband died young, leaving his wife still "fair as any the eye might scan." The widow has her name inscribed on the tomb with her husband's, thus "Forgoing Heaven's bliss if ever with spouse should she/ Again have lain." She falls in love again, but refuses to marry her new lover, who reproaches her "that one yet undeceased/ Should bury her future." After her priest advises her not to marry, she is torn between her new lover and her fear of damnation. Her lover, growing cool, gives her "till Midsummer morn to make her mind clear," but the burden of decision is too much for her. On the fateful day she is found in the church, "facing the brass there, else seeing none,/ But feeling the words with her finger, gibbering in fits." The conflict is clear—fidelity to a sacred vow versus love for a man—and from the point of view of Hardy the modernist, whose works include frequent attacks on marriage conventions, judgment is easy; the widow would seem to be the victim of an oppressive ecclesiastical institution.

But the situation is more complicated, for there are hints of impulsiveness and of a tendency toward self-dramatization in the widow which contribute to obscuring the conflict. These qualities are implicit in her act of including her name on her husband's tomb inscription. On impulse, she publicly displays her fidelity. Certainly Hardy makes clear that she is concerned with public opinion, for her fear of social scorn, he reveals, is as important to her as her fear of damnation:

> Moreover she thought of the laughter, the shrug, the jibe
> That would rise at her back in the nave when she
>   should pass
> As another's avowed by the words she had chosen to
>   inscribe
> On the changeless brass.

She lacks the full courage that her love should provide her. The priest is aware of the worldly dangers in her situation; for him, "more perceptions moved than one." Hints of what

112

his perceptions might be appear in the description of how the widow fell in love with her new suitor:

> And her heart was stirred with a lightning love to its pith
> For a newcomer who, while less in years, was one
> Full eager and able to make her his own forthwith,
>   Restrained of none.

That her "lightning love" might be a dangerous impulse is supported by her suitor's being a newcomer, younger than she, and himself impulsive. The priest, in making his recommendation, seems to be responding as much to his judgment of their shared "impulse of passionate need" as to the sanctity of the widow's vow. It could be a fatal mistake for her to marry an eager lover younger than herself. The priest's objection to the marriage seems to be his way of protecting her from what he sees as a threat. In short, he is not merely a dogmatic oppressor, for he shows awareness that the integrity implied by faithfulness to a vow can be a protection against too-impulsive action. But the results suggest that the priest, despite his apparent decency, gave the wrong advice. His voice makes up as important a part as the young lover's insistency in the forces that drive the widow to madness. In the poem Hardy transforms a melodramatic conflict between faith and love into a study of the bewildering precariousness and complexity of choice.

An even more complicated narrative is "The Noble Lady's Tale (*circa* 1790)" (*CP*, pp. 272–277), most of which is told by the lady herself. Like "The Inscription," it records an entirely imagined incident, but the situation is based on a real marriage between an actor and a lady who lived in the parish of Stinsford in the late eighteenth and early nineteenth centuries. As a boy, Hardy often saw their memorial plaque in Stinsford Church (referred to in the poem as the "yellowing marble" in "Mellstock Quire"), and the disparities in their social stations provoked his curiosity. The poem shows that he brooded not only over the lady's willingness to marry beneath her, which is the salient fact of the story from the conventional point of view, but also over the actor's willingness to abandon his profession for her. In the poem the actor, although he had promised her to leave the stage, is troubled by a wish to perform once more. He confesses his desire to his anxious wife, and

113

she repays his honesty by releasing him from his promise despite her apprehensions:

> "I thought, 'Some wild stage-woman,
>   Honour-wrecked . . .'
> But no: it was inhuman
>   To suspect."

Although there appears to be full confidence, "faith and frankness," between the actor and the lady, both are aware of some nameless threat: "He feared it . . . I, also,/ Feared it still more." Ironically, the lady's impulse to suspect is quite natural.

In the event that follows, the threat assumes a psychological reality that ruins the lives of the couple. When the actor returns to his wife, he reports bitterly that he failed in London because he saw her concealed in the audience and lost faith in her trust:

> " 'Faith—frankness. Ah! Heaven save such!'
>   Murmured he,
> 'They are wedded wealth! I gave such
>   Liberally,
> But you, Dear, not. For you suspected me.' "

She protests that she has remained faithfully at home and did not attend the performance. Yet to his dying day he insists on blaming his failure on her, deciding that even if she was not there, the apparition was her wraith "projected . . . Thither, by [her] tense brain at home aggrieved." Neither character sees the possibility that the wraith was a projection of his own guilt, or of his unconscious awareness of her fundamental lack of trust in him.

The major irony is that the professed confidence of the two lovers in one another, their willingness to confess all, turned out to mask deep-seated, unconfessed fears and insecurities. Whether a manifestation of the wife's anxiety or the husband's guilt, a phantom arose from the psychological depths to blight their lives. Their hope for salvation lay in a full confession of their fears and suspicions, but instead, they destroyed their relationship by professing faith. The poem dramatizes how difficult it is to know when to suppress threatenting impulses, and when to give them expression. The final stanza reveals the narrator's sympathetic inability to pass conclusive judgment:

> Riddle death-sealed for ever,
>   Let it rest! . . .
> One's heart could blame her never
>   If one guessed
> That go she did. She knew her actor best.

Ironically, she did not know her actor well enough.

Both "The Noble Lady's Tale" and "The Dead Quire" are associated with the history of Hardy's boyhood parish church at Stinsford. By extension, both poems deal with mystery—one with the mystery of a Christian miracle, the other with the more natural mystery of human psychology. Thus, they record the old illusions and the new. Along with Hardy's other ballads and narratives, they also constitute an imaginative history of the Wessex countryside, preserving the memory of a society comprised of sympathetic, imaginative, complex human beings, whose sufferings merit compassionate attention.

The Burden of Guilt

In the ballads and narratives based on historical materials, Hardy portrays characters who attempt to exert their moral imagination flexibly in the face of complex circumstances, such as the burghers whose deceptions allow a man a happy death, the volunteer who attempts to reconcile duty to country with fidelity to wife, the priest who aims at protecting the vulnerable widow, and the noble lady who tries to put down her fears and indulge a passionate wish of her husband. All of these characters have the qualities that Hardy celebrates in *The Science of Fiction*. In that they attempt humane action based on partial perceptions sympathetically received, they have what the artist must have: "the mental tactility that comes from a sympathetic appreciativeness of life in all of its manifestations."

It is significant that all of these people are from the country, for country people, in Hardy's view, are more fully endowed with imaginative sympathy—more fully human—than city

115

dwellers. This view helps explain Hardy's preoccupation with Wessex as a subject for poetry. As Hardy contends in the biography, children raised in the country are "imaginative, dreamy, and credulous of vague mysteries . . . [because] 'The Unknown comes within so short a radius from themselves by comparison with the city-bred.' " Of the so-called "barbarism" of the peasants, which equates persons with things and founds wide generalizations on slender analogies, Hardy comments: "This 'barbaric idea which confuses persons and things' is, by the way, also common to the highest imaginative genius— that of the poet."[7] This passage is dated 18 December 1890, while *The Science of Fiction* appeared in 1891. It seems safe to say that Hardy writes about the countryside partly because he finds there people who most fully exercise the power to deal with the mysterious "Unknowns" of life through imaginative sympathy.

Although this power usually has tragic consequences, it occasionally enables Hardy's characters to break out of the web of circumstances by making unconventional, unpredictable choices; sometimes they succeed in ignoring social norms and defying the logic of their selfish inclinations in order to create more humane and realistic personal standards of conduct. In "A Wife and Another" (*CP*, pp. 246–248), for example, the wife tells another woman, whom she suspects of a romantic involvement with her husband, that he is returning early from the war. Sensing intuitively that the woman has also received a letter, the wife steals it and discovers a plan for a secret tryst the night before her husband's return to her. She goes to the meeting place with plans to break up the affair, but, struck by the disclosure that her rival is to have a child, she has a change of heart:

> Then, as it were, within me
> Something snapped,
> As if my soul had largened:
> Conscience-capped,
> I saw myself the snarer—them the trapped.

Feeling herself the victim, she discovers that she is actually the victimizer. She releases her husband from his bonds to her and returns home, sad but confident: "I held I had not stirred God wrothfully." Her ability to sympathize with the lives of others liberates her from the web of circumstance and removes her to a higher realm of consciousness and morality.

"Her Late Husband (King's Hintock, 182–)" (*CP*, pp. 151–152) also portrays a woman who recognizes her rival's claim to her husband as greater than her own. She makes arrangements for him to be buried next to his mistress, "After whose death he seemed to ail,/ Though none considered why," while providing for her own burial in her family plot. She regards her act as conforming to a higher morality than social convention, and imagines that on Christmas, when angels walk, they will say:

> " 'O strange interment! Civilized lands
> Afford few types thereof;
> Here is a man who takes his rest
> Beside his very Love,
> Beside the one who was his wife
> In our sight up above!' "

Again, the nonconforming choice is a successful act of liberation.

"The Burghers (17—)" (*CP*, pp. 20–22), in contrast, presents the more complex case of a man whose moral scrupulosity leads him to question even his humane actions. Knowing of his wife's plans for an elopement, he schemes, with the encouragement of a friend, to surprise the lovers and kill the seducer. When the event occurs, the wife looks quickly at her lover—"Never upon me," says the husband, "Had she thrown look of love so thoroughsped!"—and then attempts to shield him from her husband's blow. "Blanked by such love," the husband pardons them and insists that his wife take with her money and all her possessions. The wife overcomes her scruples at accepting the generosity of a husband she is abandoning and takes the gifts. The poem concludes with an analysis of the complexities and ambiguities in the husband's act:

> " 'Fool,' some will say," I thought.—"But who is wise,
> Save God alone, to weigh my reasons why?"
> —"Hast thou struck home?" came with the boughs'
> night-sighs.

It was my friend. "I have struck well. They fly,
But carry wounds that none can cicatrize."
—"Not mortal?" said he. "Lingering—worse," said I.

On the surface it seems that the husband's impulse is generous
and humane, yet he realizes the potential of his action to feed
the lovers' guilt and thus leave worse than mortal wounds.
Only God can "weigh" his motive; not even he is sure of the
significance of what he has done. His act of liberation has put
the lovers eternally in his debt and opened a new realm of
possible guilt for himself. His higher morality may be a form
of more subtle enslavement.

In Hardy's ballads and narratives the characters usually fail.
They calculate humanely and sympathetically, but inaccurately;
events deceive; the power of the imagination is inadequate to
the circumstances. Yet what is most painful is not their failure
but the self-torture resulting from the sort of moral scrupulosity found in the husband in "The Burghers." Despite the relatively small and inconclusive part played by the characters in
the concatenation of events leading to death and suffering,
again and again they take upon themselves the full burden of
guilt. They imaginatively confuse cause with responsibility.
This is the most painful irony of all—that the characters, having attempted a moral action according to their best lights, tor-
ture themselves with anguished self-reproach. It is this overwhelming guilt, only partially justified, which is Hardy's most
compelling theme in his ballads and narratives of the Wessex
countryside.

"A Sunday Morning Tragedy (*circa* 186–)" (*CP*, pp. 188–191),
for example, is told by a woman in whom crushing circumstances arouse passionate energies of self-reproach. Her
daughter has been made pregnant by a man who refuses to
marry her, despite the urgings of the mother:

> I plodded to her sweetheart's door
> In Pydel Vale, alas for me:
> I pleaded with him, pleaded sore,
> To save her from her misery.

To induce abortion, the mother gives the girl an herb pur-
chased from an old shepherd, and the result is fatal. As the girl

lies on her deathbed on a Sunday morning, neighbors come to chide the family for the secrecy of her impending marriage; surprisingly, the banns were announced in church that day: " 'Ha-ha! Such well-kept news!' laughed they." The lover comes and whispers to the mother that her arguments have changed his mind: "I've felt for her, and righted all." But all is wrong. The mother goes to her daughter's bedside, and her scream draws everyone else:

> There she [the daughter] lay—silent, breathless, dead,
> Stone dead she lay—wronged, sinless she!
> Ghost-white the cheeks once rosy-red.

The circumstances causing the tragedy are shown to be complex and powerful. The young man avoids marriage because he plans to emigrate, presumably to get a job and not merely to escape a moral responsibility: " 'Poverty's worse than shame,' he said." Whether or not his motives are exclusively self-serving, in the final event he shows himself to be susceptible to a moral plea: "I've felt for her." The mother is aware of the tragic absurdities of living in a world where birth can be a curse, as indicated in her observation on the old shepherd's justification of the herb:

> " 'Tis meant to balk ill-motherings"—
> (Ill-motherings! Why should they be?)—
> "If not, would God have sent such things?"
> So spoke the shepherd unto me.

The shepherd's logic is weak—that an indication of God's providence is the existence of herbs that will kill unborn children. The mother's view seems closer to the realities: her daughter's predicament is an indication of the perplexing grimness of the human situation. Yet the most touching feature of the tale is the mother's guilt. The refrain "Alas for me!" (not for the daughter) rings again and again, and the poem ends with a self-curse: "My punishment I cannot bear,/ But pray God *not* to pity me." One can understand her feeling of guilt, for she unsuccessfully risked her daughter's life in order to avoid scandal. Yet, from an objective point of view, the ultimate responsibility was not hers. She was trapped by external complex-

119

ities—the lovers' passion, the man's poverty, the "prov-
idential" existence of abortifacients, the weight of social
pressures, her concern for her daughter's future—all of which
led to her well-intentioned act. Yet she assumes the burden
of responsibility. Throughout she believes in the "innocency"
of her daughter, who in her view died "wronged, sinless"; but
she cannot forgive herself, even though she is a victim of the
same circumstances.

"Her Death and After" (CP, pp. 34–38) provides an even
more painful example of the tragically scrupulous moral imagination at work, for it describes the guilt of a man whose well-
intentioned actions are successful. He is called to the deathbed
of a woman dying in childbirth, who had refused his suit and
married another man. The woman realizes now the mistake
of her marriage and fears that her husband, a man of cruel
impulses, will mistreat her child, who was born lame. On her
deathbed she repents her fidelity to traditional morality:

> "As a wife I was true. But, such my unease
> That, could I insert a deed back in Time,
> I'd make her yours, to secure your care;
> And the scandal bear,
> And the penalty for the crime!"

Her fears are realized: the husband remarries, and he and his
new wife mistreat the child. The speaker continues to visit the
wife's tomb, and one evening he encounters the husband in
"the Cirque of the Gladiators," Dorchester's Roman Ring,
"Whose Pagan echoes mock the chime/ Of our Christian time."
In that morally ambivalent place, the speaker makes a strange,
unconventional choice. The husband demands that he stop visiting the wife's grave:

> "There's decency even in death, I assume;
> Preserve it, sir, and keep away;
> For the mother of my first-born you
> Show mind undue!"

On a desperate impulse, the speaker claims that the child is
his—"God pardon—or pardon not—the lie"—and offers to
care for it. If necessary, he is even willing to fight a duel. The

husband then sends him the child, whom the speaker raises and loves—but not without feelings of guilt:

> And I gave the child my love,
> And the child loved me, and estranged us none.
> But compunctions loomed; for I'd harmed the dead
>   By what I said
> For the good of the living one.

> —Yet though, God wot, I am sinner enough,
> And unworthy the woman who drew me so,
> Perhaps this wrong for her darling's good
>   She forgives, or would,
> If only she could know!

There is no question in the reader's mind but that the man is a saint, not a sinner; that he is more worthy of the woman's love, not less; that his action merits forgiveness, not condemnation; and that he should feel moral satisfaction, not guilt. But the poignancy of the poem results from his inability to feel free and confident in his action and to accept the girl's love without "compunctions." He has fulfilled the wishes of the woman he loved, risked his life to save another human being from suffering, and found the consolation of loving companionship. Yet he feels guilty for telling a lie that impugns the good name of a dead person, even though the woman herself confessed on her deathbed that she would willingly endure scandal to save her child.

The ending is typical. Again and again Hardy's narratives conclude on a note of guilt. The characters submit to circumstances and feel guilty; they attempt to act according to conventional moral principles and feel guilty; they act courageously and boldly to liberate themselves from conventions and circumstances, and the result is guilt. Guilt drives the wife in "At Shag's Heath" to suicide. Guilt causes the protagonists in "San Sebastian" (*CP*, pp. 17–19) and "A Sunday Morning Tragedy" to bring down curses on their own heads. Guilt makes a wandering outcast of the trampwoman. Thoughts of her guilt obsess the mind of Jenny as she dies at the end of "The Dance at the Phoenix" (*CP*, pp. 38–42). In "The Peasant's Confession" (*CP*, pp. 26–30) a man expresses his guilt for subverting Napoleon's chances at Waterloo in order to prevent the battle from taking place on his own land. "The Sacrilege" (*CP*, pp. 375–379), describing a man's vengeance on a predatory woman who led his brother to his death, ends with the vision of her hair floating in the water and the sound of her dying scream haunting him "Until his judgment-time." "The Carica-ture" (*CP*, pp. 728–729) concludes with a man driven insane by his guilt for a trivial but cruel act. "The Flirt's Tragedy" (*CP*, pp. 195–198), another tale of love and infidelity, ends with the guilt of a wronged man who failed in his attempts to repair the excesses of his vengeance:

> But pass by, and leave unregarded
>   A Cain to his suffering,
> For vengeance too dark on the woman
>   Whose lover he slew.

In poetically recording the history of the Wessex countryside, Hardy tells tales of people trapped by their errors, their uncer-tainty as to proper moral values, their failure of perception, their inability to foresee consequences and to predict the effects of change and chance. But the most interesting theme is the tragic scrupulosity of the moral imagination. Hardy delineates the limitations of his characters' responsibility for their condi-tions, makes allowances for their good intentions, and forgives them for their mistakes—that is, he brings into play his own sympathetic imagination. But the characters themselves see only their errors, their failures, their moments of temporary malice. Too often they take full responsibility for circumstances that are partially outside their control, and act as unforgiving judges of their own lives. For them, the imaginative sympathy is a burden; their high and flexible sense of morality, their aspi-rations for the better, their desires to be expansively human bring them grief. In Hardy's verse narratives the characters' afflictions come from chance and circumstance and bitter ironies of situation, but no external forces punish them as unremittingly as their own consciences.

122

PHILOSOPHICAL FANTASIES
5

"Hap," "The Impercipient," "A Sign-Seeker," and "A Meeting with Despair" from *Wessex Poems*, with their earnest visions of a world devoid of intentioned structure, either benign or malicious, and presided over by random forces operating unconsciously, foreshadow Hardy's creation of a new kind of poem, which might be called, to borrow from one of his own titles, a philosophical fantasy. In poems of this sort, appearing plentifully and for the first time fully developed in *Poems of the Past and the Present* (1902), Hardy writes fanciful dramas in which the leading actors are usually personified forces of nature. The forms of the dramas are various. In one poem, God, a man-projected figure dying because knowledge is gradually revealing the imaginative nature of all religious myth, gives advice to man as he perishes. In another, God's mourners assemble at his funeral to lament their loss and express their perplexity in the face of a world without supernatural comfort. In other poems, God lives but acts unconsciously; or he is conscious but lacks a moral sense; or he has an incipient moral sense, but it has not yet evolved to the level of man's; or he has developed a morality but has forgotten the earth. Nature is a sleep-worker, oblivious to the suffering of her creatures; or she is awake, sensitive, and anxious about her creation, but blind, so that she must depend on unfeeling Doom to execute her intentions; or she is fully conscious and all-seeing but impotent to control the forces that she has launched in her acts of creation. These poems exhibit Hardy's imagination at play with religious and philosophical ideas.

Cosmic Injustice

In Hardy's poetry there is significant variation in the views presented, as illustrated by the various attitudes expressed toward the possibilities for humane progress. Some poems indicate that the pain-inducing flaws in the nature of things are ever-present and eternal. "The world is as it used to be," says God in "Channel Firing" (CP, pp. 287–288) to the dead, who have awakened at the sound of gunnery practice and think it Judgment Day. "Will the world ever saner be . . . In our indifferent century"? asks a voice from the grave, "And many a skeleton shook his head." In "A Night of Questionings" (CP, pp. 688–690), the dead on the eve of All Soul's Day ask, "What of the world now?" The modern speaker can only reply that as far as he knows, nothing has changed. At the conclusion of the poem he addresses the ghost of a hanged man:

> "Men have not shown,
> Since you were stretched that morning,
> A white cap your adorning,
> More lovely deeds or true
> Through thus neck-knotting you;
> Or that they purer grow,
> Or ever will, I trow!—
> No more I know."

In contrast to the vision of an eternally suffering, unchanging world, other poems suggest a movement downward, a process of historical deterioration. "At the Entering of the New Year" (CP, pp. 605–606), with the speaker's impassioned plea that the year should not come into being ("O stay without, O stay without"), implies the view that history has degenerated to a condition of unendurable suffering and disillusionment, and that time should stop before things get worse. The speaker who addresses Nature in "Genetrix Laesa" (CP, p. 733) seems likewise to see the end of all hope:

> Why should man your purblind blinking
> Crave to cure, when all is sinking
> To dissolubility?

A third view in the poems assumes the possibility of progress. It may be that the animating force of nature, whether it is called God or the Immanent Will or Nature herself, is gradually becoming conscious, rational, and humane, as Hardy suggests in "Agnostoi Theoi" (*CP*, pp. 171–172):

> Perhaps Thy ancient rote-restricted ways
> Thy ripening rule transcends;
> That listless effort tends
> To grow percipient with advance of days,
> And with percipience mends.

The speaker in "The Graveyard of Dead Creeds" (*CP*, p. 687) hears a voice prophesying a new set of beliefs " 'That shall make tolerable to sentient seers/ The melancholy marching of the years.' " History may be moving toward humane fulfillment, it may be deteriorating into hopelessness, or it may be plodding on in endless, monotonous defeat and suffering. All three views are expressed, with variations and modifications, in Hardy's poetry. For this great problem of man's fate he has no solution.

Despite their variety of form and idea, the philosophical fantasies usually attribute the cause of human suffering to the nature of things. The ballads, whose characters repeatedly experience overwhelming guilt for catastrophes beyond their control, dramatize one way of responding to the crushing complexities of existence: to assume personal responsibility for their effects. Throughout his work Hardy dramatized this alternative. The novels present many figures who attempt to take the responsibility for themselves and the lives of others; when they fail, as they usually do, they tend to experience guilt. Gabriel Oak in *Far from the Madding Crowd*, Clym Yeobright in *The Return of the Native*, Giles Winterborne in *The Woodlanders*, and Tess in *Tess of the d'Urbervilles* are manifestations of this type. Clym, for example, feels himself to be fully accountable for the death of his mother, an event caused by a complex web of circumstance and motive that was to a large extent beyond his control. Late in the novel he stares at his mother's chair, idealizing her ("the sublime saint whose radiance even his tenderness for Eustacia could not obscure") and blaming himself: "It was all my fault . . . O, my mother, my mother! would to God that I could live my life again, and endure for you what you endured for me!"[1] His guilt exceeds his causal responsibility for the catastrophe, just as his idealization of his mother exaggerates the reality of her character. His response represents an extreme.

The other extreme response is to blame all catastrophe on the skewed nature of things, as Hardy tends to do in the philosophical fantasies and in many statements in his notebooks: "The emotions have no place in a world of defect, and it is a cruel injustice that they should have developed in it." Again, this was a response Hardy frequently dramatized. Characters like Sergeant Troy in *Far from the Madding Crowd*, Eustacia Vye and Wildeve (and to a great extent Mrs. Yeobright) in *The Return of the Native*, and Fitzpiers and Mrs. Charmond in *The Woodlanders*, tend to ignore their causal responsibility for their plights and to blame their suffering on the injustice of circumstance. When Sergeant Troy, for example, finds that the rain has demolished the plot of flowers he planted on Fanny Robin's grave in a self-indulgent, sentimental gesture, he feels that the nature of things is thwarting his change of heart: "to find that Providence, far from helping him into a new course, or showing any wish that he might adopt one, actually jeered his first trembling and critical attempt in that kind, was more than nature could bear."[2] Finding nothing in external circumstances to reinforce the flimsy promptings of his moral sense, he abandons all responsibility, sets aside the memory of the country girl he seduced, and flees, conscience-free, from Bathsheba, his wronged wife.

Sue Bridehead in *Jude the Obscure* continually wavers between her sense of nature's injustice and her sense of guilt. After Father Time kills her children and takes his own life, Sue says, "There is something external to us which says, 'You shan't!' First it said, 'You shan't learn!' Then it said, 'You shan't labour!' Now it says, 'You shan't love!' " Something outside her seems to thwart her life. Yet she also feels guilty for encouraging Father Time in his gloomy view of the world and decides that her children's death was a punishment for her sinful relation with Jude: "My babies have been taken from me to show me this . . . What, *what* shall I do! I am such

126

a vile creature—too worthless to mix with ordinary human beings!" Jude's reply indicates Hardy's awareness of the destructive potential of obsessive guilt: "It is monstrous and unnatural for you to be so remorseful when you have done no wrong!"[3] Indeed, Sue's abandonment of Jude and sacrifice of herself once again to Phillotson, actions based on her sense of guilt, are "monstrous and unnatural." Obsessive guilt and a sense of deterministic cosmic injustice are the two extremes. Both views render life an arena of meaningless suffering. The problem is to find a middle way.

The middle way is expressed both explicitly and implicitly in Hardy's philosophical fantasies, despite their prevailing sense of cosmic injustice. The solution is to accept one's limitations and to exert as much compassion and imaginative sympathy for human suffering as one is capable of, in hopes that the result will be amelioration and change. The acceptance of limitations is a protection against obsessive guilt, and the imperative to be compassionate defines a reasonable area of human responsibility and tempers outrage at the nature of things. The dying god in "A Plaint to Man" (*CP*, p. 306), for example, points out the implication of his death:

> The truth should be told, and the fact be faced
> That had best been faced in earlier years:
>
> The fact of life with dependence placed
> On the human heart's resource alone,
> In brotherhood bonded close and graced
>
> With loving-kindness fully blown,
> And visioned help unsought, unknown.

Time in "The Lacking Sense" (*CP*, pp. 106–107) urges man to assist blind Mother Nature "where thy creaturely dependence can or may." The "Drinking Song" (*CP*, pp. 864–866) which explodes history's hopeful myths about the benevolence of nature, ends with the pledge to "do a good deed nevertheless!" In "Surview" (*CP*, pp. 660–661) Hardy makes explicit what he took to be the intended lesson of his work and, characteristically, chides himself for his failure of communication:

"You taught not that which you set about,"
Said my own voice talking to me;
"That the greatest of things is Charity."

In the "Apology" to *Late Lyrics and Earlier,* Hardy puts this view in prose: "Whether the human and kindred animal races survive till the exhaustion or destruction of the globe, or whether these races perish and are succeeded by others before that conclusion comes, pain to all upon it, tongued or dumb, shall be kept down to a minimum by loving-kindness, operating through scientific knowledge, and actuated by the modicum of free will conjecturally possessed by organic life when the mighty necessitating forces—unconscious or other—that have 'the balancings of the clouds,' happen to be in equilibrium, which may or may not be often."[4] The web of qualifications in this passage almost chokes out the possibility of the exertion of meaningful loving kindness. Yet Hardy clearly intended the statement to be a guarded expression of positive value.

More interesting but more difficult to identify than the explicit statements of belief in loving kindness are the implicit manifestations of compassion in Hardy's poetry, especially in the philosophical fantasies, which on the surface dramatize a world of defect in which emotion has no place. The workings of compassion and imaginative responsiveness in these poems, which are among Hardy's most bleakly pessimistic and grimly ironic, nevertheless illustrate his positive values and help explain the sources of his power as a poet. Many critics have read the philosophical fantasies as bald statements of deterministic, late-nineteenth-century pessimism, a philosophical position that probably seems crude, commonplace, and dated to most readers today. To read the poems in this way is to miss their imaginative texture and to ignore the various kinds of sympathy expressed by the poet and evoked in the reader.

On the most obvious level the philosophical fantasies are responses to a vision of suffering. Struck by the painful flaws in the world as he sees it, Hardy cries out that God seems to be dead, or Nature blind, or the First Cause unconscious. If any myth is to account for the blood and tears, it must be the myth of a defective creator. Moreover, the poems manifest an informed imagination consciously at work to create an order of its own by means of controlled artistry. They blend moving drama with good-humored wit, earnest pathos with black comedy, impassioned statement with verbal cunning. The structure of emotion repeatedly belies the grim message of the philosophy. Hardy often lavishes on the semiallegorical figures representing the forces of nature the kind of loving care and sympathy that God ought to have for his creatures and man can have for his fellows. Often the characters have lives of their own, psychologically complex and humanly engaging. Paradoxically, these poems dramatizing the inappropriateness of emotion in a flawed world are urgent with sympathy and compassion. In the ballads, the neutral stance of the narrator protects and conceals Hardy himself. In the philosophical fantasies, Hardy's indictment of cosmic injustice protects him by the surface strategy of putting all responsibility at nature's feet. Yet in both sets of poems Hardy indirectly expresses and evokes emotional commitment.

Drama and Compassion

One of Hardy's notions that offended elements in his reading public is the idea that the traditional, consoling religious creeds have become untenable; God is dead. "The Problem" (*CP*, p. 109) is the statement of a man who grasps this reality:

> Shall we conceal the Case, or tell it—
>   We who believe the evidence?
> Here and there the watch-towers knell it
>   With a sullen significance,
> Heard of the few who hearken intently and carry an
>   eagerly upstrained sense.
>
> Hearts that are happiest hold not by it;
>   Better we let, then, the old view reign:
> Since there is peace in that, why decry it?
>   Since there is comfort, why disdain?
> Note not the pigment so long as the painting determines
>   humanity's joy and pain.

Hardy appropriately employs the common rhetorical technique of concealing the basic fact to which his speaker responds, the "it" of the problem, and places the burden of interpretation on the reader in an otherwise fairly straightforward poem. Hardy himself follows his speaker's advice in not telling the case, and presumably only those who are already familiar with the evidence will perceive what the poem is about. The few who listen carefully, whose attention is directed upward, hear the knell announcing a death from the watch-towers, elevations from which the clearest views are obtained. The listeners are active, earnest seekers—they "hearken intently," their sense is "eagerly upstrained"—and they grasp the reality. Yet their spokesman in the poem feels sympathy rather than scorn for their benighted fellows who do not hear the knell; he shrinks from the impulse to "decry" and "disdain." Those who believe that what is dead is still alive are happier for this belief—indeed, are happier than the speaker—finding peace and comfort in it. Since the painting—the set of false beliefs —has such power to determine joy and pain, it is futile to point out that it is a human construct, done in pigments, artificial colors. The word "knell," which is the key signal to the meaning of "it," sounds the note of death and hints perhaps at the issue of Christ's resurrection, but certainly at the death of God. The true seers, directing their attention ironically toward heaven, hear the announcement of God's death while the false, earthbound believers persist in the comforting assumption that He is still alive.

"The Problem" is interesting for its ironies, for the appropriateness of the visionary dramatic situation to indirectly revealing the fact of God's death, and for the jarring disparity between the earnestness of the tone and the crudeness of the prosody—the jog-trot rhythm, created by the falling meter, the varied length of the foot, and the heavily accented, blunt alliterative groupings. But at the heart is compassion, which is expressed for the benighted faithful and evoked for the realistic searchers. The speaker is caught between the imperative to be sincere and realistic, on the one hand, and his desire to protect his fellows from the loss of peace and comfort, on the other. His is a real problem, a quandary that demands sympathy. The poem, with its bleak, pessimistic vision of "sullen significance," eschews bitterness and scorn. Instead, it evokes compassion on two clear levels, and because of his feelings for others, the iconoclast appears to be a sympathetic figure.

"God's Funeral" (*CP*, pp. 307–309), which expresses a more bizarre allegory for the death of God, is charged with greater emotion. The speaker sees a "slowly-stepping train" of mourners bearing a "strange and mystic form," an ever changing figure which, in all of its shapes, "symboled . . . Potency vast and loving-kindness strong." In contrast to "The Problem," most people here seem to be aware of the death of God and join in a lament, beginning:

> "O man-projected Figure, of late
> Imaged as we, thy knell who shall survive?
> Whence came it we were tempted to create
> One whom we can no longer keep alive?"

They show their consciousness both of having themselves created in God an image of power, justice, and mercy as an expression of their own moral vision, and of having made the mistake of believing in a myth of their own making. As the lament continues, they sketch the history of God's evolution:

> "Framing him jealous, fierce, at first,
> We gave him justice as the ages rolled,
> Will to bless those by circumstance accurst,
> And longsuffering, and mercies manifold."

They describe "How sweet it was" to have a merciful God to address in prayer and express their intense feelings of spiritual isolation at God's death:

> "And who or what shall fill his place?
> Whither will wanderers turn distracted eyes
> For some fixed star to stimulate their pace
> Towards the goal of their enterprise?"

In contrast to the views presented in "The Problem," where the benighted faithful—the many—fail to hear the death-knell, it is ironic that in this poem the few, including the speaker, who stand aloof and have a clearer vision see hints of hope for the future that the mourners ignore:

131

> to my growing sight there seemed
> A pale yet positive gleam low down behind,
>
> Whereof, to lift the general night,
> A certain few who stood aloof had said,
> "See you upon the horizon that small light—
> Swelling somewhat?" Each mourner shook his head.

Despite this reversal in situation, "The Problem" and "God's Funeral" have the same emotional core. The speaker here shows no disdain for the mourners' failure to see the "positive gleam," nor does he decry the myths they mistakenly believe in. Instead, he is a model of complex sympathy; his consciousness opens outward, participating in their feelings. As soon as he sees the procession, he cannot resist joining it:

> And by contagious throbs of thought
> Or latent knowledge that within me lay
> And had already stirred me, I was wrought
> To consciousness of sorrow even as they.

The words "throbs," "stirred," "wrought," and "consciousness" suggest a vibrant coming alive through feeling, a latency made active. As in "The Problem," some people refuse to believe in the death of God, saying: "This is a counterfeit of straw,/ This requiem mockery! Still he lives to us!" The speaker does more than sympathize with their plight, he feels it; their loss is also his:

> I could not buoy their faith: and yet
> Many I had known: with all I sympathized;
> And though struck speechless, I did not forget
> That what was mourned for, I, too, long had prized.

The problem here is not "Shall we conceal the Case, or tell it?" but how shall we bear the suffering and perplexity of lost faith—"how to bear such loss I deemed/ The insistent question for each animate mind." And while the speaker in "The Problem" makes a recommendation ("Note not the pigment"), the speaker here is left with nothing to say ("And though struck speechless"). On the surface there seems to be no solution except the dumb, perplexed, mindless acceptance expressed in

132

the last lines of the poem: "Thus dazed and puzzled 'twixt the gleam and gloom/ Mechanically I followed with the rest." Yet there is a sense of affirmative possibility in the drama of the poem, of which the speaker is only dimly aware in the symbolic "positive gleam" on the horizon, but which the reader can see more clearly. Man's high moral vision may have the power to stand in its own right without the supporting myth of a beneficent God. The speaker himself, as he says, exhibits the "Will to bless those by circumstance accurst,/ And longsuffering, and mercies manifold" embodied in the highest form of the man-projected myth. He can open his heart to the sorrow of the mourners, and participate sympathetically in their procession; at the same time, because he has experienced the same psychological need, he can sympathize with the benighted few who ignore reality. He can perceive the gleam of hope seen by the far-sighted visionaries, yet "creep and grope" with the mourners, "Sadlier than those who wept in Babylon," bearing with them the burden of their suffering. The dying God in "A Plaint to Man" points out the "fact of life with dependence placed/ On the human heart's resource alone." The speaker in "God's Funeral" demonstrates the capacity of his heart: his is the "Potency vast and loving-kindness strong" imaged in the myth of God. The ultimate pathos of the poem results from his failure to recognize that "positive gleam" in himself.

"The Problem" and "God's Funeral" present allegorical dramatic situations that evoke sympathy for the plight of man in a world without divinity, and exemplify in submerged, indirect ways the human powers which may have the potential to compensate for the death of God. In other poems the dramatic situations have more than allegorical relevance, and the characters have curious and interesting lives of their own. In a note from the mid 1880s Hardy records the germ idea for several of his philosophical fantasies: "Poem. We have reached a degree of intelligence which Nature never contemplated when framing her laws, and for which she consequently has provided no adequate satisfactions. [This, which he had adumbrated before, was clearly the germ of the poem entitled 'The Mother Mourns' and others.]"[5] There are seeds of drama in this idea of a female god, capable of framing laws, whose creations have evolved in unintended directions. These seeds flower in a highly theatrical moment in "The Mother Mourns" (*CP*, pp. 101–103). The poem is a soliloquy of Mother Nature, who laments the unforeseen results of her initial acts of creation. She is like the capricious heroines of Hardy's novels, such as Bathsheba Everdene, or Sue Bridehead, who half-consciously seek the admiration of men, only to set off, unwittingly, stronger emotions, whose consequences result in their own suffering. The Mother also resembles Mrs. Yeobright, whose love and aspirations for Clym are transformed in his character, to her dismay, into self-sacrificing idealism and a similarly ego-blinded love for another woman.

The stage is set by a speaker wandering at night in a forlorn mid-autumn landscape. He hears "A low lamentation,/ As though from a tree-god disheartened," which he discovers to be the "Weary plaint" of "Nature herself." Her complaint is against her creature, man. She begins, like a parent suffering under the criticism of ungrateful children, by piteously and futilely denying that she ever intended her offspring to grow up to think for themselves:

> —"I had not proposed me a Creature
>   (She soughed) so excelling
> All else of my kingdom in compass
>   And brightness of brain
>
> "As to read my defects with a god-glance,
>   Uncover each vestige
> Of old inadvertence, annunciate
>   Each flaw and each stain!"

She berates herself for permitting this to happen: "Why loosened I olden control here . . .?" She goes on to catalogue man's offenses: "He holds as inept his own soul-shell—/ My deftest achievement." He no longer sees the sun as a "Sanct-shape," the moon as the "Night-queen," the stars as "august and sublime ones." He sees nature as immoral, and love as a mere biological device necessary for the perpetuation of species. Indeed, man makes the ultimate charge against Mother Nature, the perpetual boast of the young when they look at the sorry mess that their parents have made of the world:

134

" 'Give me,' he has said, 'but the matter
And means the gods lot her,
My brain could evolve a creation
More seemly, more sane.' "

The catalogue of offenses finished, Mother Nature once
again laments her mistake, but this time it becomes clear that
her original goals in creating man included self-interest. Her
ulterior motives, which she fails to admit fully, she nevertheless now regrets:

—"If ever a naughtiness seized me
To woo adulation
From creatures more keen than those crude ones
That first formed my train—

"If inly a moment I murmured,
'The simple praise sweetly,
But sweetlier the sage'—and did rashly
Man's vision unrein,

"I rue it!"

She enjoyed being surrounded by sycophantic flunkies, and
at least one of her reasons for creating man was her desire for
more intelligent praise of her own work. Her error was pride.
She should have left well enough alone and been content with
the lower creatures than man:

"From them my waste aimings and futile
I subtly could cover;
'Every best thing,' said they, 'to best purpose
Her powers preordain.'—

"No more such!"

Now the flunkies are disappearing, Nature observes, for man,
having "aped mine own slaughters," is destroying the lesser
animals. Her only recourse is to vow to restrict her creations
in the future to ugliness and deformity:

"Let me grow, then, but mildews and mandrakes,
And slimy distortions,
Let nevermore things good and lovely
To me appertain;

"For Reason is rank in my temples,
    And Vision unruly,
And chivalrous laud of my cunning
    Is heard not again!"

If man will not be chivalrous to her, she will live up to his criticisms with a vengeance.

The poem has come a long way from the germ idea for while it expresses a pessimistic philosophical vision, it also exposes character, that of a parent lamenting the ungratefulness of her children, cataloguing their wrongs, reproaching herself for her own miscalculations, revealing her vanity, and shaping revenge. This progression, with parallel shifts in tone from sorrow to self-recrimination to hostility, is psychologically credible. The casting of this all-too-human character in the role of Mother Nature surveying the mess she has made of her work also creates a disparity that has its comic side. This humor, together with the theatrical bleakness of the speaker's introduction and the grotesqueness of the diction and syntax, make for an odd mixture of melodramatic posturing, realistic psychology, philosophic fancy, and linguistic unruliness. Hardy once wrote, "The business of the poet and novelist is to show the sorriness underlying the grandest things, and the grandeur underlying the sorriest things." His statement about farce and tragedy is also relevant here: "If you look beneath the surface of any farce you see a tragedy; and, on the contrary, if you blind yourself to the deeper issues of a tragedy you see a farce."[6] "The Mother Mourns" considers a grand issue, the origin of human consciousness, but finds that origin to be a sorry one, the mixed motives of an imperfect creator. Moreover, there are both sorriness and grandeur in the character of the abused parent, whose children, born partly as the result of her desire for love, respect, and admiration, employ their intellectual and emotional powers to reveal her defects and to despise her. To cast this familiar human figure in a lofty role, allowing her unwittingly to expose her pettiness and vanity, has the effect of farce. From another point of view Mother Nature is a tragic figure, because her actions have had the result of trapping her in a world she cannot control. In this poem, then, philosophy has generated dramatic vision. Hardy's idea of a flawed world served him as a stimulant to the creation of a playfully mixed theatrical moment.

Hardy himself makes reference to the playfulness of his philosophical fantasies in a letter to Alfred Noyes, in which he emphasizes the distinction between "the expression of fancy and the expression of belief . . . My imagination may have often run away with me; but all the same, my sober opinion —so far as I have any definite one—of the Cause of Things, has been defined in scores of places, and is that of a great many ordinary thinkers: that the said Cause is neither moral nor immoral, but *un*moral." The letter reveals that Hardy saw the potential for humor in certain conceptions of God: "no doubt people will go on thinking that I really believe the Prime Mover to be a malignant old gentleman, a sort of King of Dahomey—an idea which, so far from my holding it, is to me irresistibly comic." He describes the poems "New Year's Eve" and "God's Education" (earlier titled "His Education") as representing "fanciful impressions of the moment"; that is, they are essentially works of the imagination.[7] These two poems, as well as several others— "God-Forgotten" in particular—illustrate Hardy's playful treatment of the idea of an unmoral God, and show that he sometimes irresistibly regarded such a god as comic. He creates dramatized moments which, as in "The Mother Mourns," blend sorriness and grandeur, tragedy and farce.

In "New Year's Eve" and "God's Education" Hardy casts as the first creator characters who are quite different from the mourning mother, and dramatizes quite different situations. In neither poem is there any reference to the progression of thought or feeling within the consciousness of a single character. Instead, both poems by means of dialogue dramatize the disparity between the judgments of the sensitive human creature and the indifference of the creator. "New Year's Eve" (*CP*, pp. 260–261) begins:

> "I have finished another year," said God,
> "In grey, green, white, and brown;
> I have strewn the leaf upon the sod,
> Sealed up the worm within the clod,
> And let the last sun down."

137

God is presented as a neat and orderly housekeeper, announcing the completion of his duties in clear, simple language that has the tone of calm domesticity often found in Emily Dickinson's poetry, especially in the coy last line, "And let the last sun down." God is an agent of order, concerned with the placement of each leaf and worm. When the human speaker interrupts to question the meaning of it all, the language of the poem becomes more contorted and harsh:

> "And what's the good of it?" I said . . .
>
> "Yea, Sire; why shaped you us, 'who in
>   This tabernacle groan'—
> If ever a joy be found herein,
> Such joy no man had wished to win
>   If he had never known!"

God leaves it to man to find the explanation for himself:

> Then he: "My labours—logicless—
>   You may explain; not I:
> Sense-sealed I have wrought, without a guess
> That I evolved a Consciousness
>   To ask for reasons why."

This is a bald statement of the germ idea of Nature's amorality, but the poem expands beyond mere statement. God, it turns out, is no mechanical monster, although "sense-sealed"; he has the quite human ability to be struck by surprise:

> "Strange that ephemeral creatures who
>   By my own ordering are,
> Should see the shortness of my view,
> Use ethic tests I never knew,
>   Or made provision for!"

The moment is half-comic, again mixing farce and tragedy. Man has asked why he was created, since he is vulnerable to such suffering, and God's response is to express curiosity that man should have the intelligence and sensitivity to ask such a question. But God's moment of surprise is brief, and he resumes his role of orderly housekeeper:

> He sank to raptness as of yore,
>   And opening New Year's Day
> Wove it by rote as theretofore,
> And went on working evermore
>   In his unweeting way.

Although the poem asserts the amorality of God, it does so by dramatizing a confrontation between a morally earnest human being and a hard-working, indifferent, and mildly perplexed creator. Both the temporal setting of the poem, beginning with the end of the old year and ending with the inevitable commencement of the new, and the arrangement of the poem, each speaker being allowed two stanzas, create a satisfying sense of order and completion.

"God's Education" (CP, pp. 261–262) develops a similar contrast, but with greater intensity and more startling effect. In "New Year's Eve" God merely tidies things up and the human speaker asks a relatively abstract question. Here God, observed by the speaker, has a specific destructive effect on a human life. He contributes to the aging and death of a woman:

> I saw him steal the light away
>   That haunted in her eye:
> It went so gently none could say
> More than that it was there one day
>   And missing by-and-by.

> I watched her longer, and he stole
>   Her lily tincts and rose;
> All her young sprightliness of soul
> Next fell beneath his cold control,
>   And disappeared like those.

The language describing the quiet, barely perceptible transformation from light, color, and sprightliness to inert bleakness is simple, graceful, and controlled, again reminiscent of Emily

Dickinson. The speaker's feelings are submerged in the objective description of what he saw. He saves his emotion for God, of whom he asks the old question, why:

> I asked: "Why do you serve her so?
>   Do you, for some glad day,
> Hoard these her sweets—?" He said, "O no,
> They charm not me; I bid Time throw
>   Them carelessly away."

In the first two stanzas there was a correlation between line and phrasing, whereas in this third stanza, the phrasing breaks up the lines, resulting in a sense of passion and conflict. The dash in the third line after "sweets" suggests either that the speaker's outrage has led him to inarticulateness, or that God has interrupted him. In any case, God speaks, as it were, with a callous shrug of the shoulders. The speaker refuses to let it pass and earnestly addresses him again:

> Said I: "We call that cruelty—
>   We, your poor mortal kind."
> He mused. "The thought is new to me.
> Forsooth, though I men's master be,
>   Theirs is the teaching mind!"

The bitter, half-comic irony in God's final words is even more exasperating than his carelessness. A woman is dying, which a man protests with deep concern, and God, calmly musing, is struck only with the thought that man could teach him a lesson. Here the poem ends. There is no final stanza, as there is in "New Year's Eve," to resolve the feelings in contemplation of the ongoing processes of existence. The poem begins in quiet, controlled sorrow and ends on a note of exasperating irony.

"God-Forgotten" (CP, pp. 112–113) includes Hardy's most fully realized and humanized statement of an indifferent divinity. In this philosophical fantasy he also most successfully blends pathos and humor, tragedy and farce. The earnest questioner speaking in the poem is a representative of all mankind:

> I towered far, and lo! I stood within
> The presence of the Lord Most High,
> Sent thither by the sons of Earth, to win
> Some answer to their cry.

The speaker's reverence, the Biblical overtones of the language, and the sense of elevation in the dramatic scene produce expectations of a serious confrontation between Earth's spokesman and a lofty deity. One expects a just and righteous God, or a merciful, compassionate God—certainly some version of the Biblical deity concerned with every detail in the drama of his creation. God's words come as an anticlimax:

> —"The Earth, sayest thou? The Human race?
> By Me created? Sad its lot?
> Nay: I have no remembrance of such place:
> Such world I fashioned not."

The messenger insists that God spoke "the word that made it all," in reference again to God in his Biblical manifestations. God thinks for a moment, and "dimly" recalls "Some tiny sphere I built long back/ (Mid millions of such shapes of mine)/ So named." Adam and Eve in the garden, the temptation, fall, and redemption of man, are reduced to dim memories of a careless and unsuccessful experiment:

> "It lost my interest from the first,
> My aims therefor succeeding ill;
> Haply it died of doing as it durst?"

With passion the speaker contradicts him: "Lord, it existeth still." God is roused to anger: "Dark, then, its life!" He has heard nothing from earth, which is earth's fault: "Of its own act the threads were snapt." At one time it had asked for "gifts of good" but then went silent, in contrast to the rest of creation: "All other orbs have kept in touch." God's self-righteous annoyance leads him to inconsistency. On the one hand, he would have listened if earth had kept in touch, but on the other, it is presumptuous of earth to assume that such a successful and busy creator would have time to pay attention to its petty concerns:

141

"And it is strange—though sad enough—
Earth's race should think that one whose call
Frames, daily, shining spheres of flawless stuff
Must heed their tainted ball!"

God has second thoughts, feeling "grieved" that earth should suffer "pangs distraught,/ And strife." But then he contradicts himself once more: earthlings should have known that *"Not to Mend/* For Me could mean but *Not to Know."* His solution is swift: "Hence, Messengers! and straightway put an end/ To what men undergo."

God here is an amusing figure—busy, careless, self-righteous, self-contradictory. His moods are capricious: he is now forgetful, curious, annoyed, angry, compassionate, decisive. He resembles a comic mayor of Casterbridge of cosmic proportions, like Michael Henchard all ego, something of a braggart whose wilfullness too often overcomes his sense of moral principle. But unlike Henchard, he is immune to the effects of his own mistakes. The comedy lies both in the exaggeration resulting from the brevity and compactness of the passages revealing God's alternating moods, and in the shocking disparity between his character and the traditional, Biblical concept of divinity. But this comic God appears in a serious setting; his impulsive self-righteousness contrasts with the consistent earnestness of the questioner and with the real suffering referred to in the poem. Black humor is not the final effect, however, for the last stanza brings the reader back to earth:

Homing at dawn, I thought to see
One of the Messengers standing by.
—Oh, childish thought! . . . Yet often it comes to me
When trouble hovers nigh.

The speaker dismisses his dramatic vision as mere fantasy, a "childish thought." There is comfort in imagining that one can visit God, remind him of earth's plight, and provoke him to send a messenger to ameliorate that suffering; but to do so is to let the imagination overreach itself. "When trouble hovers nigh" it is unrealistic and self-defeating to expect help; usually no one comes.

142

Style

In "The Mother Mourns," "New Year's Eve," "God's Education," and "God-Forgotten," which illustrate the variety of dramatic conception in the philosophical fantasies, the assumption is that men "have reached a degree of intelligence which Nature never contemplated when framing her laws." The common irony in these poems is that in comparison with the creature man, the creator, God or Nature, is morally deficient. The poems tend to generate sympathy for suffering mankind. In other philosophical fantasies, such as "The Lacking Sense," "Doom and She," and "The Subalterns" from *Poems of the Past and the Present*, the forces of nature are shown to have a superior morality, which is thwarted in its effect by overpowering circumstances. In "The Lacking Sense" and "Doom and She," Nature's blindness subverts her good intentions; in "The Subalterns," the elements of nature are enslaved by greater powers. In a curious way, these three poems generate sympathy for the forces that ravage men's lives. Yet despite their similarities, they also have crucial differences in verbal texture, tone, and rhetorical structure that make them as distinct from one another as *The Return of the Native, The Woodlanders,* and *Jude the Obscure.* Although there is no hint of comedy in these poems, they exhibit Hardy's stylistic playfulness.

"The Lacking Sense," as a stage direction indicates, is inspired by a local Wessex scene, *"A sad-coloured landscape, Waddon Vale."* The very face of nature seems to express grief and melancholy, which leads the speaker to wonder why. He addresses Time, who can be expected to know the history of Nature's plight:

> "Oh Time, whence comes the Mother's moody look amid
>   her labours,
> As of one who all unwittingly has wounded where she
>   loves?
>   Why weaves she not her world-webs to according lutes
>   and tabors,
> With nevermore this too remorseful air upon her face,
>   As of angel fallen from grace?"

Time answers by attacking the speaker's simile, saying "Her look is but her story: construe not its symbols keenly." The fact of the matter is that "yea surely has she wounded where she loves." She looks sad because of her "sense of ills misdealt for blisses," and she reproaches herself: "Self-smitings kill self-joys." The sadness of the landscape is a direct expression of Nature's sense of guilt. This explanation leads the speaker to another question: "And how explains thy Ancient Mind her crimes upon her creatures . . . ?" Time is surprised at the question, for in his view, Nature's shortcoming is obvious: she is "sightless." As he explains it:

> "[this] bar to her omniscience
> Brings those fearful unfulfillments, that red ravage
>   through her zones
>   Whereat all creation groans."

After this bald statement of the bitter situation, Time continues to address the speaker through two additional stanzas, which are laden with complex irony and emotion. Time presents Nature as a pathetic figure, loving her children, laboring strenuously with her blind, deliberate caution ("pathetic strenuous slow endeavour"), sensing helplessly her blunders, but nevertheless dealing out pain to her creatures. Men may think that they are doomed by some original, primitive curse, but the fate of Mother Nature, given her capacity to love, her power to create, and the purity of her intentions, is even more profoundly touching, according to Time: "her primal doom pursues her, faultful, fatal is she ever." Time concludes with a tender instruction:

> "Deal, then, her groping skill no scorn, no note
>   of malediction;
>   Not long on thee will press the hand that hurts the
>   lives it loves;
> And while she plods dead-reckoning on, in darkness
>   of affliction,
>   Assist her where thy creaturely dependence can or
>   may,
>   For thou art of her clay."

At the end of the poem, men are presented not merely as victims, but as free agents, capable of some modicum of assistance to Nature, an assistance warranted by their status as children of this loving, beneficently intentioned, fatally doomed mother. The very nature of things demands not malediction but help.

"The Lacking Sense" is an experiment in diction and prosody. There is a curious ambiguity in the meter. Although it appears to be iambic, in many of the lines the rising meter seems to dissolve into languid falling trochees. This impression is reinforced by the feminine rhymes:

"O Time, whence comes the Mother's moody look amid her labours."

"She whispers it in each pathetic strenuous slow endeavour."

The first four lines of each stanza resemble gradually descending, pulsating arcs, conveying the thought and emotion downward toward the low points expressed in the truncated fifth lines ("As of angel fallen from grace"; "Whereat all creation groans"). The series of mournful descents carries the reader to the concluding blunt statement of reality: "For thou art of her clay." The stanza, of Persian origin, consists of four seven-stress lines and a concluding three-stress line. The rhyme scheme, which is regular from stanza to stanza, is asymmetrical. The first line rhymes with the third, the rhyme, always feminine, being interrupted by the blank second line. The fourth line rhymes with the fifth, the rhyme, always masculine, coming out of cadence abruptly at the end of the shorter line. The second, unrhyming lines repeat, in one form or another, the main paradox of the poem:

"In her wonderworks yea surely has she wounded where she loves."

"These fallings from her fair beginnings, woundings where she loves."

"Not long on thee will press the hand that hurts the lives it loves."

This repeated idea of hurting the object of one's love is common in love poetry, and the combination of it, the long line, the ambiguous, mournful rhythms, and the elaborate stanza form of exotic origin is directly reminiscent of late-nineteenth-century aestheticist poetry. But in "The Lacking Sense" these elements are not related, as they might be in Dowson or Swinburne, to an expression of the delicious anguish of the wounded lover, but to a dramatized considera-tion of the relationship between man and nature. There is a disparity between the matter usually associated with the style employed and the actual subject of the poem. This disparity is further accentuated by the musical reference in the first stanza, where the speaker asks, "Why weaves she not her world-webs to according lutes and tabors . . . ?" He imagines a possible musical accompaniment for Nature's work, which would provide a context of pace, order, measure, and har-mony—exactly the kind of context that is provided for the poem by the long lines punctuated with a regularly appearing short line, the asymmetrical rhyme scheme, and the refrain-like repetitions of the second lines. But there is a jarring dishar-mony between the elements in Nature's tapestry, her "world-webs," as well as a disparity between her intentions and the results of her actions. The gentle, intimate sounds of the quiet-voiced lute and the tappings of a tabor are sadly out of place as background music for Nature's work, just as the elaborate prosodic structure is at variance with the poem's subject. There are stylistic variations within the poem itself. Hardy contrasts the melodic assonance and regularity of lines like "With never-more this too remorseful air upon her face" with the awk-ward dissonances of lines like "The sense of ills misdealt for blisses blanks the mien most queenly." The poetic techniques thus echo and heighten the contrasting concepts in the poem, enforcing the disparity between the jarring realities of Nature's "world-webs" and the imagined beauties of order and justice. It is as if Hardy were tearing gaping wounds in the stylistic heritage of Swinburne, which he so much loved.

"Doom and She" (*CP*, pp. 108–109) introduces a wholly dif-ferent world of poetic technique:

> There dwells a mighty pair—
> Slow, statuesque, intense—
> Amid the vague Immense:
> None can their chronicle declare,
> Nor why they be, nor whence.

146

These lines, instead of moving like descending arcs of mourn-fulness, march forward at a slow, steady pace toward the heavy beats of the final syllables; one hears not the tapping of a tabor but the strokes of a base drum, not the voluble eloquence of passion but the laconic, measured voice of author-ity, not lament but proclamation. The alliteration in "The Lack-ing Sense" assists the movement and often helps establish a sense of metrical ambiguity, which contributes to the falling effects of the lines, as in the phrase "moody look amid her labours." By contrast, in "Doom and She" the alliteration tends to enforce the measured distance between phrases and to sup-port the unambiguous iambic beat: "Amid the vague Immense." The introduction of Latinate, polysyllabic words in "Doom and She" has the effect of slowing the pace still further and, though metrically disruptive, tends to emphasize the sense of stately progress, as in the phrases "Slow, statuesque, intense" and "Or multitudinous moan." The same kind of dic-tion in "The Lacking Sense" seems to accelerate movement and heighten the iambic-trochaic ambiguity, as in "With nevermore this too remorseful air upon her face," and "She whispers it in each pathetic strenuous slow endeavour."

The sense of measured statement in "Doom and She" is created primarily by the short, three-stress lines, most of which contain complete phrases or utterances; the reader com-prehends the poem in terse, measured units of meaning. This feeling of balance and measure is reinforced by a system of weighted dualities evident in the title and in the rhetorical organization:

> Mother of all things made,
> Matchless in artistry,
> Unlit with sight is she.—
> And though her ever well-obeyed
> Vacant of feeling he.

The stanza begins with "Mother" and ends with "he." Mother Nature is described in three lines, Doom in two, but one of his is the long line. Two points are made about each character: she is unexcelled as an artist, but blind; he is a perfect servant, but lacks feeling. The implications of the dual nature of each of the pair are worked out in the rest of the poem, with Mother

147

Nature asking a question, and Doom replying with a question of his own. She has heard moans and groans from the earth, as if from " 'a world of strife,' " and asks Doom, "A throb in every word," to view the fates of her creatures. He sees, but cannot recognize states of feeling or morality. His reply reveals his perplexity:

> "World-weaver! What *is* Grief?
> And what are Right, and Wrong,
> And Feeling, that belong
> To creatures all who owe thee fief?
> Why is Weak worse than Strong?"

At the end of the poem, Mother Nature is left in a state of perplexed meditation, "brood[ing] in sad surmise" about her unanswered questions. The last lines return to the realities of nature:

> —Some say they have heard her sighs
> On Alpine height or Polar peak
> When the night tempests rise.

In early versions, Hardy used Wessex names in the next to the last line of the poem, first "On High-stoy Hill or Pilsdon Peak," then "On Pilsdon Pen or Lewsdon Peak." That he finally settled on "Alpine height or Polar peak" is in keeping with the stateliness created by the measured pace of the poem, and confirms the differences in tone and stature between the blind mothers in "The Lacking Sense" and "Doom and She." In contrast to *"A sad-coloured landscape, Waddon Vale,"* which is a human place with a human name, the reference in "Doom and She" is to anonymous natural objects of monumental grandeur. The mother in "The Lacking Sense" has a "moody look," a "too remorseful air upon her face"; in "Doom and She" she is heard on barren mountaintops sighing in the winds of tempests. The one mother is "groping," her endeavours "pathetic strenuous slow"; the other is "matchless in artistry." The one moves blindly on with her work while Time and a man discuss her activities; the other pauses to address her servant. The one is a pathetic, blundering figure; the other is grand, heroic, and her plight closer to romantic tragedy than to pathos. "The Lacking Sense" ends with a reference to the human condition and a recommendation to man, while "Doom and She" ends with a distant view of the brooding mother. The one poem is an outpouring of sadness, a lament on nature's inadequacies and their consequences for human beings. The other focuses on the grand and tragic paradoxes of nature itself, imaged in a hopelessly entrapped artist. Doom and Nature are the earnest questioners, paradoxically flawed, caught in the toils of their own fated natures.

"The Subalterns" (*CP*, p. 110) is another variation on the theme of the elements of nature as trapped in the service of forces larger than themselves, but here the tone is gently whimsical rather than pathetic or tragic. The speakers exhibit a sympathetically human desire to be thought well of. John Crowe Ransom noted the satisfying visual form of the poem, its use of Common Measure, the religious echoes in the language of the speakers, and the way the poem reflects Hardy's ideas.[8] But its most remarkable feature is the relative simplicity and colloquial naturalness of the diction and phrasing:

I
"Poor wanderer," said the leaden sky,
  "I fain would lighten thee,
But there are laws in force on high
  Which say it must not be."

II
—"I would not freeze thee, shorn one," cried
  The North, "knew I but how
To warm my breath, to slack my stride;
  But I am ruled as thou."

III
—"To-morrow I attack thee, wight,"
  Said Sickness. "Yet I swear
I bear thy little ark no spite,
  But am bid enter there."

IV
—"Come hither, Son," I heard Death say;
  "I did not will a grave
Should end thy pilgrimage to-day,
  But I, too, am a slave!"

V
We smiled upon each other then,
And life to me had less
Of that fell look it wore ere when
They owned their passiveness.

These lines display inversion ("knew I but how"), ellipsis ("But am bid enter"), archaism ("attack thee, wight"), and an occasional harshness of diction ("shorn one"). Yet they have very little alliteration or assonance and, compared with the two other poems, relatively little sense of line, as a result of the frequent enjambment ("cried/ The North"; "how/ To warm"; "I swear/ I bear"). There is nothing in "The Lacking Sense" to mitigate the sadness of the landscape, and in "Doom and She" the night tempests swirling around "Alpine height or Polar peak" seem all the more chilling as a result of the tragic stateliness of the poem. But at the end of "The Subalterns" the characters smile at one another, and the reader smiles, too, at the skillful way in which Hardy has humanized and domesticated the forces of nature ("Come hither, Son," says Death). The benign energy of the poem, manifested in the gentle seriousness of the actors, has the effect of lessening the "fell look" of life and, somehow, making it more humanly comprehensible.

In the philosophical fantasies Hardy thus creates his own personal myths to account for the nature of things. Characteristically, the surface belies the depths. Despite their deterministic pessimism, which seems to assign responsibility for suffering to external forces, the philosophical fantasies illustrate a sympathetic vision and demand compassion from the reader. They also exhibit imaginative craftsmanship in their variety of dramatic conception, style, and tone, and in their complex characterizations of the quasimythical figures. Instead of simply crying out against cosmic injustice in these poems, Hardy humanizes the forces of nature.

POEMS OF THE PAST

6

All of the poems considered so far involve significant distancing features. In the poems of ironic circumstance, Hardy exposes grim disparities in the lives of others with a minimum of personal involvement or revelation. The ballads and narratives purport to record received legends and histories rather than stories invented by the author. The philosophical fantasies present imagined dramas which on the level of realism no one could be expected to take seriously. But throughout his career Hardy wrote personal and confessional poetry as well, and as he grew older, he dealt more and more frequently with the materials of his own life. He continued to write satires, ballads, and philosophical fantasies, but he also wrote a growing body of personal lyrics presented as examinations of his own experience and feelings.

One of the dominant images emerging from Hardy's poetry is that of an old man, living with memory, meditating on the personal past and searching for its meaning. A case in point is "The Ghost of the Past" (*CP*, pp. 290–291):

> As daily I went up the stair
> And down the stair,
> I did not mind the Bygone there—
> The Present once to me;
> Its moving meek companionship
> I wished might ever be,
> There was in that companionship
> Something of ecstasy.

In this poem the past is a comfort. But memory—subject, like everything else, to chance and change—fades away:

> It looms a far-off skeleton
> And not a comrade nigh,
> A fitful far-off skeleton
> Dimming as days draw by.

Through poetry Hardy attempts to put the flesh back on the bones, to arrest his fading memory and reveal the significance of his own history, for to understand the personal past is to have a grasp on reality. Yet the reality recollected is often a cause for sadness. Sometimes Hardy remembers moments of high happiness, and it saddens him that they cannot be relived or fully revived through poetry. Sometimes he recollects blows endured, injustices suffered, and the ravagings of time and circumstance. He himself is the dupe of life's ironic disparities. Even more painful, he remembers moments of severe damage inflicted by himself on others, moments that can never be repaired or atoned for; these haunting memories he would prefer to escape. Time may be said to be the distancing feature in Hardy's personal poems, but often the past is a searing presence in his consciousness.

Although the attitudes toward the past in Hardy's poetry are complex and contradictory, they fall generally into three basic modes. These modes appear with considerable purity in two of the narratives, "The Revisitation" and "My Cicely," and in "Poems of Pilgrimage," a set of meditations on historical places.

Reality and Illusion

"The Revisitation" and "My Cicely," both of them monologues of characters who revive the past, illustrate two contrasting ways of dealing with personal history, ways that are directly related to the thematic conflict in Hardy's work between guilt and a sense of cosmic injustice. In "The Revisitation" (*CP*, pp. 177–181), an old soldier returns to a town where he was once stationed in his youth, the location of a painful love affair. It is July, the same month as that "joyless hour of discord" in the past which led to the soldier's "bitterest loss," the loss of the girl he had passionately loved. The soldier is convinced that even the "month-night was the same." Haunted by memories, unable to sleep, compelled by a mysterious sense of romance, he sets off through the night across the countryside to the old trysting place, the scene of the discord. His physical journey, a pilgrimage to the location of the determining event in his life, brings him to ancient and ominous relics of the larger historical past as well:

> Round about me bulged the barrows
> As before, in antique silence—immemorial funeral piles—
> Where the sleek herds trampled daily the remains of
>> flint-tipt arrows
> Mid the thyme and chamomiles.

This landscape is ambivalent, combining the pastoral harmony and peace signaled by the sheep and flowers with the violence and death associated with the human relics. It could be a place of union or of disruption.

For the soldier, time seems to have collapsed. Even the birds, described in vivid, concrete language, seem to be the same ones that witnessed the moment of parting:

> their pale pinions like a fitful phosphorescence
> Up against the cope of cloud,

> Where their dolesome exclamations
> Seemed the voicings of the self-same throats I had heard
>> when life was green,
> Though since that day uncounted frail forgotten
>> generations
> Of their kind had flecked the scene.

The speaker, "living long and longer/ In a past that lived no more," is hardly surprised when his lost Agnette, whose name has obvious pastoral connotations, appears in the darkness. They talk—"It is *just* as ere we parted!" she says, with unwitting irony—and they fall asleep together. When the soldier awakens in daylight, he is shocked at the way Agnette has aged. "Time's transforming chisel" has made "crease where curve was, where was raven, grizzle—/ Pits, where peonies

153

once did dwell." She notices his "quite involuntary dismay" and takes offense:

"Yes, Sir, I am *old*," said she,
"And the thing which should increase love turns it quickly
    into scorning—
And your new-won heart from me!"

She departs hastily before the soldier can call her back. Ironically, time has in fact collapsed: they meet in love and forgiveness only to part once again in anger and bitterness.

The cause of their parting and its relation to the past are both complex and obscure. It is clear that the two lovers' feelings for one another had been strong enough to determine the course of their lives. The narrator characterizes himself as "one fated mateless/ From those far fond hours till now," and Agnette, also still single, confesses that she often comes to the fateful spot in order to think of her former lover. It is also clear that, although Agnette broke off the relationship—the narrator refers to the time "when One who went, came not again"—they shared responsibility for the breech, for they pledge "mutual forgiveness" before falling asleep. Certainly they share responsibility for the present rupture. The soldier shows real shock at Agnette's appearance, and she interprets his reaction as "a warning/ Of the worth of man's devotion"; that is, she questions his fidelity. Yet her judgment may be too harsh, for she leaves without giving him a chance to reply, revealing "the too proud temper . . . that had parted us before." The soldier himself is unable to overcome his aversion to her and bring himself to follow. Perhaps he is repulsed by her appearance, as he honestly suggests: "But it *may* be (though I know not) that this trick on us of Time/ Disconcerted and confused me." More likely, however, he is held back by a bitter sense of hurt at her candid, blunt, and all-too-accurate attack on him. Although his expression of shock was certainly natural, from one point of view trivial, and "quite involuntary," she points out a larger significance in it that he cannot deny. Once again she makes him feel inferior and guilty, as he did in the past:

Well I knew my native weakness,
Well I know it still. I cherished her reproach like
    physic-wine,
For I saw in that emaciate shape of bitterness and
    bleakness
A nobler soul than mine.

There are hints in the poem as to their previous relationship. The speaker was a soldier, a transient, temporarily stationed near Agnette. She was an older woman (her "years out-count" his) and the daughter of a propertied man ("the downlands were her father's fief"). Probably their different social stations made marriage unlikely. Perhaps she with her "too proud temper" demanded conformity to a standard of obedience and fidelity that he, with his "native weakness," the impulsiveness of a roving soldier, could not achieve. Certainly it is his fidelity that she now questions. In any case, whatever parted them in the past parts them in the present. She takes offense and leaves in passionate haste; he remains alone, guilty, emotionally dessicated: "Love is lame at fifty years" are his last words. Thus, the possibilities for romance implied by the pastoral features of the landscape are illusions, whereas the violence, death, disparity, and disruption hinted at in the ancient relics are the reality. The two lovers' shared impulse to visit their old meeting place on the anniversary of their parting suggests the workings of a mysterious, cosmic force; but the real mystery is that, while "Time's transforming chisel" continues in its inevitable ravagings, nothing changes. To revisit the past is to be brought face to face once again with the starkness of reality. The soldier's reaction is to accept his "native weakness" and the lameness of love in an old man, to submit to the inevitability of history, and to remain isolated, guilty, and loveless.

"My Cicely" (CP, pp. 45–48) is another first-person narrative of a man who revisits the past, but his response is to deny reality and insist on illusion. Living in the city, he hears that an old sweetheart has died in the far West of England, and he impulsively decides to make a pilgrimage to her grave. At the graveside he learns that he has been deceived by a confusion of names and that "his" Cicely still lives, but in blighted circumstances. Having married beneath herself, she now serves as a barmaid in an inn, where the narrator had stopped quite by chance on his way down the highway. Returning to the city in disillusionment, he decides to believe that the dead woman was, after all, his Cicely:

> Far better
> To dream than to own the debasement
> Of sweet Cicely.

Thereafter he shuns the West Highway, "lest I disturb my choice vision."

The structure of events and the choice of language show that the whole experience is highly colored by the speaker's fantasizing imagination. He rearranges the chronology of events for dramatic effect, beginning at the climactic moment at the graveside, when he learns that the buried woman is not his Cicely:

> "Alive?"—And I leapt in my wonder,
>   Was faint of my joyance,
> And grasses and grove shone in garments
>   Of glory to me.

His self-dramatizing propensities are evident: first he "leapt," then he "was faint." He describes his moment of ecstasy in language that recalls Wordsworth and Shelley: "wonder," "joyance," "garments/ Of glory." In a flashback the speaker then recalls his life in the city, and again his language has the effect of heightening and romanticizing his experience. The city is a place of "frenzy-led factions," where he "squandered green years and maturer," not merely by wasting time but by worshiping false gods, by "bowing the knee/ To Baals illusive and specious." News of Cicely's death reminds him of his love for her; yet his was not mere love but a "passion the planets had scowled on,/ And change had let dwindle." The man who in the previous stanza confessed his sinful idolatry now presents himself as a victim of the cosmos and the forces of change. In view of the speaker's powers of self-dramatization, it is no wonder that the news of Cicely's death relifts his passion "To full apogee" and impels him to gallop on horseback down the West Highway to her graveside. The cosmic victim turned idolator becomes passionate pilgrim.

The speaker embellishes the description of his journey with ominous and portentous detail. The trip into the past and into the West is also a journey back through England's history, past romantic historic landmarks into the land of Roman invasion and pagan mystery. He passes the "House of Long Sieging," associated with a heroic moment in the wars of the seventeenth century; the "thin steeple" of Salisbury; the "bleak hill-graves of Chieftains"; the vast prehistoric earthworks of Maidon Castle; "Nine-Pillared Cromlech," a mysterious, miniature version of Stonehenge; and so on. The journey becomes increasingly gloomy, sinister, and mysterious as it progresses. He makes frantic haste, changing his "blown bearer" along the way, and travels alone into the darkness, hearing "only the creak of a gibbet/ Or waggoner's jee." With this exhaustive pilgrimage behind him, fraught with the meanings and associations he has invested in it, he is well prepared to be lifted from the depths of melancholy to the heights of joy at the news that Cicely lives. He feels "heart-heavings/ And new ecstasy," and seems to imagine new romantic possibilities. The report of Cicely's ruination, therefore, he takes as another cosmic blow:

> More ghastly than death were these tidings
> Of life's irony!
>
> For, on my ride down I had halted
> Awhile at the Lions,
> And her—her whose name had once opened
> My heart as a key—
>
> I'd looked on, unknowing, and witnessed
> Her jests with the tapsters,
> Her liquor-fired face, her thick accents
> In naming her fee.
>
> "O God, why this seeming derision!"
> I cried in my anguish:
> "O once Loved, O fair Unforgotten—
> That Thing—meant it thee!

> "Inurned and at peace, lost but sainted,
>   Were grief I could compass;
> Depraved—'tis for Christ's poor dependent
>   A cruel decree!"

The irony, as he sees it, is that someone he once loved but never forgot (not quite true, as shown earlier in the poem, where he says that "change had let dwindle" her memory) should have turned into a "Thing." This is a cause of grief he cannot compass, a cruel blow for "Christ's poor dependent." Better that she had died to sustain his illusions. Thus, at the end of the poem the speaker invents a new illusion as his means of protest against reality. People may call him "Frail-witted, illuded," but he believes that it is better to dream than to accept the grim facts of life.

The speaker's failures in morality are obvious:

> Moreover I rate it unseemly
>   To hold that kind Heaven
> Could work such device—to her ruin
>   And my misery.

There is considerable presumption in his notion that the powers should have singled him and Cicely out for special ironic punishment, and there is further presumption in his protest, for by Christian standards, one who has wasted his life in a frenzied city worshiping false gods would seem to deserve punishment. Throughout, the speaker ignores moral concerns and dwells on his own feelings, except when assuming a moral position from which to judge the heavens. He shows a failure of compassion by measuring the importance of Cicely's fall exclusively in terms of its effect on him. He blithely calls her a "Thing," with her "liquor-fired face, her thick accents," without ever expressing any sympathy for her. He saves all his sympathy for himself.

The speaker's failings have not generally been noted, because the poem is primarily one of affect—albeit a very strange affect. The speaker is a kind of "epicure in emotions," on the order of Sue Bridehead, Edred Fitzpiers, Eustacia Vye, and other of Hardy's self-dramatizing characters.[1] He indulges his own feelings, regarding himself as the central actor in a cosmic drama. Since the world has importance for him only as it affects him, his feelings are at the center of the poem. But what saves him from a harsh judgment is the possibility that in important ways his response to reality may be valid. It may be, according to a common modern notion, that life has meaning only to the extent that one imagines it for oneself.

In this respect, the position of "My Cicely" in *Wessex Poems* is significant. "A Sign-Seeker" (*CP*, pp. 43–44), immediately preceding it, is a monologue of the nineteenth-century man who finds in reality none of the signs of immortality he hopes for: "When a man falls he lies." The poem following "My Cicely" is "Her Immortality" (*CP*, pp. 48–50), which shows that a dead sweetheart exists only in the memory of the living lover:

> When I surcease,
> Through whom alone lives she,
> Her spirit ends its living lease,
> Never again to be!

Within this context, the self-dramatization of the speaker in "My Cicely" makes sense. In a world without signs he must imagine them for himself. In a world of ever-threatening oblivion, he must remember and reimagine the past. A lovely girl has suffered ruin. The nineteenth-century sign-seeker would probably view it as one more disheartening example of "Death's sudden finger, sorrow's smart," but the speaker in "My Cicely" insists on the way of "Her Immortality," preserving imaginatively the memory of the girl. More than that, on the basis of the slim facts of her fall and the way in which he discovered it, he has imagined a full-blown drama of personal emotion, interweaving a variety of themes: the contrast between city and country, the romance and fatefulness of the nation's past, issues of faith and doubt, and the disparity between appearance and reality. Paradoxically, "My Cicely" dramatizes the necessity for exercising the imagination, precisely because of the imagination's inadequacy to change the disillusioning facts of life. This may well be the source of its peculiar, bittersweet melancholy. The only meaning in the speaker's life consists in the dramatic trappings with which he embellishes its unpalatable realities.

159

Poems of Pilgrimage

The speaker in "The Revisitation" accepts the inevitability of historical reality and experiences feelings of guilt and isolation, whereas the speaker in "My Cicely" defiantly insists on imagined illusions and suffers from a sense of cosmic injustice. These two modes for dealing with the past represent the extremes found in Hardy's poetry. Yet there is a third way: the creative apprehension of the real, inspiriting meanings inherent in human history.

Just as in many of his ballads and narratives Hardy preserves memories of lives past and records significant events of local tradition, in many of his personal lyrics he revives the meaning in ancient things in an effort to establish continuity between past and present. Places, objects, landmarks, or pieces of old furniture become rich with layers of human association. As Hardy apprehends them in "Old Furniture" (*CP*, p. 456), for example:

> I see the hands of the generations . . .

> Hands behind hands, growing paler and paler,
>   As in a mirror a candle-flame
> Shows images of itself, each frailer
>   As it recedes, though the eye may frame
>   Its shape the same.

In this poem Hardy sits among commonplace objects which, because they have been made sacred by human use, are for him "relics of householdry." He sees a "foggy finger" on the clock's dial, a hand dancing on an old violin, a dim face by the tinder box that glows momentarily as the fire flares up, in almost the same way as the hands and faces of Hardy's imagination emerge from obscurity into momentary clarity when he depicts them in a poem. Like his grandmother, described in "One We Knew" (*CP*, pp. 257–258), he dwells "on such dead themes, not as one who remembers,/ But rather as one who sees." Looking at an object or visiting a place in the present, he visualizes images that validate the continuity of human experience—images of similar people from generation after generation, dancing the old dances, singing the old songs, using the old tools, falling in love according to immemorial patterns, working, suffering, and dying in the same old ways. Yet "Old Furniture" ends on a characteristic note of self-effacement, when he gently chides himself for his love and respect for the past:

> Well, well. It is best to be up and doing,
> The world has no use for one to-day
> Who eyes things thus—no aim pursuing!
> He should not continue in this stay,
> But sink away.

These lines indicate Hardy's sense that there may be no place in the modern world, with its emphasis on production and progress, for one who remembers. In other poems he conceives of the resistance to history as not merely a modern social phenomenon but an implacable force, working through the nature of things to obliterate memory and meaning, like "Time's transforming chisel," which changes the beautiful Agnette into an "emaciate shape of bitterness and bleakness."

In his poems Hardy often attempts to oppose this modern tendency and this natural force with a tone of confidence that contrasts strikingly the self-effacement of "Old Furniture." The "Poems of Pilgrimage" from his second volume, *Poems of the Past and the Present,* express an assertive, creative response to the past. In them he writes as a sensitive, learned, modern man, who is nevertheless "old" with the weight of ages, keeping alive the memories of general human history associated with places and things, while adding confidently his own tender, affectionate, complex responses to the ongoing interplay of chronological levels of experience. In these poems Hardy is the pilgrim, actively seeking out the sacred monuments of the European continent and describing key episodes in his quest, most of which involve the blending of disparate levels of time, disparate geographical locations, and disparate experiences. Most of the poems in the group focus on a concrete experience, something that actually happened at a specific time in a specific place. That experience provokes an insight into the relationship between past and present.

In "Rome: On the Palatine" (*CP*, p. 93), for instance, Hardy wanders over the ruins, allowing his visual imagination "to beguile/ The outer sense," so that he seems to see each crumbling edifice in "its pristine glow/ Of scenic frieze and pompous peristyle." Then quite by chance a present event enhances his experience and stimulates his imagination to a higher vision. When an orchestra on the hill above strikes up a Strauss waltz, the music, orchestrating the scene and informing his envisioning mind, "blended pulsing life with lives long done,/ Till Time seemed fiction, Past and Present one." All the elements of the scene—the decaying ruins, "Victor Jove," "Livia's rich red mural show," "Caligula's dissolving pile," a popular piece of music, and Hardy's experiencing consciousness—become unified in a moment transcending time, and history is transformed into felt experience.

Likewise, the poem "In the Old Theatre, Fiesole" (*CP*, pp. 92–93) blends past and present, as well as disparate places. The history of Rome is also felt and experienced as the history of Hardy's native countryside. Walking through the Circus, "Where Rome and dim Etruria interjoin," Hardy is approached by a child, who shows him an ancient coin. The effect is to raise for him "In swift perspective Europe's history." In his explanation of this effect, the Anglo-Saxon diction is appropriate to the shift in geography:

> For in my distant plot of English loam
> 'Twas but to delve, and straightway there to find
> Coins of like impress . . .
>   her act flashed home
> In that mute moment to my opened mind
> The power, the pride, the reach of perished Rome.

To the "opened mind," history presents itself in moments of vision.

The "Poems of Pilgrimage" manifest confidence not only in the meaning of history but also in the creative role of the historian. "Rome: At the Pyramid of Cestius near the Graves of Shelley and Keats" (*CP*, p. 95) attempts an imaginative blending of levels of the past in order to testify in the present to the sanctity of human creative effort. Hardy, meditating on the obscurity of an ancient Roman, Cestius, concludes that to have one's tomb marking the way for "pilgrim feet" to the graves of "two immortal Shades" is "an ample fame." The "purpose" of the pyramid "was exprest/ Not with its first design," but when the two English poets were buried nearby. It is as if the man Cestius has an ongoing destiny, moving toward fulfillment only after his death and generations have passed, a destiny discovered by Hardy on a visit and defined in the poem. Cestius' history expands and takes on new meaning because of his association with Hardy the poet-historian as well as with Keats and Shelley.

Hardy makes a pilgrimage not only to places but also to moments in time, as in "Lausanne: In Gibbon's Old Garden: 11–12 P.M., *June 27*, 1897 (*The 110th anniversary of the completion of the 'Decline and Fall' at the same hour and place*)" (*CP*, p. 96). In the poem, Gibbon's spirit "seems to pass," but Hardy describes the moment as if it actually occurred:

> He [Gibbon] contemplates a volume in his hand,
> And far lamps fleck him through the thin acacias.
>
> Anon the book is closed,
> With "It is finished!"

Gibbon then turns and addresses Hardy from the past, questioning him about the present:

> "Still rule those minds on earth
> At whom sage Milton's wormwood words were hurled:
> *'Truth like a bastard comes into the world*
> *Never without ill-fame to him who gives her birth'?"*

Gibbon's past struggles with the enemies of truth are reinforced by Milton's words, which were known to him as a learned historian, and also stand as Hardy's comment on the world as he sees it in 1897. Hardy presents here the intellectual equivalent of the "hands of the generations" in "Old Furniture"—"Hands behind hands, growing paler and paler." Levels of the past, creatively employed by an envisioning poet, merge to illuminate the meaning of the present. Again and again Hardy is concerned with anniversaries in his poetry, as if each recurrence of the date of a significant event provides the occasion for a further fulfillment of that event's meaning, another reflection of the candle flame. The poet, by adding new dimensions of meaning, refuels the moment and keeps it aglow.

The most tender and touching of the "Poems of Pilgrimage"
is "Shelley's Skylark *(The neighbourhood of Leghorn: March 1887)"*
(*CP*, p. 92), which further illustrates how the creative historian
in the present expands the significance of the past:

> Somewhere afield here something lies
> In Earth's oblivious eyeless trust
> That moved a poet to prophecies—
> A pinch of unseen, unguarded dust.

The earth, without eyes or feeling, is unworthy of its sacred
trust, just as the skylark—frail, small, ephemeral, and of the
earth—seems an unworthy thing to move a poet to prophecy.
It "only lived like another bird . . . Lived its meek life; then,
one day, fell—" without knowing of its immortality. Hardy
imagines it in the "loam," in the "myrtle's green," and in the
"coming hue/ Of a grape," that is, in changing temporal situations that dissipate its glory. He wants it preserved. Tenderly,
whimsically, he calls on the fairies to "go and find/ That tiny
pinch of priceless dust" and then to bring for it:

> a casket silver-lined,
> And framed of gold that gems encrust;
>
> And we will lay it safe therein,
> And consecrate it to endless time;
> For it inspired a bard to win
> Ecstatic heights in thought and rhyme.

Like Cestius, the skylark has an ongoing destiny. First Shelley
immortalized it; then Hardy, aware of the disparity between
its frail, earthly condition and the ecstatic heights of poetry it
inspired, consecrated it anew in a tender, eloquent poem. He
helps to save it from "Earth's oblivious eyeless trust," from
the resistance in nature to memory and meaning. Again there
are interlocking chronological layers of interpretation and significance; again, the past is regenerated and expanded in
meaning by a creative act of the imagination in the present.
Reality is not merely stark and grim, nor is meaning mere illusion.

"Poems of Pilgrimage," however, ends not with "Ecstatic
heights in thought and rhyme" but with references to tragedy

and suffering, and the final poem pictures the historian not as one who expands the significance of the past, but as one who objectively records and vicariously experiences the ancient tragedies. The entire group of poems is coherently organized. In "Genoa and the Mediterranean" (CP, p. 91), the first poem, Hardy describes entering that city by means of "Torino's track" and seeing the sordid ugliness of its back streets. In terms of his feminine personifications of the city, he sees not "the Beauty but the Dowd." Although he later experiences Genoa's "soul-subliming powers," the poem concludes:

> But, Queen, such squalid undress none should see,
> Those dream-endangering eyewounds no more be
> Where lovers first behold thy form in pilgrimage to thee.

The collection of poems moves as a whole from places of "soul-subliming" power to "dream-endangering" sights. "Shelley's Skylark," which comes second, is followed by several poems of confident affirmation. In the fourth from the last poem, "Lausanne: In Gibbon's Old Garden," with its ironic vision of the rewards for those who bring truth into the world, the tone of the group darkens, and dreams are again endangered. In the third poem from the last, "Zermatt: To the Matterhorn (June–July 1897)" (CP, pp. 96–97), Hardy addresses the mountain on the thirty-second anniversary of its conquest, which took the lives of four of the seven climbers:

> [His] mind takes flight
> To that day's tragic feat of manly might,
> As though, till then, of history thou hadst none.

Yet the mountain had a previous history that made it a fitting site for tragedy:

> Yet ages ere men topped thee, late and soon
> Thou didst behold the planets lift and lower;
> Saw'st, maybe, Joshua's pausing sun and moon,
> And the betokening sky when Caesar's power
> Approached its bloody end; yea, even that Noon
> When darkness filled the earth till the ninth hour.

The mountain has beheld moments of awesome power and tragic suffering—moments held sacred in human memory— played against the background of enduring geological forms and planetary motions. This context dwarfs the seven climbers' "tragic feat of manly might," and indicates that violence and suffering are eternally present to the human condition.

The next to the last poem of the series, "The Bridge of Lodi" (*CP*, pp. 97–99), continues the mood of tragedy. It evokes the violent episode of human history that most engaged Hardy throughout his life, the Napoleonic wars. A tune about the battle of Lodi that was "a strange delight" in his childhood haunts him when he makes his adult pilgrimage to the Continent, so that none of the sights of northern Italy could "woo [him]/ From the spot englamoured so." Returning to the place of the battle in order to relive it in his imagination, he finds the local people enthralled by "transitory/ Marketings in cheese and meat":

> —Not a creature cares in Lodi
> How Napoleon swept each arch,
> Or where up and downward trod he,
> Or for his outmatching march!

It may be that the people of Lodi, in forgetting the past, "Are but viewing war aright," but Hardy feels the memory to be worth preserving:

> Nay; I'll sing "The Bridge of Lodi"—
> That long-loved, romantic thing,
> Though none show by smile or nod he
> Guesses why and what I sing!

The battle seems glamorous and romantic to him alone. He keeps the story alive on the basis of personal whim. Absent is the confidence of the creative historian.

The last poem of the group, "On an Invitation to the United States" (*CP*, pp. 99–100), presents a more chillingly reductive view of the historian's role. In this poem Hardy declines the opportunity to visit "a modern coast":

> Where the new regions claim them free
> From that long drip of human tears
> Which peoples old in tragedy
> Have left upon the centuried years.

For, wonning in these ancient lands,
Enchased and lettered as a tomb,
And scored with prints of perished hands,
And chronicled with dates of doom,
Though my own Being bear no bloom
I trace the lives such scenes enshrine,
Give past exemplars present room,
And their experience count as mine.

In the early "Poems of Pilgrimage," Hardy manifests his faith in the historian's ability to expand creatively the meaning of the past. In "On an Invitation to the United States," all Europe becomes a tomb enshrining the doomed, and the hands of the generations, instead of being real presences, are evident only in the feeble prints they left behind. Here Hardy regards history as tragic, and the chronicling of it as a means of living vicariously while his own being bears "no bloom"; he objectively describes "past exemplars" in order to fill an empty personal life. This self-effacing view, conceiving of himself as one whose life has been thwarted, blighted, and drained of meaning, is characteristic of many of Hardy's personal poems.

The Personal Past

Other poems scattered throughout Hardy's verse involve the landmarks of the Wessex countryside. "The Roman Road" (*CP*, p. 248) presents a view of the same West Highway romanticized by the speaker in "My Cicely." In this poem Hardy describes a stretch of road that runs "straight and bare" across the heath, seeming to invite by its austere blankness an effort of imaginative interpretation. Looking at the road, Hardy thinks of "thoughtful men" who:

delve, and measure, and compare;

Visioning on the vacant air
Helmed legionaries, who proudly rear
The Eagle, as they pace again
The Roman Road.

In the "Poems of Pilgrimage" Hardy takes the position of the "thoughtful men," examining the relics of history external to

167

himself, delving, measuring, comparing past and present.
Here, in Wessex, a personal memory overshadows history:

> But no tall brass-helmed legionnaire
> Haunts it for me. Uprises there
> A mother's form upon my ken,
> Guiding my infant steps, as when
> We walked that ancient thoroughfare,
> The Roman Road.

This poem has an objective quality akin to the self-effacement in "On an Invitation," a certain tactful restraint and quiet refusal to make explicit interpretation. The public, historical reality of the ancient relic is forced into the background by personal memory, where it exists as a vague, obscure, but resonant context for the central remembered moment, like a counterpoint melody heard in the distance or a mysterious complex of hints of meaning. The road once traversed by helmeted legions is haunted for Hardy by the image of his mother guiding his infant footsteps. Hardy merely exposes the contrast, without judging or interpreting it.

Few critics have been more successful than G. M. Young in describing sympathetically the qualities of self-effacement and restraint evident in poems like "Old Furniture," "On an Invitation," and "The Roman Road." He wrote of Hardy's pessimism that it is "primarily that of the disappointed man, who cannot find the serenity which naturally attends on satisfaction and achievement, and feels himself ill-adjusted to an ill-adjusted world. It is the vast projection of an inner discord, untuning the music of the spheres." The diction here is suggestive. Hardy is "disappointed" rather than wounded, thwarted, or disillusioned. His aim is "serenity" rather than happiness, vision, or moral certainty, and it is something that "he cannot find," not something malignantly denied him. He and the world are "ill-adjusted," not profoundly flawed, and although Hardy makes a "vast projection" of his problem on the world of his vision, his problem is "inner discord," not anxiety, or a shattered, divided consciousness. Young found in Hardy's poetry "the tone of an ageing man watching the fire die down, and thinking of old tunes, old memories: moments remembered at railway stations and lodging-houses; sunsets at the end of London streets, water coming over the weir, the rain on the downs. But what we hear is the voice of an age, of a generation carried beyond sight of its old landmarks, and gazing doubtfully down an illimitable vista, of cosmic changes endlessly proceeding, and ephemeral suffering endlessly to be renewed. Twilight was coming on: an evening chill was on the air."[2] Hardy is like a quiet, passive old man, watching, remembering, and "gazing doubtfully" at the past.

Young's poignant characterization is only partially accurate, however, for Hardy presents himself in a variety of guises, ranging from the guilt and emptiness found in "The Revisitation" to the sense of victimization found in "My Cicely," and he is frequently able to regard the past with serenity, recognizing and affirming the "old landmarks," as in many of the "Poems of Pilgrimage," where he is an active seeker rather than a passive observer. The restraint, humility, and self-effacement found in the poems can often be shown to be qualities of a self-protective stance, designed to conceal passion and affirmation. In some of his personal poems there is a note of profound agitation, hinting at something deeper than disappointment. His voice can be savagely condemnatory, or it can whine with self-pity. Often Hardy does not merely remember but participates once more in a remembered experience, feeling again the pain of the experience itself. While he frequently gazes down a vista of endless change, he sometimes sees, intead of mere change, radical discontinuity. He presents himself not only as one who sits by the fire meditating but also as a lonely wanderer across the landscape, haunting pathetically, futilely, the old environs, while haunted himself by pursuing, inescapable ghosts from the past. He frequently appears not merely as an observer but as a victim—a victim of time and change, of natural forces beyond his control, or of human misunderstandings. Sometimes he appears as a victim of himself, in poems expressing both explicitly and implicitly his sense of guilt for past sufferings of himself and others. He is often not merely an old man gazing and remembering, but an old man burnt out, wrung dry by suffering, eager for death, haunted by memories that he cannot keep down, struggling quietly to hold sorrow at a distance. And finally, he sometimes sees himself as one whose life history evidences a clear structure of ineffaceable positive meaning.

"Life offers—to deny!" writes Hardy in "Yell'ham-Wood's Story" (*CP*, p. 280), and in his personal poems he often presents himself as a victim of life's denials and of the persecution in store for those who accurately perceive the harsh realities. He is a victim of time, which leaves old men with memories of happy moments never to be relived. He longs once again to dance the old dances with the alluring women, as in "Concerning Agnes" (*CP*, p. 838), but the "old romance" is gone, and Agnes is dead. He returns to the old places, as in "In a Former Resort after Many Years" (*CP*, p. 666), to find everything changed. His mind, which in his youth was "like an open plain," has become "as a gallery protrait-lined,/ And scored with necrologic scrawls," echoing feeble voices from underground. Memories of dancing now halted, singing now silent, and bright eyes now dulled haunt him in "Song to an Old Burden" (*CP*, pp. 790–791). With such recollections, he can sing and dance no more, for to dance "around around around" now seems "tedious." The dancers whirled their lives away in downward spirals toward an "all-ignoring" sleep. The old man, having seen it all happen, will not get caught up in it again. It is clear that the "burden" of the song is not only the refrain but also the dead weight of the past, which cannot be recaptured and relived, but which tediously oppresses those who have the misfortune to survive to old age. Everything changes, everyone is a victim of time, everyone sees himself replaced. As Hardy remarks in "Life Laughs Onward" (*CP*, p. 435), "Old succumb[s] to Young." This is a sad fate, difficult to accept. "As newer comers crowd the fore,/ We drop behind," writes Hardy in "The Superseded" (*CP*, p. 133); "But yet we think, must we, must *we*,/ Too, drop behind?" There is a wistful pathos in the ancient man echoing the childhood question, Must I, too, die?

But in other poems, like "A Wasted Illness" (*CP*, p. 139), Hardy longs for death, or like "The New Dawn's Business" (*CP*, p. 797), he expresses a readiness to die, for time does not merely steal away lovable things and bring on death, but it also ravages the lives of men, blights their hopeful expectations, drains them of hope and feeling: time makes death seem better than life. Sometimes time operates with such deceptively quiet cunning that one hardly notices its corrosive effects. According to "In a Eweleaze near Weatherbury" (*CP*, pp. 62–63), it works remorselessly with a "little chisel," boring slyly, heaping "Quaintest pains" like a pile of sawdust, almost unnoticed; and yet its effect is to deface, destroy, and cause suffering. It ravages selectively, with grim, ironic results. In the terms of " 'I Look into My Glass' " (*CP*, p. 72), it "Part steals, lets part abide," destroying the means for loving, but preserving the impulse to love. In "Memory and I" (*CP*, pp. 170–171), time has taken away youth, joy, hope, faith, and love, which remain only in the memory as phantoms haunting imagined sites in ruination and decay: a "crumbled cot," "gaunt gardens lone," "a tomb of tomes," "a ravaged aisle," the "ageing shape/ Where beauty used to be." Time has killed the poet spiritually before his physical death, leaving him a "Dead Man Walking" (*CP*, pp. 202–203):

> but a shape that stands here,
> A pulseless mould,
> A pale past picture, screening
> Ashes gone cold.

The exact moment of his "death" is not clear. Observing the "goal of men" contributed to his demise, as did the passing of his friends and kinfolk, and the kindling of his "Love's heart" in hate for him. Whatever the cause, "I live not now."

Sometimes it seems as if Hardy's "death" were occasioned by a clearing of vision, as if becoming aware of the realities of life through growth and maturation were, ironically, a process of dying. In "To Outer Nature" (*CP*, p. 54) he describes how the world appeared to his youthful eyes, when he never doubted that it was "wrought" by love for his pleasure. He longs to see life once again imbued with iris hues, "But such re-adorning/ Time forbids with scorning." In "Shut Out That Moon" (*CP*, p. 201) he wants to keep the illusionary attractions of nature out of his sight, to "prison" his eyes and thought in a small, shuttered, lamplit room. In his youth he was too hopeful, too sensitive, too responsive; hence his disillusion is all the greater: "Too fragrant was Life's early bloom,/ Too tart the fruit it brought!"

In direct contrast are poems in which Hardy presents himself as one who never expected much, who knew all along that life offered to deny. In "Childhood among the Ferns" (*CP*, p. 825) he describes how he once sat out a rainstorm in a natural shelter made by a grove of ferns and felt pride in his "spray-roofed house." A little rain comes through, but he makes pretense that he is not rained upon and feels safe, secure, and happy: "I could live on here thus till death," he says. The source of his sense of security is not so much the successful shelter as the ability of his imagination to overcome slight inadequacies. As a child, one can easily find a fairly secure place and wish away a little rain. He likes his isolation and is willing to settle for his mild success. Even as a child, he senses that the world he will grow up to will be much more difficult to deal with successfully, and he wonders, "Why should I have to grow to man's estate,/ And this afar-noised World perambulate?" This poem, published in *Winter Words*, is consistent with another from the same volume, "He Never Expected Much" (*CP*, p. 846). Hardy, looking back over his life on his eighty-sixth birthday, remarks that the world has "kept faith" with him:

> Upon the whole you have proved to be
> Much as you said you were.
> Since as a child I used to lie
> Upon the leaze and watch the sky,
> Never, I own, expected I
> That life would all be fair.

The world, he feels, offered him "Just neutral-tinted haps and such," and his reconciliation to this meager promise enabled him to "stem such strain and ache/ As each year might assign."

There are other poems in which the death of youth, joy, hope, faith, and love seem general and cosmic rather than merely personal. The radical discontinuity between youth and age merges into a radical discontinuity in social, intellectual, and religious history. Just as Hardy seems to have died as he grew older, whole systems of perception, thought, and social organization seem also to have died. In "The House of Hospitalities" (*CP*, p. 192), he remembers a place where generosity and social ritual in celebration of a religious event blended in a moment of harmony and personal happiness as he and his friends "broached the Christmas barrel" and sang old songs.

172

But the house, a symbol for a whole way of life, has now sunk into oblivion, becoming a place of spiders and moles. He haunts its location at midnight, when he in turn is haunted by ghosts who "smile" on him wistfully and pathetically.

In "Yuletide in a Younger World" (CP, p. 822), Hardy records what it was like to celebrate Christmas Eve at a time when people "believed in highdays," "heard still small voices," and "Caught the fartime tones of fire-filled prophets." The poem ends with the question, "Can such ever have been?" It now seems so foreign, distant, and unlikely as hardly to have happened at all. One can no longer believe in the things believed in then. This sense of discontinuity is also quietly present in "The Oxen" (CP, p. 439). As the clock strikes twelve on Christmas Eve, "An elder" tells the "flock" of people around him that the oxen are kneeling in the barn outside. The speaker, however, is not an "elder" but a member of the skeptical modern world, who looks back longingly toward a disappearing age:

> So fair a fancy few would weave
>   In these years! Yet, I feel,
> If someone said on Christmas Eve,
>   "Come; see the oxen kneel
>
> "In the lonely barton by yonder coomb
>   Our childhood used to know,"
> I should go with him in the gloom,
>   Hoping it might be so.

Much as he might hope to the contrary, the speaker knows what would happen should he put the legend to the test. In this poem the past has not simply ended; it is exposed as basically false—the oxen never knelt in reverence on Christmas Eve, as the speaker and his audience know full well, and what people of the past took to be reality was nothing but a "fair fancy." The old beliefs have been exploded, and a whole society has changed.

Having experienced the destructive effects of time and the discontinuities of history, and thereby losing faith, hope, joy, and love, Hardy discovers that testifying to these experiences and exposing reality for what it is render him vulnerable to hostile attack. Like the impercipient, Hardy often presents

173

himself as one who, denied the beneficent vision for which he longs, must suffer persecution for his honesty. He urgently wishes to affirm more than he can, as expressed in "The Darkling Thrush" (CP, p. 137), where the song of a bird testifies to a "Hope" of which the speaker is "unaware," or in "On a Fine Morning" (CP, p. 118), where the speaker tries to force himself to regard shadows as "Part of a benignant plan." In "To Sincerity" (CP, p. 262), "custom" tells the speaker:

> "Say ye rejoice, though grieving,
> Believe, while unbelieving,
> Behold, without perceiving!"

Yet in "To a Lady Offended by a Book of the Writer's" (CP, pp. 57–58), Hardy insists that "Truth will be truth alway," even if people refuse to accept it. Even his vision makes him a victim.

"In Tenebris" (CP, pp. 153–155), a group of three poems, sums up Hardy's personal myth of victimization. Since life has drained him of all feeling, and ignorant optimists only jeer at his accurate vision of reality, it would have been far better for him to have died long ago, before suffering a spiritual death in life. The first poem posits some crippling blow in the past, some death of feeling and aspiration, which blasted hope and prepared the speaker for physical death, the "wintertime" that "nighs" in the poem. Having "died" once, he does not fear the end. Having once seen "Flower-petals flee," he cannot be harrowed by another winter. Already enervated, he fears no loss of strength. Love cannot wound a man who has already lost his heart:

> Black is night's cope;
> But death will not appal
> One who, past doubtings all,
> Waits in unhope.

The word "hopelessness" would imply a negative vision, as well as a state of feeling, such as anguish or desperation. Hardy therefore coins the word "unhope" to specify a condition beyond hope or hopelessness, beyond anguish or desperation. He is spiritually dead.

174

The second poem deals with his idea of personal persecution. The "many and strong" who populate the world fill the air with ignorant shoutings "That things are all as they best may be, save a few to be right ere long." Hardy, who does not share their "vision," their "lusty joys," or their ignorant optimism, feels like one "shaped awry." Yet in contrast to the enervation of the first poem, here the galloping rhythm and the vigorous, colloquial texture of the language reflect an energy of defiance:

> The stout upstanders say, All's well with us: ruers have
>   nought to rue!
> And what the potent say so oft, can it fail to be
>   somewhat true?
> Breezily go they, breezily come; their dust smokes around
>   their career,
> Till I think I am one born out of due time, who has no
>   calling here.

The satiric, ranting tone suggests confidence. There is no doubt in the speaker's mind that to disturb the order as he does is a proper mode of life. The last stanza indirectly offers a positive strategy of hope based on honest realism:

> Let him in whose ears the low-voiced Best is killed by the
>   clash of the First,
> Who holds that if way to the Better there be, it exacts
>   a full look at the Worst,
> Who feels that delight is a delicate growth cramped by
>   crookedness, custom, and fear,
> Get him up and be gone as one shaped awry;
>   he disturbs the order here.

The irony is marked: it is the "stout upstanders" who are "born out of due time," who are "shaped awry," and who should "be gone." The insistent repetition of the word "here" at the end of each quatrain suggests a stubborn determination on the part of the speaker to hold his ground. He may have presented himself in the first lyric as waiting in "unhope," but in the second he is a model of rectitude, actively, aggressively mocking the petty, ignorant optimism of his persecutors.

The third poem returns to the note of resignation found in the first, and presents the view that hope and joy are destined to result in disillusion and pain. If only the speaker had died before learning "that vision could vex or that knowledge could numb,/ That sweets to the mouth in the belly are bitter, and tart, and untoward." He describes three moments, any one of which could have been his last. The first was a morning in late March, "when the half-sunny hours told that April was nigh," and he cleared the snow from the crocuses, "Fashioned and furbished the soil into a summer-seeming order," and glowed "in gladsome faith that I quickened the year thereby." He should have died then, before the cruel, spiritual winter of disillusionment blighted his faith. The second moment was when he wandered Egdon Heath with a woman, confident in "her watching and ward . . ./ Deeming her matchless in might and with measureless scope endued." This seems to be the same moment of innocent security in his mother's care that overshadows history in "The Roman Road." The third moment was less serene and confident, when immediately following his childhood "baptism of pain," he awoke, after drowsing by "the chimney-nook quoin," with "no listing or longing to join" the world "wheeling on." Any of these moments—of joy, of security, of disillusionment—should have been his last: "Then might the Voice that is law have said 'Cease!' and the ending have come." Instead, he lived on to become the dead man walking described in the first lyric. After rising to defiance in the second poem, he sinks back into the shadows, himself a shade, haunted by memories of constructive moments made painful by the thwartings and denials that ensued. The three poems, which ironically begin in age and end in childhood, enact a structure of weary circularity.

Hardy's personal poems reveal a considerable variety in his attitudes toward himself. As he wrote elsewhere, "the road to a true philosophy of life seems to lie in humbly recording diverse readings of its phenomena as they are forced upon us by chance and change." Yet the contradictions in the poems are remarkable. It is unlikely that a man drained dry of feeling would summon the energy to denounce his persecutors and codify a constructive philosophy of life. One who "never cared greatly" for life could hardly claim that his youth was too hopeful, and it is unlikely that a dead man walking could become animated by memories of joyous singing and dancing, and long for the old passions.[3] What is consistent in these contradictions is the sense of victimization. As life offers only to deny, one must work out modes of vision that deal with this fact. To claim that one never cared greatly is to prepare for the worst as a way to the better. To claim that life, time, and circumstance blight all love and aspiration absolves one of responsibility for one's own suffering.

Yet there is a further and more profound inconsistency, for in a number of his poems Hardy ascribes life's denials to his own failings. In "Wessex Heights" (*CP*, pp. 300–301), Hardy gives an involved and obscure description of his own character. At moments of crisis he likes to visit lonely heights, where he can be put in touch with a purer, simpler self: "I seem where I was before my birth, and after death may be." On the plains, which in the poem are associated with human involvement, he has lost touch with this essential self:

> Down there I seem to be false to myself, my simple self
>   that was,
> And is not now, and I see him watching, wondering what
>   crass cause
> Can have merged him into such a strange continuator
>   as this,
> Who yet has something in common with himself,
>   my chrysalis.

Although this personal history shares features with the myth of a pure, hopeful childhood blighted by mature experience, Hardy refrains from making simple explanations. To say that life gives only to take away, or that time ravages and destroys, would be too easy. The processes of development are more obscure and curious, and Hardy, internally divided, has yet to discover why he can be "false" to his purer, essential self. The poem includes hints of persecution, to the effect that, being destined to be different, he was therefore misunderstood:

> Down there they are dubious and askance; there nobody
>   thinks as I,
> But mind-chains do not clank where one's next neighbour
>   is the sky.

Yet the people on the plains are not "stout upstanders" mocking him for his honesty; rather, they are "dubious and askance," and in their midst he seems strangely out of place. He has no confidence in his own superiority.

What bothers him most about the plains are his memories associated with particular places, those phantoms that pursue and haunt him:

> In the towns I am tracked by phantoms having weird
>   detective ways—
> Shadows of beings who fellowed with myself of earlier
>   days:
> They hang about at places, and they say harsh heavy
>   things—
> Men with a wintry sneer, and women with tart
>   disparagings.

His view of himself as a man hunted by detective phantoms, who know precisely where to find him in order to sneer and disparage, suggests a deep, inner uncertainty. In his specific descriptions of the haunters, memories of apparent happiness removed by time merge into memories of failure. He cannot go to the "great grey Plain," for there a haunting figure "makes my breast beat out of tune," which is probably a reference to his mother guiding his infant footsteps on Egdon Heath. Elsewhere ghosts "chide" him and say things "I would not hear"; they touch a sore spot he would rather forget. Climactically, he mentions "one rare fair woman," apparently still alive, in whose mind he is "but a thought." Curiously, he seems never to have expressed his love to her: "Yet my love for her in its fulness she herself even did not know." Apparently his actions were not adequate to his feelings. Thus, it was he himself, not time, who denied and betrayed. In order to escape these memories of his shortcomings and the accusing voices, perhaps even to escape the memory of his mother, he seeks Wessex Heights. The high places are a refuge from the pain resulting from his awareness of his own inadequacy to the complicated involvements of life; there "ghosts . . . keep their distance; and I know some liberty." Ironically, he uses his "liberty" to muse on the haunting ghosts in the distance. He can rise above involvement, but he can never achieve ultimate freedom from the past. Submerged in the poem, spoken by a man haunted by the inescapable consciousness of his own falseness to his purer self, is a note of profound guilt.

In many poems Hardy presents himself as the victim of his own inadequacies. Like the protagonist in "Self-Unconscious" (*CP*, pp. 311–312), he understood things too late, preoccupied as he was with his own petty dreams and designs:

> Yes, round him were these
> Earth's artistries,
> But specious plans that came to his call
> Did most engage
> His pilgrimage,
> While himself he did not see at all.

In "The Rambler" (*CP*, pp. 252–253), he traverses the countryside oblivious to the landscape before his face because of painful memories of things missed in the past:

> The tones around me that I hear,
> The aspects, meanings, shapes I see,
> Are those far back ones missed when near,
> And now perceived too late by me!

In "Surview" (*CP*, pp. 660–661) his own voice chides him for his failures of vision and compassion:

> *"You held not to whatsoever was true . . .*
>
> *"You slighted her that endureth all . . .*
>
> *"You taught not that which you set about,"*
> Said my own voice talking to me;
> *"That the greatest of things is Charity . . ."*
> —And the sticks burnt low, and the fire went out,
> And my voice ceased talking to me.

This self-accusing old man, sitting alone by a dead fire, is responsible for his own spiritual dessication. No external blow has caused his death in life.

"In Front of the Landscape" (*CP*, pp. 285–287) is Hardy's fullest and most complex presentation of himself as a lonely, guilt-haunted wanderer of the countryside. The speaker is in a

turmoil of violent feeling about the past, and his visions of that
past force themselves on his mind with such insistency that
the landscape he is viewing becomes to him an illusion, and
his vision reality. This change in the level of reality is evident
in the metaphorical structure of the poem. Although the subject is allegedly the countryside, the controlling image is the
sea, with its tides and eddies standing for the turbulence of
the speaker's mind, and its eroding force standing for the
destructive effects of time:

> Plunging and labouring on in a tide of visions,
>   Dolorous and dear,
> Forward I pushed my way as amid waste waters
>   Stretching around,
> Through whose eddies there glimmered the customed
>   landscape
>   Yonder and near
>
> Blotted to feeble mist.

The old landmarks remain in his sight—the "Ancient chalk-
pit," the "milestone"—but they now seem to be "a ghost-like
gauze," while the ghosts who haunt the speaker have become
real: "I could see them, feel them, hear them, address them."
He sees "speechful faces," some dolorous and some dear,
some smiling, some bathed in tears—"Harrowed by wiles," as
if they themselves were headlands worn down by the brine
waters of anguish. Others, "shaken by fierce unreason,/ Rigid
in hate," are "Dreaded, suspect." In one of these visions of
the past the real sea plays an actual part:

> a headland of hoary aspect
>   Gnawed by the tide,
> Frilled by the nimb of the morning as two friends stood
>   there
>   Guilelessly glad—
> Wherefore they knew not—touched by the fringe of an
>   ecstasy
>   Scantly descried.

His imagination finally carries him to the graveyard, the resting
place of the people whose memories impress his mind with
such lifelike immediacy:

> down to where lay the beheld ones;
> —Yea, as the rhyme
> Sung by the sea-swell, so in their pleading dumbness
> Captured me these.

J. Hillis Miller asserted that the regular beat of the sea defines the elgiac rhythm of the poem.[4] Just as the "sea-swell" sings a rhyme when each wave breaks against the headlands, the long lines of the poem tend to rise and swell in extended rhythmical units, followed by the abrupt, emphatic short lines. The poem also strikes an exotic and faintly archaic note in its use of complex alliterative patterns:

> O they were speechful faces, gazing insistent,
> Some as with smiles,
> Some as with slow-born tears that brinily trundled
> Over the wrecked
> Cheeks that were fair in their flush-time, ash now
> with anguish,
> Harrowed by wiles.

The rich repetitions and blendings of sound approximate the effect of the Welsh figure of speech *cynghanedd,* which consists of the intensified repetition or "chiming" of sounds in condensed phrases, as in Gerard Manley Hopkins' "a lush-kept plush-capped sloe" from "The Wreck of the Deutschland," or his "World broods with warm breast and with ah! bright wings" from "God's Grandeur." There is little doubt that Hardy was introduced to the figure by his friend William Barnes, and he seems to be employing it in the third and fifth lines above. Also, the frequent breaking of lines into smaller units consisting of heavily accented alliterative phrases echoes the elegiac pace of Anglo-Saxon alliterative poetry. These muted stylistic references to the native poetry of pagan England are appropriate to a poem that concerns a lonely wanderer across the ancient landscape, haunted by sounds of the sea and by the faces of the dead.

The poem is not an elegy, however, for at the heart of Hardy's anguish is not his sense of loss, but his guilt. Like the two friends on the headland who felt glad without knowing why, and only "scantly descried" the ecstasy of the moment they shared, Hardy again and again missed an opportunity:

Much had I slighted, caring not for their purport,
　Seeing behind
Things more coveted, reckoned the better worth calling
　Sweet, sad, sublime.

The situation in the past is directly analogous to the situation in the present. In the past, his imagination diverted him with visions of something better than the real opportunities before his very eyes. In the present, he looks at the actual landscape, but is haunted by visions of those opportunities missed. Thus, he sees "ghosts avenging their slights by my bypast/ Body-borne eyes." These ghosts are now more real—showing with "fuller translation"—than they were in the past, because then he selfishly ignored them. As a result of his own guilt the past blots out the present, "killing the daytime/ As by the night." The past lives on as the embodiment of Hardy's cruel failings. He wanders over the landscape, as he says, "seeing nought . . . Save a few tombs," because he saw so little in the past when those buried dead were alive in the flesh. The continuity between past and present in this poem is tragic; the speaker, haunted by guilt, will never be able to come to terms with those whose suffering resulted from his negligence.

In both the poems of victimization and the poems of guilt the subject is generally the speaker's own unique history. He may be ravaged by time and circumstance, or he may be a victim of himself, but at least the circumstances of the story are his alone. But a more threatening possibility arises in "The Pedigree" (CP, pp. 431–432). As Hardy ponders his family tree, "The branches seemed to twist into a seared and cynic face" with his discovery that his life, determined by the patterns of behavior and consciousness of his forebears, is merely a mechanical reenactment:

Said I then, sunk in tone,
"I am merest mimicker and counterfeit!—
　Though thinking, *I am I,*
And what I do I do myself alone."

The poem suggests that each human being endlessly and futilely reenacts patterns of suffering and despair, blinded by the illusory sense of his own individuality to the inevitable hopelessness of his situation. Hardy attempted to triumph over this sense of meaninglessness, as well as over his feelings of guilt and victimization, in the poetic response to his most personal subject, his love affair with his first wife.

LOVE POEMS

7

In the early spring of 1870, when Hardy visited St. Juliot, Cornwall, in order to make plans for restoring a church, he met Emma Lavinia Gifford, the sister-in-law of the rector, and fell in love with her. Thereafter he broke off a relationship with a distant cousin, Tryphena Sparks, courted Emma, and married her in 1874. They experienced a period of marital happiness, followed by a deepening division caused in part by Emma's sense of social superiority, her jealousy of her husband's literary success, and her dissatisfaction with life in Dorset, where the Hardys settled for good in the 1880s. Emma died in 1912. Although she was seventy-three years old at the time and had been in poor health, her death came to Hardy as an unexpected shock.

Poems inspired by Emma had appeared as early as "Ditty" in *Wessex Poems* and, in significant quantity, in "More Love Lyrics" in *Time's Laughingstocks*. But it was not until Emma died that Hardy felt completely free to examine his own emotional life history. There were many stimulants to recollection. Hardy went through Emma's effects and read her personal papers, including those now published under the title *Some Recollections*, which describe her early life and her meeting with her husband.[1] He revisited the places of courtship and romance, and noted the anniversaries of significant events. The immediate outpouring after Emma's death—"Poems of 1912–13" in *Satires of Circumstance*—was only the beginning of a flood. Poems in his last four volumes examine and re-examine the events and feelings in the various stages of his relationship

184

with Emma. In these lyrics Hardy's stance is less guarded, more confessional and revelatory, than anywhere else in his poetry.

A difficulty in examining Hardy's love lyrics results from their being scattered throughout the *Collected Poems*. It almost seems that his final effort to conceal himself was to hide his most personal poems amidst a mass of disparate verse. Carl J. Weber collected many of the love poems that seem definitely related to Emma and arranged them coherently to reflect the stages of Hardy's romance—the courtship, the period of early, happy wedded life, the growing division, Emma's death, and the aftermath.[2] But to those poems should be added others that, despite disparities between the situations described and the historical, biographical facts, are similar in theme, tone, and technique. It is appropriate to include even those love poems in which there are glaring discrepancies in fact between the verse and the known biography, such as "First Sight of Her and After," "The Shiver," and "A Broken Appointment," for the sorts of situations depicted and the kinds of emotions conveyed relate them closely to the poems about Emma. The result is an extensive lyric history of the relationship between a man and a woman based generally on Hardy's relationship with his first wife. In terms of the structure of this history and the themes and methods of the poems, the group is closer to Frost's *A Boy's Will* or even to Tennyson's *In Memoriam* than to Mrs. Browning's *Sonnets from the Portuguese*, with which it has been compared, for it deals with union, division, guilt, grief, and reconciliation, and relates personal history to philosophic crisis. Yet comparisons are at best suggestive, for Hardy's personal love lyrics, taken together, make a cohesive group of poems unique in English and American literature.

The Operations of the Mind

In order to explain the basic issues in Hardy's love poems, it is important to distinguish between the three ways in which the mind operates on reality in his poetry, although he never makes the distinctions explicit. These operations might be called perception, projection, and imaginative apprehension.

Perception refers to the way an uninformed mind sees in the external world of things and events, and even in the internal world of the consciousness, merely constant, purposeless change, indifference, disorder, and meaninglessness. This is the mode of the speaker's mind at the end of "The Revisitation" (CP, p. 181): "Love is lame at fifty years," he says, resigning himself to the disheartening realities. Projection assumes the accuracy of mere perception, but imagines a meaning to compensate for the lack of meaning in reality. It fills the empty stage with self-projected drama. It is this operation which creates fable and melodrama, which imagines intention in the workings of the external world as an alternative to perceiving indifference, and which conceives of nature not as fact but as symbol embodying an imagined meaning. The speaker in "My Cicely" (CP, pp. 45–48) willfully projects an illusion on the reality he experiences by insisting that the depraved barmaid is not the woman he once loved. The speaker in "God-Forgotten" (CP, pp. 112–113) hopefully imagines a successful visit to God, although at the end of the poem he sees this projection as a "childish thought." The speaker in "Hap" (CP, p. 7) cannot sustain his projected view of himself as the central actor in a cosmic drama, for he is in reality subject to meaningless chance and change. In his personal poems Hardy sometimes sees himself as a victim of circumstance, whereas in other poems he shows an awareness of his own responsibility for suffering, and it may be that his sense of victimization is a projection designed to deny the reality of his guilt. In contrast to the interrelated faculties of perception and projection, imaginative apprehension grasps perceived reality as a rich experience, with the result that a real event takes on the quality of created vision. This is Hardy's mode in the affirmative "Poems of Pilgrimage." Imaginative apprehension actively envisions reality, rather than projecting fantasies on a blank screen. Its animating power is akin to love, and hence is of central importance in the love poems.

"A Dream or No" (CP, pp. 327–328), a poem in which Hardy recalls his meeting with Emma in Cornwall, involves all three operations of the mind. Emma has died, and Hardy, revisiting St. Juliot where he first met her, calls into question the reality

186

of his remembered experiences with her. Mere perception yields "nought":

> But nought of that maid from Saint-Juliot I see;
>   Can she ever have been here,
>   And shed her life's sheen here,
> The woman I thought a long housemate with me?

Death—indifferent, inevitable—seems to have robbed the romance of its reality. Hardy's memories of romantic moments on the Cornish coast now appear to be merely "dreams." He feels that much of his life "claims the spot as its key," yet perhaps this feeling is a delusion, produced by "Some strange necromancy." The ending of the poem even questions the reality of the landscape itself:

> Does there even a place like Saint-Juliot exist?
>   Or a Valency Valley
>   With stream and leafed alley,
> Or Beeny, or Bos with its flounce flinging mist?

Although uninformed, neutral perception reveals that these spots do exist, there may be no real places "like" the ones Hardy envisions, places transformed by the "life's sheen" of a lovely girl into a countryside radiant with romance. Hardy's life with that girl may really have formed a significant pattern that has as its "key" the location of their first meeting, or he may merely have imagined it. Death may expose the illusion of meaning, or life may really consummate itself in an experience so glorious that it endures as long as the mind has the power to re-envision it. Reality may be blank and meaning mere projection, or Hardy's dreams may be his magical grip on the significant actuality of past experience.

"At Castle Boterel" (*CP*, pp. 330–331), another retrospective poem, answers affirmatively the question asked in "A Dream or No." Hardy describes his revisiting, as an old man, a place that was significant to his early romance. The actual, concrete situation presented in the poem is an image of his spiritual condition. As he departs from the place in the rain, he looks

187

"behind at the fading byway," just as in many of the love poems he looks back to a past that fades as his distance in time from it increases. Driving away, he sees "Distinctly yet/ Myself and a girlish form." In a vision he then re-enacts an old occurrence. The action is simple and commonplace, as is the language. He objectively describes what happened as if he is really seeing it in the present:

> We climb the road
> Beside a chaise. We had just alighted
> To ease the sturdy pony's load
> When he sighed and slowed.

This language could be prose. Words are few, as if not necessary to validate or heighten the reality, no more than it is necessary to recall the words spoken in the past: "What we did as we climbed, and what we talked of/ Matters not much, nor to what it led." What matters is the actuality of the experience. Although it lasted only a minute, it was:

> Something that life will not be balked of
> Without rude reason till hope is dead,
> And feeling fled.

With "rude reason," in other words, life can be "balked of" the significant moment. Uninformed rational perception would regard it as a commonplace event in the transitory lives of two ordinary people. But for a memory informed with hope and feeling, the moment cannot be denied. It is not simply a neutral fact but has a quality that infuses the indifferent landscape with significant history:

> But was there ever
> A time of such quality, since or before,
> In that hill's story? . .
>
> Primaeval rocks form the road's steep border,
> And much have they faced there, first and last,
> Of the transitory in Earth's long order;
> But what they record in colour and cast
> Is—that we two passed.

188

The rocks are not symbols, nor are they transformed into symbol. They are real things, which have endured unchanging while much change has occurred around them. But for Hardy, as for the readers of the poem, one transitory moment has become an unchangeable part of the recorded history of the scene.

Hardy's mind, re-envisioning the past, triumphs over neutral place and destructive time:

> And to me, though Time's unflinching rigour,
>   In mindless rote, has ruled from sight
> The substance now, one phantom figure
>   Remains on the slope, as when that night
>   Saw us alight.

Rude reason or mere perception would detect only the mindless ravagings of time, but the apprehending mind sees a phantom, without substance but nevertheless real, actually there on the slope as it was in substance that night long ago. The ending of the poem is a reminder that the speaker himself is subject to "the transitory in Earth's long order":

> I look and see it there, shrinking, shrinking,
>   I look back at it amid the rain
> For the very last time; for my sand is sinking,
>   And I shall traverse old love's domain
>   Never again.

Death approaches; he will never physically return to "love's domain." But love's domain, instead of being a mere projection, is a reality, recreated by memory, a domain inhabited by a figure that Hardy actually sees "shrinking, shrinking," a figure substantiated in the poem by the simplicity and directness of the language. In this poem, Hardy's vision is real, the partial reincarnation of a magical moment blending hope, feeling, love, and physical actuality.

"Under the Waterfall" (CP, pp. 315–317) illustrates the transformation of experience into something akin to art. The speaker, undoubtedly Emma, explains that plunging her arm into a basin of water always recalls "the sweet sharp sense of a fugitive day/ Fetched back from its thickening shroud of gray."

Again there is the sense of time creating an ever-increasing gap between memory and reality, and again the bridge between the two is a simple physical experience. It stimulates thoughts in the speaker of the one thoroughly happy, romantic experience of whose reality she is absolutely certain. Central to that experience is a natural sound, which becomes poetry:

> "the only prime
> And real love-rhyme
> That I know by heart,
> And that leaves no smart."

The "rhyme" is the sound of a waterfall. By implication, other rhymes either recall pain, or are unreal, diluted by dreams and fancies. The waterfall is described in a vivid passage which emphasizes its enduring physical reality—its size, the solidity of the rocks where it falls, its transcendence over human history and even over changing geological forms:

> "the purl of a little valley fall
> About three spans wide and two spans tall
> Over a table of solid rock,
> And into a scoop of the self-same block;
> The purl of a runlet that never ceases
> In stir of kingdoms, in wars, in peaces;
> With a hollow boiling voice it speaks
> And has spoken since hills were turfless peaks."

The scene described was the location of a picnic long ago, when the two lovers, as the speaker says, "under a sky/ Of blue with a leaf-wove awning of green," ate their lunch "By the runlet's rim" and, after drinking together from the same glass, let it fall into the pool. Because the speaker then reached her arm into the water in an attempt to retrieve the glass, whenever she puts her hands into a basin in the present, it assists her imaginative recall:

> "The basin seems the pool, and its edge
> The hard smooth face of the brook-side ledge,
> And the leafy pattern of china-ware
> The hanging plants that were bathing there."

190

The feel of water and smooth hardness and the sight of the foliage pattern on the edge of the basin provide enough elements from the past to stimulate the recreation of a vivid, concrete experience. This memory is no dream.

Memory here is evoked by something natural united with something humanly constructed, water in a leaf-decorated basin, and the language of the poem repeatedly transforms something natural and changing into the permanence of art. The sound of the waterfall is a "real love-rhyme." The blue of the sky and the green of the foliage "paint the scene." The commonplace glass is elevated to a romantic, mythic vessel: "that chalice of ours." It fell into a "little abyss," where it remains "intact":

> "its presence adds to the rhyme of love
> Persistently sung by the fall above.
> No lip has touched it since his and mine
> In turns therefrom sipped lovers' wine."

The moment is thus not only a remembered actuality, recorded in words that lend it the quality of art, but the scene itself endures as a work of art, whether anyone remembers it or not. The glass is still there, a love-chalice intact and untouched, safe at the bottom of the pool, presided over by the waterfall eternally murmuring its rhyme, surrounded by the permanent rocks, decorated by the blue of the sky and the green of the foliage. It is not a dream, nor has dream given meaning to fact; fact, instead, has become art. Place is anything but neutral, and human experience triumphs over time.

It is in the love poems that Hardy's faith in the reality of imaginative apprehension appears most clearly. Again and again he perceives real visions as he surveys the romantic past. Moreover, the whole history of his love relationship becomes real vision; he sees form, progression, and actual meaning in what otherwise might appear as a commonplace youthful romance leading to a disappointing marriage. What happened to Hardy after Emma's death is similar to what happens to the lovers in his poems after their first meeting: the new lover is informed with imaginative apprehension and perceives the world in new ways, in which nature arranges itself into

191

dramatic and pictorial scenes; nature and art merge, fact becomes meaning, and his life reveals a pattern. Likewise, Emma's death seems to have aroused in Hardy the kind of "hope" and "feeling" noted in "At Castle Boterel," enabling him to rise above "rude reason" to envision life with her as forming a meaningful pattern, to which her youthful dwelling place in Cornwall is the key.

The transformation of life into art is evidenced by the figurative language. Hardy continually makes use of the vocabulary of artistic form. " 'By the Runic Stone' " (*CP*, p. 442), for example, describes *"Two who became a story."* In "Ten Years Since" (*CP*, p. 685), Hardy laments that at Emma's death their mutual history "shut like a book." The characters in "The Last Time" (*CP*, p. 650) "read no finis" in the episode, "As at closing of a book." The interlude in "A Two-Years' Idyll" (*CP*, pp. 594–595) seems sadly like "A preface without any book,/ A trumpet uplipped, but no call." Sometimes the episodes in the story seem to come "back in pantomime" ("The Place on the Map," *CP*, pp. 302–303). At other times the characters see "scenes slide past" (" 'Between Us Now,' " *CP*, pp. 124–125). Or the drama unfolds, as in "A Procession of Dead Days" (*CP*, pp. 609–610), in a series of scenes played in dumbshow in Hardy's mind: each "Enters . . . into view," enacts its meaning, and surrenders the stage to the next.

The metaphor of theatrical drama pervades the love lyrics. In "At the Word 'Farewell' " (*CP*, pp. 405–406) a significant moment is seen as a "prelude" to a "drama." In "The Dream Is—Which?" (*CP*, p. 615), "a curtain drops between" Hardy and his vision; and in " 'She Charged Me' " (*CP*, p. 343), the speaker sees that a final "curtain would drop upon us two" at the end of "our play of slave and queen." Music also plays a part. In "Lines to a Movement in Mozart's E-Flat Symphony" (*CP*, p. 430), Hardy attempts explicitly to accompany pantomimic scenes with musical, onomatopoeic refrains. In "The Rift" (*CP*, p. 589), the two lovers' affections correspond "As rhyme meets rhyme," until feeling "changed its chime/ From those true tones."

Portions of this story of happiness and division seem to be written on other things, sometimes as "magic . . . lineaments"

("The Change," *CP*, pp. 426–427), sometimes "scrawled/ Dully on days" ("A Two-Years' Idyll"). Returning to the old places, Hardy sees a "lucid legend," "written everywhere/ Unto me" ("Ditty," *CP*, pp. 13–14), much as the cliffs in "At Castle Boterel" preserve a record "in colour and cast." Messages seem to be engraved on faces as well as on the landscape. In "Your Last Drive" (*CP*, pp. 319–320), Hardy castigates himself for not having "read the writing upon your face." Sometimes the writing is clear: for example, the events described in " 'I Rose and Went to Rou'tour Town' " (*CP*, p. 486) "Wrote sorrows on my face," and in "The Frozen Greenhouse" (*CP*, p. 698), "Her scared young look" was "The very symbol/ Of tragedy." Sometimes the language of the poems transforms the landscapes into scenes akin to painted and drawn pictures. Hardy notes "the fair colour of the time" of early love in "The Musical Box" (*CP*, pp. 453–454). This same time is "Enringed with a purple zone" in "The Change," and appears as if "drawn rose-bright" in "The Phantom Horsewoman" (*CP*, pp. 332–333). In young love the lover's "form" stands out against the "background," before "the duller/ Loomings of life" have defined themselves ("Green Slates," *CP*, p. 675), and this period seems embowed with "rainbow-rays" ("Looking at a Picture on an Anniversary," *CP*, p. 501); "life would show . . . no finer glow," no "rosier pink" than it did then ("Best Times," *CP*, pp. 646–647). "The Figure in the Scene" (*CP*, p. 447) and " 'Why Did I Sketch?' " (*CP*, pp. 447–448) describe actual pictures, and other poems, such as "Beeny Cliff" (*CP*, p. 330), with its description of the "chasmal beauty" of the cliff looming against the sky, paint pictures in words. Again and again Hardy apprehends the story of his love as if it were a work of art.

The distinctions between the operations of the mind are useful in understanding Hardy's imaginative grasp on the total meaning of his own love story. The poems describing the period leading up to the first meeting of the two lovers are, for the most part, projections; Hardy imagines a cosmic significance in the dramatic preface to the story. For the most part the poems in which imaginative apprehension operates at the time being described portray scenes from the period of early love in Cornwall. After the couple's meeting, love irradiates the world, which glows and sings and becomes transformed into art. The power of love, which animates imaginative apprehension, begins, however, eventually to fail. The characters fail in "reading" one another properly. They project meanings that are not actually there. Nature becomes a grim, neutral, ironic backdrop for bitter disappointment. Art and experience divide. After Emma's death, Hardy's powers are reanimated. He reaffirms his faith in the reality of those early, key moments, but it is a faith tempered by regret, guilt, and remorse at the mutual responsibility of the two lovers for the loss of that early magic. Past and present are fused in a poetry of faith and regret.

The Meeting

In describing the first stage of romance, the lovers' meeting, Hardy presents an ironic drama of predestined love balanced by predestined separation. In poems that capture the self-dramatizing tones of a youthful, romantic lover, he imagines cosmic meanings in the moment of meeting. There are some poems of memory rather than imagination. ."St. Launce's Revisited" (*CP*, pp. 335–336), for example, describes Hardy's actual recollection of the specific place where he changed from train to horsecart for the last stage of his journey to St. Juliot. The poem expresses his sadness that nothing is the same, all "banished/ Ever into nought!" In contrast, most of the poems about the first meeting create a sense not of sadness at the passing of things, but of awe at the mysterious significance of the moment. Indeed, the meeting itself is never presented. No concrete descriptions are given, for instance, of the place where the lovers first meet, or of their appearance as they first stand face to face. Instead, Hardy deals with the feelings of the relevant characters as they approach the meeting, and the effect of the moment on them immediately afterward. The drama lies in the contrast between before and after, intensified by a sense that the moment is the focus of energies beyond the characters' control.

The most obvious evidence that this situation is one of drama, the structure primarily of Hardy's imagination rather than of his memory, is that the three main poems dealing with the event regard it from the points of view of three different

194

people: the young man, his new lover, and his former lover.[3] The young man is speaking in "The Wind's Prophecy" (*CP*, pp. 464–465). Moving westward across the countryside toward the coast, he thinks he is leaving his love behind, but the mysterious voice of the wind contradicts him: "Nay; toward her arms thou journeyest." The young man thinks of his present lover's "ebon loops of hair," her "city home," and her place in the east; whereas the wind speaks of her "tresses flashing fair," her "sea-bord" home, and her dwelling in the west. The man's final ironic utterance is a prayer that the girl in the east should be faithful to him:

> "I roam, but one is safely mine,"
> I say. "God grant she stay my own!"
> Low laughs the wind as if it grinned:
> "Thy Love is one thou'st not yet known."

It is the young man who is destined to be the unfaithful lover.

In this poem, nature, described in vivid language, plays an active role in the drama. The landscape is relevant not alone as a backdrop to a significant event, like the rocks and foliage in "Under the Waterfall," which enshrine permanently the happy moment, or the sound of the waterfall, which is a "real love-rhyme" as opposed to merely a symbol of love. Nature in "The Wind's Prophecy" takes on an ominous, symbolic value. The wind speaks. In addition to personification, Hardy makes frequent use of metaphor and simile to heighten the violent contrasts between light and dark, dullness and color, height and depth, action and passivity:

> I travel on by barren farms,
> And gulls glint out like silver flecks
> Against a cloud that speaks of wrecks,
> And bellies down with black alarms.

The "distant verge morosely gray" is broken by "clots of flying foam" ascending from "its muddy monochrome" while a "light blinks up far away." The surf at the coast sounds in "smitings like the slam of doors,/ Or hammerings on hollow floors," and while "one quick timorous transient star" appears, the waves

195

"Huzza like a mad multitude." Nature is animated to give warnings, to cheer ironically, to threaten, to hint at a mysterious hollowness. The final image is of a "headland, vulturine," whose "every chasm and every steep" are thrown into deeper, contrasting blackness as the pharos lights come on.

The violence and changefulness of the scene seem to help bring on the speaker's thoughts of his absent lover. In her there is a safe haven, a hope for stable, abiding feeling, in contrast to the ominous, ever-changing texture of the unfamiliar world into which the young man ventures. But ironically, the aspects of nature that reinforce his thoughts of her and his fears of her unfaithfulness are images suggesting characteristics of his own nature. For he, too, is about to change from dark to light, as he says, from "ebon loops of hair" to "tresses flashing fair." His affections will move sunlike across the sky from their focus in the east to a new focus in the west. His journey into the depths is in reality an ascent to a new height, and the light of his new love will throw into shadow his old. The speaker need fear neither the ominous, mysterious violence of nature nor the inconstancy of his lover; the issue is rather the stability of his own heart. That the wind knows the full meaning of his journey creates an awesome sense of predestination—of foreordained union and foreordained separation. As the new lights come on, shadows deepen.

The speaker of "The Shiver" (CP, p. 743), a girl whose lover is about to abandon her, lives in the country, whereas "The Wind's Prophecy" refers to her city home. Yet there are enough similarities between the two poems to justify considering them both as treatments of the same basic situation. The girl wakens at five in the morning, while "Stars wore west like a slow tide flowing," in order to catch a glimpse of the young man "hasting by" on his westward journey to the coast. The man's unwillingness to "bend his track" to her window because of his haste hints at his impending unfaithfulness. The girl understands the omen:

> But I wished he had tried to!—and then felt a shiver,
> Corpse-cold, as he sank toward the town by the river;
> And back I went sadly and slowly to bed.

196

She had, however, caught one glimpse of him in the distance: "A dim dumb speck, growing darker and bigger,/ Then smalling to nought." This image suggests the pattern of their whole relationship. He approaches, but not close enough to have full identity, then fades from her life. The very quality that prevents him from awakening early enough to have the time to see her before leaving—that slight failure of consideration and faithfulness—makes him receptive to what subsequently happens to him at the seaside. He returns with the cruel news:

> "But I've seen, I have clasped, where the smart ships
>   plough,
>   One of far brighter brow.
> A sea-goddess. Shiver not. One far rarer
> In gifts than I find thee; yea, warmer and fairer:—
> I seek her again; and I love you not now."

There is no mincing of words; the blow falls hard. Her "shiver/ Corpse-cold" on the morning of his departure was fully justified. He has become as indifferent to her as was the march of time signaled by "Five lone clangs from the house-clock" in the first stanza, or as the distant, ever-moving stars.

In " 'A Man Was Drawing Near to Me' " (*CP*, p. 549), Hardy imagines the state of mind of Emma, the new lover, as the young man approaches. Her mood is a combination of indifference, complacent passivity, and idle thoughtfulness. She complains that, being "Apart from aught to hear, to see," she finds the world dull. It is a "gray night of mournful drone," and outside is "the moorland dim and dun/ That travellers shun." She has no dreams, and no one to think of, "no concern at anything,/ No sense of coming pull-heart play." She is occupied by "trifles" only, "legends, ghosts." Although she sees the "seaward pharos-fire" mentioned in "The Wind's Prophecy," it is not a beacon in her life, for there is:

> Nothing to let me understand
>   That hard at hand
>   By Hennett Byre
> The man was getting nigh and nigher.

The last stanza describes the commonplace sounds and sights

that announce his arrival, and then the moment of meeting:

> There was a rumble at the door,
> A draught disturbed the drapery,
> And but a minute passed before,
>   With gaze that bore
>   My destiny,
> The man revealed himself to me.

By focusing on the contrast between her indifference and the determining significance of this meeting for her life, as indicated by the word "destiny," Hardy transforms a commonplace meeting into cosmic drama. While she sits in dullness and gloom, her fate, in the shape of the approaching man, is preparing to burst upon her consciousness, utterly unexpectedly. And yet not utterly unprepared for. Her preparation is precisely her isolation, the dullness of her life, the idleness of her thoughts, and the meaninglessness of her surroundings. Passive and inert, she waits, without even knowing it herself, to be quickened into life. In Emma Gifford's words from the passage in her recollections that seems partly to have inspired the poem, "My life's romance now began." When quoting this sentence in his biography Hardy significantly changes it in an attempt to load the moment with even greater meaning: "My life now began."[4]

Other poems, such as "The Discovery" (*CP*, p. 313), " 'I Worked No Wile To Meet You' " (*CP*, p. 574), and "Before Knowledge" (*CP*, p. 418), present the same essential situation, an unexpected fulfillment resulting from the mysteriously pre-destined convergence of two people. The mode of these poems is not so much recollection as imaginative meditation. The episodes recorded imply a pattern of almost mythic dimensions. The moment of high happiness, of revivification and rebirth, is seen in the context of mysterious, predestinating, cyclical forces. Just as in "The Convergence of the Twain" (*CP*, pp. 288–289), the Immanent Will prepares both the iceberg and the ship *Titanic* for their moment of meeting, that "consummation" which "jars two hemispheres," in these love poems destiny seems to single out the lovers and prepare them for the determining, consummating moment of their lives. Fate is both cruel and kind; it brings two people together, but leaves a third bereft. Thus, the road to that convergence is marked by an oppressive gloom and threatening omens. The poems merely imply the moment of high consummation, focusing instead on the situation's grim ambivalences. Hardy makes his vision of that meeting in the past both romantic and ominous by such means as deep shadows, howling winds, dark crevices, pounding surf, legends and ghosts, and the lonely clanging of indifferent clocks.

The Courtship

Having met, the lovers perceive the world in new frames of meaning. One change is described in "First Sight of Her and After" (CP, pp. 406–407):

> A day is drawing to its fall
> I had not dreamed to see;
> The first of many to enthrall
> My spirit, will it be?
> Or is this eve the end of all
> Such new delight for me?
>
> I journey home: the pattern grows
> Of moonshades on the way:
> "Soon the first quarter, I suppose,"
> Sky-glancing travellers say;
> I realize that it, for those,
> Has been a common day.

The outcome is uncertain, but the meeting has stirred the young man's consciousness. He is in a state of agitation and doubt: will the "new delight" cease or endure? His question sets him apart from other travelers on the road, who glance at the moon and make predictions that are certain to come true, for the new moon will wax into the first quarter. For the speaker, in contrast, the evening may be either a beginning or an end, and the future shape of his love story is unknown. On this uncommon day he has been introduced to feeling and risk, possible loss or gain. Counterpointed to the certainties of ordinary life and the inevitabilities of nature's processes, his life has taken on at least the potential of significant shape, and the world is different for him.

In " 'When I Set Out for Lyonnesse' " (*CP*, pp. 293–294), a poem explicitly related to Hardy's first trip to Cornwall, home of the ancient, romantic kingdom, the speaker knows that the lovers' meeting has been a beginning. The first stanza expresses distance, coldness, indifference, and loneliness:

> When I set out for Lyonnesse,
>   A hundred miles away,
>   The rime was on the spray,
> And starlight lit my lonesomeness
> When I set out for Lyonnesse
>   A hundred miles away.

What happens is mysterious and unpredictable, something "No prophet durst declare" nor "wisest wizard guess." Without revealing what it is, the poem dramatizes its impact:

> All marked with mute surmise
> My radiance rare and fathomless,
> When I came back from Lyonnesse
>   With magic in my eyes!

No longer does the starlight light his lonesomeness; as anyone can see by looking at him, his own eyes illuminate the world and turn its neutral order into a magical scene.

There is a difference between envisioning something that is not there and seeing what is there in a clearer, more harmonious way. In "After a Romantic Day" (*CP*, p. 607), the protagonist's love inspires in him the ability to project. He looks out the window of a railway train and sees an earthen cutting:

> The bald steep cutting, rigid, rough,
>   And moon-lit, was enough
> For poetry of place: its weathered face
> Formed a convenient sheet whereon
> The visions of his mind were drawn.

Here the lover imposes the poetry on the place. In contrast, there is little sense of projection in Hardy's poetic descriptions of actual moments in his courtship. The excitement of love, the rush of emotion, and the keen sense of possibility seem to have resulted for Hardy in a freshening of his ability to perceive creatively the external world. The sensuous vividness of those poems that recall the early period of his romance testify to this heightened sensitivity. Sounds and sights had for him real meaning as integral parts of organic experience. Furthermore, the moments described are really artlike, because art itself was central to the primary remembered experiences. Together, he and Emma created and performed. In those happy moments, they played the piano and sang, recited poems and drew sketches. In the poems dealing with his romance, Hardy makes very little of Emma's physical beauty or of the qualities of her intellect, and he seldom records the words that passed between them. As in "At Castle Boterel," the words do not matter. What matters instead are the moments of consummated harmony with one another and with nature experienced by the two, moments like the one described in "Underneath the Waterfall."

The biography reveals that Hardy thought Emma was "so living."[5] In the poems of courtship he suggests her vivacity by describing her singing and piano playing, her daring, graceful horseback riding, and her magical ability to impose her presence on the landscape. Such scenes, which he sometimes recorded quite literally in pencil sketches, also imprinted themselves on his memory as if they were actual pictures, as in "The Figure in the Scene":

> It pleased her to step in front and sit
> Where the cragged slope was green,
> While I stood back that I might pencil it
> With her amid the scene.

Despite a rainfall that streaked the picture, he continued his sketch. Just as in the past the rain immutably marked his work of art, in the present Emma's figure has for him merged permanently and organically with the place:

Yet her rainy form is the Genius still of the spot,
    Immutable, yea,
Though the place now knows her no more, and
        has known her not
    Ever since that day.

In " 'Why Did I Sketch,' " a poem inspired by the same drawing, he shows how "The picture waxes akin/ To a wordless irony." Her presence in the drawing is a grim reminder of her death, and he berates himself for the joy of the occasion that inspired him to put her figure in the scene. He makes it clear that central to the experience were the artistic, creative activities they performed together:

    Let me sooner pass from sight of the sky
        Than again on a thoughtless day
        Limn, laugh, and sing, and rhyme
    With a woman sitting near, whom I
        Paint in for love, and who may
        Be called hence in my time!

"Green Slates" shows that not only scenes actually sketched speak with wordless irony, but also moments remembered as if they were pictures. While working on the restoration of St. Juliot Church, Hardy visited a quarry with Emma in search of slates to repair the roof:

    And saw, the while I peered around there,
        In the quarry standing
    A form against the slate background there,
        Of fairness eye-commanding.

Even now, in his old age, when "duller/ Loomings of life" have descended, any green slates he sees, whether "high on roofs, or lower/ In waggon, truck, or lorry" seem to cry out: "Our home was where you saw her/ Standing in the quarry!" He remembers what he saw: a form against a background of green slate. To see the background is to remember the form. He recalls not what Emma said, nor the expression on her face, nor the quality of her smile, but a total picture, sketched in outline and simple colors.

In the poems of courtship, seeing is of the utmost importance. Hardy saw and read things not written or spoken in words, just as he read the "wordless irony" of his drawing in " 'Why Did I Sketch?' " "At the Word 'Farewell,' " which records Hardy's departure from Emma at the conclusion of his first visit to Cornwall, makes its statement entirely in terms of things seen. It begins with a word picture:

> She looked like a bird from a cloud
>   On the clammy lawn,
> Moving alone, bare-browed
>   In the dim of dawn.
> The candles alight in the room
>   For my parting meal
> Made all things withoutdoors loom
>   Strange, ghostly, unreal.

The picture is recalled in vivid detail, including the prosaic purpose of the candles indoors which bathe the outside scene in a strange, unnatural light. "The hour itself was a ghost" because of the dimness of the light, and also because of its ephemeral, flimsy meaning. The young man had not yet understood that "a Plan of the past . . . Was in working at last." He had not yet realized that what appeared to be a trivial moment was the opening of a high drama:

> No prelude did I there perceive
>   To a drama at all,
> Or foreshadow what fortune might weave
>   From beginnings so small.

The revelation comes after a brief conversation on the lawn, not by means of something said, but by means of something seen. The two exchange commonplace thoughts on his parting:

> Even then the scale might have been turned
>   Against love by a feather,
> —But crimson one cheek of hers burned
>   When we came in together.

Her blush shines out in the dullness and dimness, casting a rosy hue over the young man's life.

203

Music is also important to Hardy's memories of early love, in which sound blends with form, color, and line to create a total dramatic event. Music orchestrates the visual scenes, as in "The Change":

> In that week there was heard a singing,
>   And the white owl wondered why.
> In that week, yea, a voice was ringing,
>   And forth from the casement were candles flinging
> Radiance that fell on the deodar and lit up the path
>   thereby.

In "A Duettist to Her Pianoforte: Song of Silence" (*CP*, pp. 555–556), the speaker is Emma, addressing her dead sister's piano. The playing described took place during Hardy's first visit to Cornwall, and the way in which the duet becomes a metaphor for shared experience illuminates Hardy's poems of early love.[6] The speaker resists touching the piano, for its sound painfully revivifies scenes from the past:

> Since every sound moves memories,
>   How can I play you
> Just as I might if you raised no scene,
> By your ivory rows, of a form between . . .
>   As when each day you
> Answered our fingers with ecstasy?

The speaker is "doomed to counterchord/ Her notes no more," although she "fain would second her, strike to her stroke." She leaves the piano "hushed, hushed, hushed" rather than revive the painful vision, which is described pictorially:

> Should I fling your polyphones, plaints, and quavers
>   Afresh on the air,
> Too quick would the small white shapes be here
> Of the fellow twain of hands so dear;
> And a black-tressed profile, and pale smooth ear.

Quite literally, Hardy's and Emma's life together consisted of many duets when they joined their voices in song. When Hardy speaks in "The Rift" of the change in his relationship with Emma, his language is not purely metaphorical:

> your old gamut changed its chime
> From those true tones—of span so brief!—
> That met my beats of joy, of grief,
> As rhyme meets rhyme.
>
> So sank I from my high sublime!

There was a time when their "Tones" literally accorded, when the sounds of her playing "rhymed" with his feelings, when together they performed the old songs while emotions in two different hearts ran parallel.

In "Lines to a Movement in Mozart's E-Flat Symphony," Hardy attempts to set the allure and energy of his early love to music, and to transform verse into musical drama. In each of the four stanzas he asks to be "shown" a scene from the past, all of which involve sensuous perception and performance. The lovers hike across meadows and hills, they gaze at the sea, they look fearfully at one another, and finally they kiss. The refrainlike conclusions of each stanza set these scenes to a kind of poetic music, as in the first stanza:

> Show me again the time
> When in the Junetide's prime
> We flew by meads and mountains northerly!—
> Yea, to such freshness, fairness, fulness, fineness,
> freeness,
> Love lures life on.

This moment of vitality, freshness, and activity is followed by a scene in which passion, like the surf, swells to greater intensity then recedes into sighings. This moment, when "We looked together upon the pestered sea," involves "surging, swaying, sighing, swelling, shrinking." The third stanza portrays an hour of fear, perhaps of separation, perhaps of the dangers of passion:

> by the pinnacled tower
> We eyed each other and feared futurity!—
> Yea, to such bodings, broodings, beatings, blanchings,
> blessings,
> Love lures life on.

In the final stanza, the sense of foreboding is muted:

205

Show me again just this:
The moment of that kiss
Away from the prancing folk, by the strawberry-tree!—
Yea, to such rashness, ratheness, rareness, ripeness,
    richness,
Love lures life on.

This poem attempts to imitate symphonic form, rising in three stanzas to a crescendo of ominous tension "by the pinnacled tower," then subsiding into a condition of harmony, in the midst of a social occasion but "Away from the prancing folk." Apparently the final stanza represents the first kiss, which would seem to antedate the moments described earlier. But in weaving together symphonically the themes and motifs of youthful love, Hardy places the kiss at the conclusion. Although tension is still present, for the kiss blends "rashness" with "richness," and love is always a lure, this moment alone—"just this"—is to be remembered when all else is forgotten, as a sign of the union or harmony between two people.

It was Emma's ability as a horseback rider that most captured Hardy's imagination in his poems describing the courtship. With graceful daring she controlled the horse and mastered the landscape, and Hardy remembers these moments in vivid, colorful pictures:

O the opal and the sapphire of that wandering
    western sea,
And the woman riding high above with bright hair
    flapping free—
The woman whom I loved so, and who loyally loved me.

These first lines of "Beeny Cliff" sum up the three elements in the picture: the western sea, the riding woman, and love. Sounds orchestrate the vision: the cries of the birds above, the waves below "In a nether sky . . . saying their ceaseless babbling say," and at mid-level on the cliff, between the heaven above and the heaven below, the laughter of the two lovers. These sounds blend with the changing visual features of the scene: first the clear sun, then a "little cloud" bringing an "irised rain" and causing the ocean to be "dyed . . . with a dull misfeatured stain," and finally the sun bursting forth again, so that "purples prinked the main."

In "The Phantom Horsewoman" Hardy visits this place again, where he sees Emma in "A sweet soft scene/ That was once in play," and envisions the total picture as if "It were drawn rose-bright":

> Time touches her not,
> But she still rides gaily
> In his rapt thought
> On that shagged and shaly
> Atlantic spot,
> And as when first eyed
> Draws rein and sings to the swing of the tide.

In the last line, picture, song, and gay, controlled riding merge with the motion of the sea to produce a totally unified blending of diverse experiences, fused by love. This vision of Emma who is described in "Places" (*CP*, pp. 331–332) as riding "down, as if she must fall . . . To the charm of all," has "a savour that scenes in being lack,/ And a presence more than the actual brings." In Hardy's mind it is alive, like a poem, a picture, a song, or a "real love-rhyme." He remembers his early court-ship as a time when life quite literally became art, and when place quite literally became poetry. As he explains in "Ditty," it appears to him as if these unified, coherent scenes actually drew themselves on the countryside, although no one else seems able to read the "lucid legend":

> Upon that fabric fair
> "Here is she!"
> Seems written everywhere
> Unto me.

The Division

"For winning love we win the risk of losing," writes Hardy in "Revulsion" (*CP*, p. 11), one of his earliest poems, "And losing love is as one's life were riven." In "Song to Aurore" (*CP*, p. 845), from his last volume, *Winter Words*, he expresses the same sentiment: "We'll not begin again to love,/ It only leads to pain." To commit oneself through love is to make oneself vulnerable to suffering, for the magic fails as mysteri-ously as it comes into being. In Hardy's poems describing the

207

period of division with Emma, he shows how this magic fails. When lovers cease to love, they lose their power to identify sympathetically with one another. As a result, nature, art, and vision pull in different directions, and life falls short of its potential for fulfillment.

"Once at Swanage" (CP, p. 745) depicts the precariousness of love:

> The spray sprang up across the cusps of the moon,
>   And all its light loomed green
>   As a witch-flame's weirdsome sheen
> At the minute of an incantation scene;
> And it greened our gaze—that night at demilune.
>
> Roaring high and roaring low was the sea
>   Behind the headland shores:
>   It symboled the slamming of doors,
> Or a regiment hurrying over hollow floors. . . .
> And there we two stood, hands clasped; I and she!

The two lovers, hand in hand, face the mystery and ominousness of the external world, whose threatening indifference suggests the threat of their own possible indifference to one another. In a moment their hands may part, and either may become for the other a figure in the dangerous world they look at now with one vision, a world "greened" by the moon so that it seems weird and unnatural. Rather than being a part of the picture, as they were in the poems of early romance, they stand in contrast to it. And the scene seems not in itself to have inherent meaning, for it "symbols" ominously, portentously. The second stanza directly echoes a passage from "The Wind's Prophecy":

> From tides the lofty coastlands screen
> Come smitings like the slam of doors,
> Or hammerings on hollow floors.

Thus, either of the lovers in "Once at Swanage" might become for the other what the ill-fated dark-haired girl in that earlier poem became for the young man hastening unwittingly toward his destiny.

# #

ousLOVE POEMS

There are continual omens that the hands may part and the lovers divide. In contrast to the blending of drama and music attempted in "Lines to a Movement in Mozart's E-Flat Symphony," "The Musical Box," describing the early period of marriage, shows the disintegration of a unified vision. Bathed in the heat absorbed during the day by "the posts and walls and road," the speaker walks home, seeing his house from a distance, "And her, white-muslined, waiting there/ In the porch with high-expectant heart." It is a moment of full satisfaction, but it is undercut by the "thin mechanic air" of the music box, which drones on in the background, not in accompaniment but in ironic contrast, suggesting unheard words:

> Lifelong to be
> I thought it. That there watched hard by
> A spirit who sang to the indoor tune,
> "O make the most of what is nigh!"
> I did not hear in my dull soul-swoon—
> I did not see.

Like the lovers in "A Two-Years' Idyll," who call their interval of spontaneous happiness "Nought" and "Commonplace, scrawled/ Dully on days that go past," he fails to read the significance of the moment. While the music plays on by mechanical rote and gives a tinny ring to the quality of the experience, the bats, "whose wings, be-webbed and tanned,/ Whirred like the wheels of ancient clocks," suggest the neutral indifference of ongoing nature. Nature, artifice, and love are somehow at odds. The unifying vision is gone, and the meaning missed. While this poem and "Lines," with its reference to the lure of love, both suggest the precariousness of the future, the basic effects are significantly different. The music in "Lines" rushes the lovers toward the dangerous fullness of a realized passion; the effect is tragic intensity. The music here suggests the deadened, mechanical, indifferent inevitabilities of life; the effect is hollow irony.

In "Once at Swanage" the nighttime landscape is in itself neutral, although it looks like a witch's "incantation scene" and seems to symbolize something. There is no "real" meaning in

209

it in the sense that the sound of the waterfall is a "real love-rhyme." In the poems describing the period of division there is frequently a disparity between the things seen and the source of meaning. "Overlooking the River Stour" (*CP,* pp. 452–453) employs the same sort of crisp, concrete language and submerged metaphor found in "Under the Waterfall," but for ironic effect. The speaker sees swallows flying "in the curves of an eight," a moor-hen "Planing up shavings of crystal spray," closed flowers in a meadow "Drip[ping] in monotonous green"—the sort of detail that in the poems of early romance would blend with the figure in the foreground and resonate with unifying love. But the speaker here looks in the wrong direction. These "less things" hold his gaze, and he does not turn his head "To see the more behind my back."

In "Beeny Cliff" the "irised rain," a "less thing," bathes the scene in tender radiance, and in "The Figure in the Scene" Emma sits in the rain until Hardy finishes his sketch, and the water blot on the picture signals a blending of nature and art, past and present. Yet in " 'We Sat at the Window' " (*CP,* pp. 402–403), the rain is blank and meaningless:

> And the rain came down like silken strings
> That Swithin's day. Each gutter and spout
> Babbled unchecked in the busy way
> Of witless things:
> Nothing to read, nothing to see
> Seemed in that room for her and me
> On Swithin's day.
>
> We were irked by the scene, by our own selves.

The lovers have somehow lost their power to apprehend imaginatively, so that nature appears neutral and indifferent, an arena of "witless things." Their inability to blend vision and reality, to transform scene into meaning, is related to their failure to "read" one another:

> For I did not know, nor did she infer
> How much there was to read and guess
> By her in me, and to see and crown
> By me in her.

To borrow once again Hardy's terms from *The Science of Fiction,* both lack "sympathetic appreciativeness of life in all of its manifestations," the intuitive power "To see in half and quarter views the whole picture, to catch from a few bars the whole tune." The result is grim desolation:

> Wasted were two souls in their prime,
> And great was the waste, that July time
> When the rain came down.

J. Hillis Miller developed the view that in Hardy's world love must inevitably fail. As love grows, the loved one becomes the ordering center of a chaotic, indifferent world. When union occurs, according to Miller, the two lovers stand together looking outward into the same chaos and indifference; neither has the focus of vision formerly provided by the other at a distance. When the two focii coincide, there is nowhere to look except out again.[7] " 'We Sat at the Window' " would be an exception to the general applicability of Miller's thesis. Although the two lovers look outward into an apparently indifferent world, their failure is not inevitable. Rain can be imaginatively apprehended as an integral part of a unified experience. The unchecked babbling of gutter and spout could be heard as a "real love-rhyme" if the lovers were actually united. But in this poem they are not united, as they were in the moments of early romance, because they fail to envision one another. Each has much more to give than the other sees. In "His Heart" (*CP*, pp. 432–433), a woman "reads" her husband's heart only after his death, when it is too late: "Yes, there at last, eyes opened, did I see/ His whole sincere symmetric history." She reads his "truth," his "simple singlemindedness," his "daily deeds" done in "good faith," and his "regrets":

> There were old hours all figured down as bliss—
> Those spent with me—(how little had I thought this!)
> There those when, at my absence, whether he slept
>   or waked,
> (Though I knew not 'twas so!) his spirit ached.

211

Clearly, had the wife read his heart while her husband still lived, she would have loved him more, and her life would have had more meaning. Likewise, the lovers in " 'We Sat at the Window' " could save their lives from waste by knowing one another better—by being really unified. Their lives fail precisely because they do not stand at the same place. Why they do not is the mystery. Why they lack the vision or the desire, the energy or the skill, or whatever is necessary for them to read one another clearly and fully is an unanswered question. In the poems about meeting and early romance, Hardy shows what this mysterious power of love can do and dramatizes his faith in its reality and goodness; and in the poems describing the period of division he shows how the power can fail and what the effects can be. But he does not explain the causes.

Whatever the cause, the failure of sympathetic vision results in serious wounds for both lovers, as in "The Rift." The break here occurs at a specific time and place, "just at gnat and cobweb-time,/ When yellow begins to show in the leaf." For some reason, at this moment of frustration and uncertainty, the woman's "old gamut change[s] its chime," but the speaker fails to recognize the cause: "never I knew or guessed my crime." Nor does she seem to have any more insight into the rift than he. The speaker in "When Oats Were Reaped" (*CP*, p. 734), musing near his lover's grave, says, "I wounded one who's there, and now know well I wounded her;/ But, ah, she does not know that she wounded me!" In any case, according to "The Man with a Past" (*CP*, p. 478), "the first dart fell," and "that is why and how/ Two lives were so—/ Were so." Thus, there is a "thwart thing betwixt us twain," like that described in "The Division" (*CP*, p. 205), a poem which may or may not refer to Emma—a thing causing an infinitely greater separation than any geographical distance. The hurt endures, as in "The Wound" (*CP*, p. 436), where the wounded man suffers in blank, bewildered silence, "For I'd given no sign/ That it pierced me through." The wound also never heals in " 'I Thought, My Heart' " (*CP*, pp. 481–482):

> I thought, my Heart, that you had healed
> Of those sore smartings of the past . . .
> But closely scanning in the night

I saw them standing crimson-bright
Just as she made them:
Nothing could fade them.

Certain poems hint at the causes of the division. From the beginning, both lovers seem to have had a morbid penchant to fear the worst. A foreshadowing of what is to happen appears in a poem describing the period of courtship, "Near Lanivet, 1872" (*CP*, pp. 409–410). The two lovers, who have been walking, stop to rest at a "crossways" where Emma leans against a "stunted handpost":

She leant back, being so weary, against its stem,
    And laid her arms on its own,
Each open palm stretched out to each end of them,
    Her sad face sideways thrown.

Her white-clothed form at this dim-lit cease of day
    Made her look as one crucified
In my gaze at her from the midst of the dusty way,
    And hurriedly "Don't," I cried.

They move on "wordless" through the "west cloud's murked obscure," both somehow oppressed by what has happened:

"It struck her too," I thought, for as if afraid
    She heavily breathed as we trailed;
Till she said, "I did not think how 'twould look in
        the shade,
    When I leant there like one nailed."

I, lightly: "There's nothing in it. For *you*, anyhow!"
    —"O I know there is not," said she . . .
"Yet I wonder . . . If no one is bodily crucified now,
    In spirit one may be!"

Hardy employs here the prosaic style found in "At Castle Boterel" and "Under the Waterfall," giving the moment the concreteness of reality. The tone is objective, and the scene and events are described with neutral precision. It is perfectly natural that the lovers should stop to rest as they do, and Emma's posture is quite ordinary. This all actually happened,

213

as the factual title indicates, near Lanivet in 1872; it cannot be denied. Yet all of the neutral, objective features of the poem resonate forebodingly. That both characters spontaneously make the same associations with Emma's pose suggests a genuine ominousness, present both in the blend of their modes of perception and in the external realities at which they look. As a result, the other details of the poem seem portentous as well. It becomes significant that the handpost is "stunted," that the time is "twilight," "this dim-lit cease of day," that at sunset the western horizon should be cloudy, a "murked obscure." And it is highly significant that the scene should occur at a "crossways," a word suggesting crucifixion, turning-point, and thwarting, since all of these meanings are potential in the situation. That is, the poem presents a total, unified experience, in which the elements of nature, echoing the apprehensions of the characters, blend into a harmonious picture. But to apprehend this reality imaginatively is also to be put in touch with tragedy. The characters exit benighted by their new sense of oppression:

> And we dragged on and on, while we seemed to see
>   In the running of Time's far glass
> Her crucified, as she had wondered if she might be
>   Some day.—Alas, alas!

In "At a Fashionable Dinner" (*CP*, pp. 674–675), Emma Lavinia (here called Lavine) also speaks, again to interpret something seen. She and Hardy sit at the end of a table feeling somewhat isolated at a fashionable party: "no diners out/ Were we." Hardy attempts to make small talk:

> Then we noticed a shade extend
>   By a distant screen,
> And I said: "What to you does it seem to mean,
>   Lavine?"

Her interpretation reveals again a morbidity of mood or temperament:

> "—It is like my own body lying
>   Beyond the door

> Where the servants glide in and about
> The carpeted floor;
> And it means my death hour!—"

Hardy scoffs: "What a fancy!" and offers an alternative interpretation: "To me it is more like satin sheen." Lavine insists on her own mood:

> "—That means your new bride, when you win her:
> Yes, so it must be!
> It's her satin dress, no doubt—
> That shine you see—
> My own corpse to me!"

Thus, "the spirit of the scene/ Forsook her," and she falls out of tune with the gaiety and laughter of the party. In projecting her own gloomy mood into a neutral appearance, she becomes divided in mind from her husband.

Significantly, "Near Lanivet, 1872" and "At a Fashionable Dinner" are among the few poems in which Emma actually speaks, and then only to cast a blight on the scene. The poems describing early love establish her as a person whose vitality is expressed in action, not words. Her attractions are "Without, Not Within Her" (*CP*, p. 612):[8]

> It was what you bore with you, Woman,
> Not inly were,
> That throned you from all else human,
> However fair!

In Hardy's soul, "no thought of yours tarried/ Two moments at all"; that is, she has few serious thoughts. Rather a "strange freshness" makes her attractive, a quality, according to "Fetching Her" (*CP*, pp. 602–603), that resulted from her associations with the Cornish landscape:

> "It seems to be,
> My friend,
> That I were bringing to my place
> The pure brine breeze, the sea,
> The mews—all her old sky and space,
> In bringing her with me!"

But time takes this quality away after Emma is uprooted, like a flower, from her native place. The breeze, the birds' wings, the "shore's sibilant tune"—all "fainted soon." In Hardy's view, Emma's inner strength seems to have been the sort of mute faithfulness described in "A Woman's Trust" (*CP*, pp. 645–646), a quality "steadfast" as a star. "She waited like a little child" with "A confidence sublime as Spring's" through "cruel years and crueller." This childlike, natural faith "in his good faith with her" endures despite all the pressures marshaled against it: "Thus she believed in him!"

Yet, also like a child, she seems not to be able to express herself effectively. In " 'You Were the Sort That Men Forget' " (*CP*, p. 408), Hardy points out that she has "not the art . . . To make men see how sweet your meaning,/ Which, visible, had charmed them glad." Instead, she lets fall "words inept" which give offense. She "lacked the eye to understand" humble people with crude manners. As a result of these social insufficiencies, only Hardy remembers her, lamenting the "waste" that nature did not endow her with powers of expression and of outgoing vision. And this "slighted weakness/ Adds to the strength of my regret!" He himself lacks the imaginative compassion to overcome and compensate for her failing. Her mode, described in "Without Ceremony" (*CP*, p. 323), seems to be uncommunicative: "To vanish without a word." When she also dies without warning, Hardy searches for a meaning:

> Your meaning seems to me
> Just as it used to be:
> "Good-bye is not worth while!"

Yet sometimes good-byes are worthwhile: to say the words clarifies intentions and acknowledges the interests of other people in oneself. As Hardy writes in "Saying Good-bye" (*CP*, pp. 586–587):

> So, with this saying,
>   "Good-bye, good-bye,"
> We speed their waying
> Without betraying
> Our grief, our fear.

"Had You Wept" (*CP*, pp. 357–358) may refer to Florence, Hardy's second wife, but the behavior of the woman dramatized is consistent with Hardy's presentation of Emma in the poems about division. The moment occurs in a period of "storms" and suffering. Hardy is stubborn—"I bade me not absolve you on that evening or the morrow"—but at least he puts his unforgiving attitude into words. The woman refuses to join the encounter, to "make war . . . with those who weep like rain." She is too strong and self-contained, and her apparent invulnerability is in reality weakness: "the weak one is the strong." Had she wept, the situation could have been resolved: "Then would have come back all the joys the tidings had slain that day,/ And a new beginning, a fresh fair heaven, have smoothed the things awry." Instead, she is unable to give vent to her pain, and the result is their shared suffering: "You felt too much, so gained no balm for all your torrid sorrow,/ And hence our deep division, and our dark undying pain."

"Had You Wept" dramatizes a moment of agonizing perplexity, of mutual failure and shared guilt. Just as the poems of early love reveal the romantic significance in minor, commonplace events—a picnic, a walk along the seashore, a duet played at the piano—the poems of division reveal the painful tragedy in trivial words spoken and gestures made at apparently insignificant moments. An example is "That Moment" (*CP*, p. 778):

> The tragedy of that moment
> Was deeper than the sea,
> When I came in that moment
> And heard you speak to me!
>
> What I could not help seeing
> Covered life as a blot;
> Yes, that which I was seeing,
> And knew that you were not.

The poem attempts to formulate tragedy in its simplest everyday terms. The poet enters. The woman speaks. He grasps a meaning so obvious that he "could not help seeing" it even if he had attempted willfully not to. What makes it worse is his awareness that she does not see the painful meaning of her words. The triteness of the figures ("deeper than the sea," "Covered life as a blot"), the repetitions of key words ("that moment," "seeing"), and the metrical regularity of the brief lines turn the poem into a paradigm for tragic misunderstanding. There is no indication even that the actors are man and woman; they could be any two people who fail in their relationship with one another. Again and again, commonplace events deepen into tragedy and suffering. Each moment demands from those who experience it an imaginative apprehension and compassionate responsiveness. Mistakes are easy to make. "Words inept" so easily fall. Only constant awareness, constant effort, constant love can prevent the common tragedies of daily life.

In "That Moment" it seems to be the woman who fails; the speaker, at any rate, is in the right. In other poems the failure is Hardy's. The love poems resonate with his own guilt, and nothing makes him feel more guilty than his stubborn unwillingness to respond to Emma's half-inept gestures toward him. Sometimes, as in "The End of the Episode" (*CP*, p. 211), he congratulates himself for his forebearance and dramatizes himself as the persecuted, mute sufferer:

> Ache deep; but make no moans:
> Smile out; but stilly suffer:
> The paths of love are rougher
> Than thoroughfares of stones.

In "Tolerance" (*CP*, p. 313) he expresses bitterness that his quiet, long-suffering forebearance was not properly valued, but finds an ironic consolation in his sense of rectitude. Now his only happiness:

> Is to remember I refrained
> From masteries I might have gained,
> And for my tolerance was disdained.

But he also sees the self-protectiveness of mere tolerance, which often masks a refusal to communicate. Just as he castigates the woman in "Had You Wept" for her inability to respond, he also berates himself for his stubbornness, and feels agonizing guilt for his inflexibility.

Like "That Moment," "The Peace-Offering" (*CP*, p. 435) is a brief, prosaic poem, whose muted, calm, objective tone con-

218

trasts with the deep feelings of guilt engendered by the situation described. Again, it concerns a little matter of vast importance:

> It was but a little thing,
> Yet I knew it meant to me
> Ease from what had given a sting
> To the very birdsinging
> Latterly.

In "That Moment" the woman does not understand the meaning of her words or their effect on the listener. Here the disparity is between understanding a meaning and feeling it compassionately, as if the speaker's mind is divided against itself. He recognizes the motive of the peace-offering but mysteriously, inexplicably, he refuses to grasp it sympathetically. The "little thing," unnamed, is an enduring, real memory, not merely a dream:

> But I would not welcome it;
> And for all I then declined
> O the regrettings infinite
> When the night-processions flit
> Through the mind!

The paradoxical phrase "night-processions flit" makes poignant sense. Hardy's painful memories come in quantity at night, and with the solidity and weight of processions; yet they move about rapidly and elusively. They are there in reality; yet they cannot be grasped and dealt with like reality. Both "That Moment" and "The Peace-Offering," spare and brief, written in direct, commonplace language, leave unsaid the concrete details but affirm the inescapable actuality of suffering.

The night-processions flit through Hardy's poems describing the latter years of his life with Emma, haunting him with pain and perplexing his vision. In poems written after her death, he frequently reveals a sense of failure, regret, and guilt. In "Everything Comes" (CP, pp. 477–478), he describes how he had planted trees to shelter the house too "bleak and cold" that he had built for Emma, but they grew too late. In "The West-of-Wessex Girl" (CP, p. 542), he expresses regret for not pursuing the impulse that he had felt shortly before her death to revisit with her the places of their early romance in an attempt to revive the old feelings. He had never talked with her about the old times, as he laments in "The Going" (*CP*, pp. 318–319):

> Why, then, latterly did we not speak,
> Did we not think of those days long dead,
> And ere your vanishing strive to seek
> That time's renewal?

Emma's ghost calls him in "The Voice" (*CP*, pp. 325–326), adding to his regrets:

> Saying that now you are not as you were
> When you had changed from the one who was all to me,
> But as at first, when our day was fair.

Yet even this phantom cannot be grasped: "Can it be you that I hear?" "Or is it only the breeze . . . ?" He is left isolated, empty, perplexed:

> Thus I; faltering forward,
> Leaves around me falling,
> Wind oozing thin through the thorn from norward,
> And the woman calling.

Sometimes Emma comes, not as a vision of what she was at the time of early romance, but as a wronged woman, the image of his guilt portrayed in "The Haunter" (*CP*, pp. 324–325):

> Now that he goes and wants me with him
> More than he used to do,
> Never he sees my faithful phantom
> Though he speaks thereto.

The most painful of Hardy's missed opportunities seems to have been his failure to respond to Emma's piano playing shortly before her death. Here was a real chance to revive the old feelings, but he missed it. In "Lost Love" (*CP*, p. 299), spoken by Emma, he records her efforts to re-establish communication with him by playing the "sweet old airs":

> The airs he knew
> When our love was true—
> But he does not balk
> His determined walk,
> And passes up the stairs.

The poem ends with Emma, alone, wondering "why such/ A woman as I was born!" In "The Last Performance" (*CP*, p. 457), she plays her "oldest tunes"—"All the old tunes I know,—/ Those I learnt ever so long ago." Hardy, however, fails to listen and leaves the house. When he returns, she finishes playing and announces, "It's the very last time . . . From now I play no more." Too late he realizes that she must have known of her impending death, and he wonders how she knew.

In "Penance" (*CP*, pp. 596–597), Hardy sits alone after her death, guilt- and grief-stricken, "By that harpsichord." He thinks of her when she:

> in loneliness bending wistfully,
>> Would wake each note
>> In sick sad rote,
> None to listen or see!

He reproaches himself for his heedlessness:

> "I would not join. I would not stay,
>> But drew away,
> Though the winter fire beamed brightly. . . . Aye!
>> I do to-day
> What I would not then; and the chill old keys,
>> Like a skull's brown teeth
>> Loose in their sheath,
> Freeze my touch; yes, freeze."

In "An Upbraiding" (*CP*, p. 500) Emma's voice comes to reinforce his guilt:

> Now I am dead you sing to me
> The songs we used to know,
> But while I lived you had no wish
> Or care for doing so.

221

Song, clearly, has become a metaphor for poetry. Hardy pays lyric tribute to Emma only when it is too late.

Ultimately Hardy begins to question the meaning of those old songs, and they become a metaphor for the story of his love. In " 'I Look in Her Face' " (*CP*, p. 597), while examining Emma's picture, he asks her to " 'Sing as you used to sing/ About Love's blossoming.' " But she "hints not Yea or Nay." He asks her to sing at least " 'that Love's a pain,' " but again "dumb her lips remain." Going to another room, he hears a faint, ghostlike song, but which song it is, whether of love's blossoming or of love's pain, he cannot tell: "it seems to come from a tomb." Perplexed by guilt and pain, haunted by conflicting memories, he does not know which song Emma would sing to sum up her view of their love, and now it is too late.

At times he hears the music turn to mockery in his own memory. In "The Change" he describes the joyful singing of the period of courtship, but now, after the change, the division which has broken his heart, he questions the meaning of the song:

> Could that song have a mocking note
> As it trilled out warm from the singer's throat,
> And who was the mocker and who the mocked when
>   two felt all was well?

In "The Prophetess" (*CP*, pp. 799–800), Hardy is sure of the answer. In this poem, the lady who sings the song "The Mocking-Bird" is a "Mocking-bird in truth":

> I found I had heard
> The Mocking-bird
> In person singing there to me that day.

In "At the Piano" (*CP*, pp. 497–498), he remembers the happiness of listening while Emma played during the period of youthful love, when he was carried mentally to "some fancy-place/ Where pain had no trace." Yet he sees now that a "cowled Apparation" was present in the scene, unheeded by both the man and the woman, "and Time laughed awry,/ And the Phantom hid nigh." Time seems to have made a mockery of romance. Love is lost, vision dead, and the music rasps on in a hollow, ironic jest.

222

The Aftermath

The story does not end on a note of ironic mockery, however; indeed, there is no final note, no clear last poem in the sequence. Emma dies, leaving Hardy perplexed, as "The Going" indicates:

> Well, well! All's past amend,
> Unchangeable. It must go.
> I seem but a dead man held on end
> To sink down soon. . . . O you could not know
> That such swift fleeing
> No soul foreseeing—
> Not even I—would undo me so!

As Emma's story was Hardy's story, he pondered it again and again after her death, quite undone by his inability to recover his loss, to repair his errors, and to grasp the full meaning of the relationship. He revisited Cornwall and wrote the poems of early love that give tangible reality to his romance. Each year on the seventh of March, the day of their meeting, he would relive it all over again, as described in "Joys of Memory" (*CP*, p. 410):

> I begin again, as if it were new,
> A day of like date I once lived through,
> Whiling it hour by hour away;
> So shall I do till my December,
> When spring comes round.

He also recalls the death day and other moments of searing pain, while looking at her picture, pondering a lock of her hair, visiting her grave, or noting important anniversaries—the meeting, the marriage, the death. Thus he keeps the story alive in his mind, examining and re-examining key scenes, recording his changing moods and feelings, questioning, pondering, meditating. This is the one story whose telling does not consist of giving "past exemplars present room,/ And their experience count as mine" ("On an Invitation to the United States," *CP*, pp. 99–100), and it is therefore the one story that has no conclusive ending, for it has the rough edges, the untied ends, the diffuseness of reality. Hardy himself never even gathered the poems in a sequence. The state in which he left them—some

223

grouped in "Poems of 1912–13" and the rest scattered throughout the *Collected Poems*—mirrors the refractoriness of the experience itself.

Nevertheless, the effect of the poems expressing Hardy's
state of mind after Emma's death is, on the whole, affirmative.
Clearly, he did find a meaning in the story. He had loved
Emma, his division from her was a personal tragedy, the
responsibility for the tragedy was his as well as hers, and his
suffering was genuine. Despite his pain, he could revive his
belief in the positive meaning of the story by recalling the
period of their early romance. " 'She Opened the Door' " (*CP*,
p. 735), for example, affirms that Emma opened for Hardy
doors to the west, to romance, to love, and to the past. His
journey to the west, the land of romance, where love bathed
life in radiance, is a past worth reviving and keeping alive.
Other retrospective poems looking back at the period of early
romance are equally affirmative. "A Woman Driving" (*CP*, p.
645) resurrects and attempts to immortalize the vision, so
important in Hardy's life, of Emma, "With form erect and keen
contour," reigning the horses' heads high as she guided them
"Down that grim steep," a vision that seems to transcend time
and place:

> Where drives she now? It may be where
>   No mortal horses are,
> But in a chariot of the air
>   Towards some radiant star.

This poem sums up Hardy's faith in the scene, the moment,
the figure, and the human qualities which made that place in
Cornwall a "key" in his life; it keeps alive one of the most
vital affirmative images in his poetry.

Another such poem is "After a Journey" (*CP*, pp. 328–329),
describing an old man's visit to scenes haunted by the ghost
of his wife, who leads him "Up the cliff, down, till I'm lonely,
lost." This poem puts the memory of early romance in the context of later division:

> Summer gave us sweets, but autumn wrought division?
>   Things were not lastly as firstly well
>   With us twain, you tell?
> But all's closed now, despite Time's derision.

224

Time cannot triumph over Hardy as he is dramatized in this poem, and tragedy cannot triumph over romance. He loves his ghost and is eager to pursue it into its haunts:

> Trust me, I mind not, though Life lours,
>   The bringing me here; nay, bring me here again!
>   I am just the same as when
> Our days were a joy, and our paths through flowers.

"After a Journey" provides a corrective to the view of Hardy as a poet solely of the ironies of time and the thwartings of circumstance. It is a firm statement of his faith that neither time nor circumstance can touch him: he is just the same as he was. Like Arnold's *"Our tree yet crowns the hill"* from "Thyrsis," or Tennyson's "I have felt" from *In Memoriam,* Hardy's last two lines in this poem affirm the positive meaning in the personal past.

In "He Prefers Her Earthly" (*CP,* p. 466), the affirmation consists not of faith in the reality of romance, but in the full acceptance of Emma for what she was. In this poem Hardy chooses not to think of Emma as a dweller in the "glory-show" of "after-sunset," immortal and etherealized. As glorious as that view is, "Cliff-heads of craggy cloud surrounding it," her presence would require an unacceptable change in her mortal mold. He prefers her earthly:

> Well, shall I say it plain?
> I would not have you thus and there,
> But still would grieve on, missing you, still feature
>   You as the one you were.

There is more consolation in his memory of her earthliness, in the reality of her nature, physical as well as spiritual, than there is in the thought of her presence in the sunset. He would rather grieve for the full reality of what he has lost than find joy in the possibility of her dwelling transformed in the heavens.

"The Shadow on the Stone" (*CP,* p. 498) best sums up the entire sequence, presenting what is the dominant image of the whole group, that of an old man remembering his dead wife. Written in Hardy's prosaic style, it has the concreteness and directness of actuality, the honesty and sincerity of one who

sees reality for what it is, and the implied faith of one who
has really loved. Like the poems of early love, it depicts a real
scene and describes something that really happened, a minor,
ephemeral thing of vast meaning:

> I went by the Druid stone
> That broods in the garden white and lone,
> And I stopped and looked at the shifting shadows
> That at some moments fall thereon
> From the tree hard by with a rhythmic swing,
> And they shaped in my imagining
> To the shade that a well-known head and shoulders
> Threw there when she was gardening.

Hardy discriminates faithfully between what is seen and what
is imagined. The only word that colors reality is "broods," and
even here, although a stone cannot "brood," there is a content
of significant actuality in the word. Though not human, the
stone does have a human history, for it is associated with the
mysteries of the past and with obscure, pagan ritual. When
seen aright, it does bring the past into the present and evoke
a sense of historical continuity, obscure and evocative, on the
modern garden where it now stands. It does "brood" with the
weight of ages, thereby lending a new dimension to the experience.

The ephemeral shadows of the present play on the brooding
monument from the past, causing the observer to imagine,
clearly and specifically, the presence of one now dead:

> I thought her behind my back,
> Yea, her I long had learned to lack,
> And I said: "I am sure you are standing behind me,
> Though how do you get into this old track?"
> And there was no sound but the fall of a leaf
> As a sad response; and to keep down grief
> I would not turn my head to discover
> That there was nothing in my belief.

Here again is the impulse found so often in Hardy's poetry
to persist in imaginative, unrealistic vision, but the self-
conscious, poignant whimsicality is quite different from the

226

insistence of the stubborn believers in "The Impercipient" and "In Tenebris, II," or from the willful egotism of the speaker in "My Cicely." Hardy wants to believe that Emma has come back from the grave to visit him because he loves her so much. Turning his head would allow the old grief to arise, which would be worse than persisting in his whimsy. So he walks quietly away:

> Yet I wanted to look and see
> That nobody stood at the back of me;
> But I thought once more: "Nay, I'll not unvision
> A shape which, somehow, there may be."
> So I went on softly from the glade,
> And left her behind me throwing her shade,
> As she were indeed an apparition—
> My head unturned lest my dream should fade.

Emma cast her shadow across Hardy's later years, and he found her power irresistible. But strangely, mysteriously, his scrutiny of his history with her did not have the consistent effect of "unvisioning"; instead, he re-envisioned her in poems that transform the examination of a disappointing, commonplace relationship between a man and a woman into a subdued affirmation of the goodness and power of love.

MOMENTS OF VISION

8

"Any little old song/ Will do for me," writes Hardy in his humblest vein in " 'Any Little Old Song' " (*CP*, p. 666):

> Newest themes I want not
> On subtle strings,
> And for thrillings pant not
> That new song brings:
> I only need the homeliest
> Of heartstirrings.

In general, "Any little old song" would seem not to do for Hardy, for his poems usually attempt bold and dramatic effects. There is the brutal intensification of irony in the satires, and the sophisticated mixture of rustic realism and lyric grace in the country songs. The ballads and narratives typically present heartbreak and anguish in melodramatic scenes and situations, and the philosophical fantasies domesticate and humanize the gods with imaginative audacity. In his personal lyrics, Hardy often heightens, intensifies, and even exaggerates his inner struggles, and in the love poems he attempts to identify and recover the transcending significances in the history of his disappointing relationship with a commonplace woman. Often his poems are highly ambitious, dealing with broad ranges of emotion—hope and disillusionment, anguish and joy—and often Hardy represents his quest for meaning and self-fulfillment in broad, colorful gestures.

One humbler, less ambitious type of poem remains to be considered, what might be called, to borrow again one of

Hardy's titles, the moment of vision. Hardy produced these brief poems of the present moment more and more frequently as he grew older, with two-thirds of the poems considered here being published in the last six years of his life. Although these poems have seldom been studied in a systematic way, they represent some of Hardy's most successful and significant work. As a writer of short lyrics of the immediate moment, his only rivals among nineteenth- and twentieth-century poets are Emily Dickinson and Robert Frost. Hardy's poems of this type, which eschew posturing and self-dramatization, concealment and self-abnegation, represent the direct and measured expression of what was best in himself, his ability to remain alive to experience. In them, he quietly triumphs over chance and change, over the threats to awareness and meaning.

Bridging the Gaps

The poems that can be appropriately called moments of vision are brief and lyrical, usually written in an unpretentious, delicate style, recording an immediate response to a concrete situation. In a fashion more direct and simple than that found in Hardy's other kinds of poems, they convey a tentative personal impression emerging from a momentary experience. They refrain from dramatizing the ironic contrasts between past and present, from exposing the absurd disparities inherent in the nature of things, from indicting the cosmos or confessing guilt, and from a confident affirmation of transcendent meanings. Instead, they deal with "the homeliest/ Of heartstirrings" in the present, often in ways so gentle and subtle that the heart hardly seems to stir. Hardy's method in these poems tends to be objective description of simple facts, things clearly seen; yet the descriptions invite the reader to bridge the gaps between apparently disparate and unrelated things so as to achieve a sense of meaning. Typically, these poems appeal to the human desire for meaning within the context of apparent meaninglessness and indifference.

In many of the moments of vision, the relation between the reader and the poem is analogous to the relation between man and the cosmos. So little is offered, and yet so much seems to be there. "The Fallow Deer at the Lonely House" (*CP*, p. 566),

229

for example, is a poem of pure description, depending heavily for its effect on the delicacy of the language and the elegance of the form. The situation described, however, seems to demand interpretation:

> One without looks in to-night
>   Through the curtain-chink
> From the sheet of glistening white;
> One without looks in to-night
>   As we sit and think
>   By the fender-brink.
>
> We do not discern those eyes
>   Watching in the snow;
> Lit by lamps of rosy dyes
> We do not discern those eyes
>   Wondering, aglow,
>   Fourfooted, tiptoe.

The human beings described in the poem seem to be in a superior position. They sit comfortably by the fire, curtained off from the cold indifference of external nature, "the sheet of glistening white." They have established a safe, secure area of human habitation. In addition, they engage in that mental activity which is said to distinguish human beings from the rest of life: they think. Yet the lamps which illuminate their room blind them to the world outside; they "do not discern." Submerged in the cold snow of the night is a feeling consciousness of which they are unaware; the comfortable, warm, protected human beings, lost in their own meditations, are being observed.

The poem seems to hint that the men and the deer share something in common, yet it also reminds one of the gap between the two forms of life; the language suggests, then retracts the suggestion. The eyes of the deer wonder with humanlike curiosity and are "aglow" with the same light that bathes the human beings in "rosy dyes." "Fourfooted" in the last line delicately reminds the reader that the creature almost humanized by the word "wondering" is a dumb animal, but the final word, "tiptoe," reinforces the gentle ambiguity of the situation. For a moment the silent observer is like a furtive, wondering child, approaching on tiptoe to spy on his parents through a chink in the curtain. Yet we know it is only a deer, a part of indifferent nature, standing outside in the snow. Perhaps the affinity between man and the animal hinted at in the poem is illusory, a mere trick of language. Perhaps the gaps between forms of life are unbridgeable, and the situation in the poem is a metaphor for the isolation of the human consciousness. Yet there is a hint that for the people in the poem to "discern" the wondering eyes would be to capture a meaning and bridge a gap. It may be that what is called "indifferent nature" embraces all things in a community of existence and consciousness, that the blank, cold, white curtain is the matrix for a myriad living sparks of curiosity and aspiration akin to man's own nature. It may be that human beings themselves have rendered nature indifferent through acts of self-isolation and through attitudes of self-centered callousness. The situation described appears to raise these issues, although to settle them on the basis of this slender poem would be to impose on it a burden of meaning that it cannot bear. The poem shimmers with suggestiveness, while the meaning remains elusive, perhaps even illusive.

The situation in "The Reminder" (*CP*, p. 252) is analogous, but here the speaker, sitting comfortably by his cosy fire, looks out the window and makes a connection:

> While I watch the Christmas blaze
> Paint the room with ruddy rays,
> Something makes my vision glide
> To the frosty scene outside.
>
> There, to reach a rotting berry,
> Toils a thrush,—constrained to very
> Dregs of food by sharp distress,
> Taking such with thankfulness.
>
> Why, O starving bird, when I
> One day's joy would justify,
> And put misery out of view,
> Do you make me notice you!

Here the human being broadens his vision, only to be reminded of his own precariousness. He sees his affinity with another of

231

earth's creatures, who, like himself, seeks food, warmth, and comfort. Yet the question arises as to what impels him to gaze at the bird. One can only speculate. It could be some force urging the expansion of consciousness, insisting on the broadest possible view of things, or a malign power working to deny men their moments of comfort, or merely an idle whim. Whatever the case, the speaker expands his view only to reach a new limit; he bridges a gap, only to face a larger mystery.

It may be that the terms of analysis used here overstate the meaning of "The Reminder," but "An August Midnight" (*CP*, p. 134), another brief poem of the present moment, explicitly evokes larger contexts. In no other poem does Hardy as skillfully raise cosmic issues on the basis of a random moment. Here the outsiders enter the human world through an open window, lured in by lamplight, and the speaker achieves a humble moment of vision with broad implications:

I

A shaded lamp and a waving blind,
And the beat of a clock from a distant floor:
On this scene enter—winged, horned, and spined—
A longlegs, a moth, and a dumbledore;
While 'mid my page there idly stands
A sleepy fly, that rubs its hands . . .

II

Thus meet we five, in this still place,
At this point of time, at this point in space.
—My guests besmear my new-penned line,
Or bang at the lamp and fall supine.
"God's humblest, they!" I muse. Yet why?
They know Earth-secrets that know not I.

The mysterious convergence—not of the twain, but of the many—is presented in homely, domestic language. Again, the terms of the description tend to humanize the insects. They enter the scene like actors coming on stage, and the cosmic arrangement seems to be designed to accommodate them as well as the human being: "in this still place/ At this point of time, at this point in space." Even if they have nothing else in common with human beings, they at least share temporal and spacial placement. Fancifully, however, the language suggests broader grounds for community. The fly is "sleepy" and "rubs its hands"; the speaker describes the group benignly as his "guests." Yet they are most unhuman in appearance— "winged, horned, and spined"—and they behave in most uncivilized ways—they "besmear" the speaker's writing, and they foolishly attempt to destroy themselves. Misguided, they abuse the hospitality of their host. The moment would seem to offer very little to the speaker, but he sees something in it, something real, the product of perception rather than fancy. With gentle irony, he learns a lesson not of human superiority but of humility. It is an indisputable fact that the insects are aware of "Earth-secrets" unknown to the speaker. The poem ends on a note of delicate tension. The human beings and the insects have something in common beyond their situation in time and space—consciousness—for they all know secrets of nature. A gap nevertheless remains between them, because their secrets are unknown to one another. As vision expands, the mysteries multiply.

Again and again in these brief moments of vision Hardy calls attention to the coexistence of things, often with subtle, ambivalent effect. People, creatures, and natural objects converge in points of time and space, and to the receptive human consciousness they suggest connections beyond mere spatial and temporal propinquity. On the one hand, there would appear to be nothing in the fact that two things exist side by side; any connection between them would seem to be random, gratuitous. On the other hand, testifying to an awareness of coexistence seems to be a way of grasping a meaning. To bridge the gap between disparate things helps to make a community of the indifferent cosmos.

In "The Felled Elm and She" (*CP*, p. 829), Hardy looks at the rings in a tree trunk and associates them with the stages in the life of a woman. Although it seems far-fetched to find a connection between these two of nature's creations, the facts are indisputable: when the tree "put on that inmost ring/ She . . . was a little thing," and when the tree was "quite hollow within/ She was felled—mere bone and skin." Strangely, the two shared the moment of death:

233

You too, lacking strength to grow
Further trunk-rings, were laid low,
Matching her; both unaware
That your lives formed such a pair.

The last lines almost make it a cause for sadness that these two fellow-creatures lived and died unaware of their parallel existence. Yet the relationship between them seems to be merely fortuitous. The effect is like the optical illusion of drawn cubes, which seem to jump out from the page when seen from one point of view, but seem to recede behind the plane of the page when seen from another. Now meaning emerges; now it retreats.

Meaning is always elusive. The world hints, and man can only guess. In "A January Night" (*CP*, p. 438), Hardy describes a tempestuous evening of rain and violent wind. The weather is the product of mere chance, yet a coincidence raises a troubling question:

Is it the spirit astray
Of the man at the house below
Whose coffin they took in to-day?
    We do not know.

"In the Garden" (*CP*, p. 499), one of the most subtle and poignant of the moments of vision, presents a similar situation. The dead person referred to is Hardy's sister, Mary:

We waited for the sun
To break its cloudy prison
(For day was not yet done,
And night still unbegun)
Leaning by the dial.

After many a trial—
We all silent there—
It burst as new-arisen,
Throwing a shade to where
Time travelled at that minute.

Little saw we in it,
But this much I know,
Of lookers on that shade,
Her towards whom it made
Soonest had to go.

As a result of the last stanza, Hardy's language throughout the poem resonates with significance, and the commonplace, inconsequential details of the scene vibrate with gentle irony. Because of the human circumstances, an altogether natural event, the bursting of the sun through the clouds on a rainy afternoon as if "new-arisen," appeared at the time to be something of a triumph. But from the larger context of a lifetime, this natural moment seems to have been an occasion of grim portent. The scene apparently has little to offer, yet from a new perspective much can be grasped there. Like the language of the poem, reality itself shimmers with suggestiveness. As a result, the silent waiting of a handful of people around a sundial becomes associated with the universal waiting for time to bring on death.

For Hardy, the quiet waiting for death merges with affirmation of life. To understand death in its broadest context is to be aware of the community of existence. In "Waiting Both" (*CP*, p. 665), Hardy bridges the gap between the most disparate of nature's creatures:

A star looks down at me,
And says: "Here I and you
Stand, each in our degree:
What do you mean to do,—
    Mean to do?"

I say: "For all I know,
Wait, and let Time go by,
Till my change come."—"Just so,"
The star says: "So mean I:—
    So mean I."

The affinity that Hardy recognizes with the star has a grim basis: both await extinction. Yet the poem affirms order and

community. Each creature has its "degree," and death is a process of "change." The star is distant and inanimate, and its
temporal span is measured in eons; but it in effect joins hands
with the human being, and together they stand outfacing their
inevitable destinies.

" 'I Am the One' " (*CP*, p. 799), another of the brief, quiet
poems, makes a similar statement. The creatures of earth mis-
judge the speaker: "Oh; it's only he," they say; "He is one for
whom/ Nobody cares . . . he quizzes not/ Our misery." Hardy
rejects the utter self-effacement expressed in these estimations
of his character and has the stars come to his defense:

> I hear above: "We stars must lend
>   No fierce regard
>   To his gaze, so hard
>   Bent on us thus,—
> Must scathe him not. He is one with us
>   Beginning and end."

In that all things begin and end, they are one. The sign-seeker
in *Wessex Poems* feels anguish at his inability to find evidence
that death is "Not the end!" The benign sense of the community of existence found in the brief moments of vision makes
the quest for immortality irrelevant.

Most of these poems, written, on the whole, late in Hardy's
life, deal directly or indirectly with death, yet with a homely
gentleness and domesticity that makes it comprehensible and
acceptable. Hardy sees connections between death and things
that are understandable—the stars and seasons, the trees and
flowers. At the deepest level, his living consciousness at work
within the context of an awareness of death is quiet testimony
to the goodness of life. In "The Six Boards" (*CP*, p. 781), he
presents what could have been a morbid thought: he imagines
the formation of his own coffin. "Six boards belong to me," he
writes; "Some morning I shall claim them." Yet he sees the
coffin as a friendly companion who will share eternity with
him:

> Those boards and I—how much
> In common we, of feel and touch
> Shall share thence on,—earth's far core-quakings,
>   Hill-shocks, tide-shakings—

Yea, hid where none will note,
The once live tree and man, remote
From mundane hurt as if on Venus, Mars,
    Or furthest stars.

Here the twain converge in friendship, and a human life is set
in the context of the cosmos and eternity. Imagining his own
death, Hardy manifests a tender, benign acceptance by showing "how much/ In common" he shares with six pieces of
wood.

These poems about death abound with images of life. Hardy
thinks of even the graveyard in terms of living things, as in
"Lying Awake" (*CP*, pp. 823–824):

You, Morningtide Star, now are steady-eyed, over the
    east,
    I know it as if I saw you;
You, Beeches, engrave on the sky your thin twigs, even
    the least;
    Had I paper and pencil I'd draw you.

You, Meadow, are white with your counterpane cover of
    dew,
    I see it as if I were there;
You, Churchyard, are lightening faint from the shade of
    the yew,
    The names creeping out everywhere.

The poem builds quietly to a crescendo of imaginative power.
The images, concretely realized, reflect the faint beginnings of
dawn. The progression is from the stasis of the "steady-eyed"
star, through the passive change of appearance in the faintly "lightening" churchyard, to the final image of quiet
activity—"The names creeping out everywhere." These images
are alive in the active mind of the man lying awake in the
darkness. His remembering consciousness animates these indifferent things so that the rising sun seems to bring with it
resurrection. It seems for a moment that the dead can live, that
names, mere words, can somehow "creep," for Hardy makes
the dead words come alive in his visualization of the things of
nature. In the last line, the poem seems to stand up and walk
in the faint light of dawn, and this mediation on lifeless things

237

becomes a recreation of life. Here Hardy bridges the final gap, and makes death seem "Not the end!"

The Best He Could

Again and again Hardy's poetry testifies to the importance of daily life. Again and again he shows his keen, sympathetic understanding of the kindly variousness of experience, and of life's potential to achieve quiet fulfillment day by day in brief, diverse perceptions of goodness and beauty and in homely acts of outgoing sympathy. Consummations come, but they are few and far between, and are usually followed by let-down and depression, disillusionment and suffering. In the meantime, there is the daily life of ordinary experience, offering little, but nevertheless something. The road to a "true philosophy" lies in "humbly recording diverse readings" of life's phenomena, and each life is a collection of brief, barely significant, felt experiences, blended together to produce a richness of consciousness and memory.

Sadly, most people take a lifetime of such experience with them to the grave, where it is obliterated and forgotten:

> Not only I
> Am doomed awhile to lie
> In this close bin with earthen sides;
> But the things I thought, and the songs I sang,
> And the hopes I had, and the passioned pang
> For people I knew
> Who passed before me,
> Whose memory barely abides;
> And the visions I drew
> That daily upbore me!

In this poem, " 'Not Only I' " (*CP*, p. 744), the speaker lists significant moments entombed and obliterated forever, among them "the joyous springs and summers . . . the jaunts with blithe newcomers," the "little achievements for blame or praise;/ Things left undone; things left unsaid":

> Compressed here in six feet by two,
> In secrecy
> To lie with me
> Till the Call shall be,
> Are all these things I knew,
> Which cannot be handed on.

Hardy, of course, in writing poetry, resists the obliteration of death. He "hands on" as much as he can—the record of his whims and fancies, his homely acts and little achievements, his glimmering perceptions of possible meanings, his moments of vision. These records of a living consciousness continually alert to experience escape the grave, and with them Hardy quietly triumphs over death. But Hardy's triumph is not merely personal. His poems are kindly, instructive acts. He shows that, even though on the grand scale life may offer only to deny, on a smaller scale life offers something undeniable and positive.

Of central importance to daily life is man's effort to make the most of things, exerted humbly in the face of thwarting circumstance. In "The Casual Acquaintance" (*CP*, p. 647), Hardy remembers a man whose goodness he did not properly recognize: "Would I had known—more clearly known—/ What that man did for me." He imagines the man saying, " 'Twas nothing new;/ We all do what we can." In "The Best She Could" (*CP*, pp. 686–687), Hardy responds whimsically to the sadness of an autumn day. The leaves are falling—"Nine leaves a minute/ Swim down shakily"—but Hardy insists on finding in their loss a benevolent meaning:

> And still the day seems to say,
> "Saw you how Dame Summer drest?
> Of all God taught her she bethought her!
> Alas, not much! And yet the best
> She could, within the too short time
> Granted her prime."

Characteristically, the enjambment minimizes the importance of the key phrase of the poem: "the best/ She could." Hardy has no faith that the best one can do is good enough, but still it is better than nothing.

This concept of human effort, of doing one's best, is at the heart of Hardy's moments of vision. He eschews not only the ambitious, bold effects of his more grandiose poems but pessimism, bitterness, and despair as well. He responds sympathetically to a given moment, exploring it to its limit. Little may be there, but what there is he will attempt to grasp and preserve. To do so is a small act of imaginative kindness and sympathy, the sort of act for which men are remembered and cherished. In "The Souls of the Slain" (*CP*, pp. 84–87), the dead heroes of the Boer wars return in spirit to England to witness their relatives' and friends' reactions to their heroism: "We bear homeward and hearthward/ To feast on our fame!" They learn, however, that they are remembered for quite different reasons:

> —"Alas! then it seems that our glory
> Weighs less in their thought
> Than our old homely acts,
> And the long-ago commonplace facts
> Of our lives—held by us as scarce part of our story,
> And rated as nought!"

This grandiose, quasimythical poem makes an accurate and simple point: the individual human heart cherishes apparently trivial deeds and gestures, the small things done and said, the humble efforts of people who are doing the best they can.

Clearly, it is not only in his brief poems of the present moment that Hardy exerts imaginative sympathy in the face of a refractory world. All of Hardy's poems in one way or another are moments of vision. They exhibit vision in three senses of the word: in the sense of accurate perception, of a dreamlike apprehension of the imagination, and of a hopeful, confident awareness of real possibilities. Thus, Hardy sees clearly; his imagination creates visions, some grim and ghast, some beautiful and good; and he has vision, a sense of what life could be. Hardy's poetic visions represent the exertion of a humane spirit against the grain of things—against conventional public opinion, against the weight of traditional illusions, against chance and circumstance, against the ravagings of time and the obliteration of death. To have visions—and to have vision—is to be fully human.

The fullness of Hardy's humanity is evident in "Afterwards" and "To an Unborn Pauper Child," two of his finest poems. The one is subtle, restrained, tentative, the other bold, passionate, ironic. Yet both affirm the power and goodness of sympathetic humanity; both deal with moments of vision; and both represent the best that Hardy could do, as an artist and as a human being.

In "Afterwards" (*CP*, p. 521), the last poem of the volume *Moments of Vision* (1917), Hardy writes an epitaph for himself. He expresses his wish to be remembered as one who notices important little things, but the interrogative rhetoric states the wish with delicate indirection:

> When the Present has latched its postern behind my
> tremulous stay,
> And the May month flaps its glad green leaves like
> wings,
> Delicate-filmed as new-spun silk, will the neighbours say,
> "He was a man who used to notice such things"?

Hardy seems to be gently cross-examining himself, seeking assurance that his responsiveness has made its mark. Will he be remembered as a man of clear, precise, sympathetic vision? The affirmative testimony of his neighbors would be enough. He never answers the question in the poem, but the memorable precision of language answers it for him. His eye is keen and discriminating, and his mind ready with vivid, quietly eloquent words. In May, all nature plumes itself as if with wings, "Delicate-filmed as new-spun silk." The image is an example of precise, appreciative realism, which Hardy himself called "artificiality distilled from the fruits of closest observation."[1] It will be said of a man who writes like this that he has noticed carefully the little meaningful things in the world around him.

Throughout the poem Hardy shows a loving awareness of the fleeting quality of life, of the fragility and delicacy of the lovely things of this world, of the shimmering variousness of experience. His stay upon earth is "tremulous"; his consciousness vibrates with susceptibility and, like the "delicate-filmed" new leaves of spring, exists in a temporary state of precariousness and vulnerability. Yet it grasps its impressions with firmness and discrimination:

If it be in the dusk when, like an eyelid's soundless blink,
The dewfall-hawk comes crossing the shades to alight
Upon the wind-warped upland thorn, a gazer may think,
"To him this must have been a familiar sight."

In contrast to the soundless, graceful swoop of the hawk across the shadows to alight on its perch, a movement as quick as the blink of an eye, Hardy describes in the third stanza a hedgehog traveling "furtively over the lawn" in the "nocturnal blackness, mothy and warm." This observation emphasizes his sympathy for conscious life in any form: "One may say, 'He strove that such innocent creatures should come to no harm,/ But he could do little for them; and now he is gone.' " Again he affirms the significance of the humble, hopeful effort, however insufficient it might have been. In the fourth stanza he indicates his cognizance of the "mysteries" by referring to the "full-starred heavens that winter sees." Characteristically, the poem ends in the graveyard; Hardy wishes to be remembered as one who paused for a moment of quiet recollection at the news of another's death:

And will any say when my bell of quittance is heard in
the gloom
And a crossing breeze cuts a pause in its outrollings,
Till they rise again, as they were a new bell's boom,
"He hears it not now, but used to notice such things"?

The positives affirmed by this poem lie mainly in the precision of language, the loving accuracy of perception in noticing the smallest and apparently least significant of things, the sympathy for life in all of its manifestations, the sense of awe at nature's mysteries. But in a subtle, muted way, the structure of the poem also exerts a positive thrust. The progression is from a bright May day to dusk, to "nocturnal blackness," to the stars in winter, to the "outrollings" of a death knell, which,

after pausing, rise again "as they were a new bell's boom."
Ambivalently, the descent into darkness, coldness, and death
is countered by a look upward toward the skies, and a renewal
of life in a sound in the air. In recording his awareness of small
things, Hardy cannot refrain from including references to ex-
pansiveness and renewal. In a humble poem on death, Hardy
includes hints of broad, hopeful meanings. He does the best he
can.

The upward thrust against the downward pressure, the turning back against the forces of circumstance, the hopeful impulse in the face of inevitable obliteration—these are characteristic gestures in Hardy's poetry. Indeed, Hardy's poetry as a
whole can be seen as just such a gesture, enacted in a lifetime
of creative effort. By keeping the consciousness alive to the
world, whether the process is called noticing or imaginative
apprehension or the recording of impressions or the exertion of
loving-kindness, one resists significantly the thwartings and
blightings of circumstance. In "Afterwards" the resistance is
subtle, muted, barely noticeable. In "To an Unborn Pauper
Child" it becomes an explicit consideration. In "Afterwards"
Hardy writes in his quiet, prosaic style. In "To an Unborn
Pauper Child" he exploits his harsh style with stunning effect,
providing a complex, benignly ironic view of the human condition.

"To an Unborn Pauper Child" (CP, pp. 116–117) is bold in
effect, primarily because of the studiously contrived harshness
of the language. In it, Hardy responds directly to a present
moment; he sees a pregnant pauper woman and addresses her
unborn child:

I
Breathe not, hid Heart: cease silently,
And though thy birth-hour beckons thee,
Sleep the long sleep:
The Doomsters heap
Travails and teens around us here,
And Time-wraiths turn our songsingings to fear.

Although the stanza form is absolutely regular throughout the
poem and Hardy counts syllables meticulously, the diction and

243

phrasing continually violate one's sense of prosodic order. The first line, with its stressed monosyllables, has six natural accents jarring against the four metrical stresses, and the alliteration in "hid Heart" and "cease silently" seems abrupt, even violent. Although the second line is naturally iambic, the frequency of *th* sounds produces an effect of awkward clogging. The fifth line establishes a sense of iambic alternation, but the metrical irregularity of the final line, reinforced by the heavy alliteration and the grotesque coinage of the word "songsingings," undermines the prosody.

Throughout the poem, Hardy puts pollysyllabic Latinate words in contexts where they seem unscannable, and he juxtaposes lines loaded with such words with lines dealing exclusively in monosyllables:

II

Hark, how the peoples surge and sigh,
And laughters fail, and greetings die:
        Hopes dwindle; yea,
        Faiths waste away,
Affections and enthusiasms numb;
Thou canst not mend these things if thou dost come.

With the strange syntax and diction of the line "Affections and enthusiasms numb," the poem itself seems to atrophy. Lyric turns into worse than bad prose. This effect of poetry turned sour and curdled is continued by the high incidence of consonants in the monosyllables of the final line. Yet the prosodic structure remains rigidly regular in terms of syllable count and rhyme. Clearly, by his skillful use of language Hardy is making of this poem a flawed, defective object, a manifestation of a world into which no one should be born.

In the third stanza, Hardy wishes he could warn the child of the world's defects, but in the fourth he realistically rejects the possibility:

III

Had I the ear of wombèd souls
Ere their terrestrial chart unrolls,
        And thou wert free
        To cease, or be,
Then would I tell thee all I know,
And put it to thee: Wilt thou take Life so?

244

IV

Vain vow! No hint of mine may hence
To theeward fly: to thy locked sense
    Explain none can
    Life's pending plan:
Thou wilt thy ignorant entry make
Though skies spout fire and blood and nations quake.

Again these lines exhibit a contrived violence of language: the high incidence of monosyllables, the alternation of metrical regularity and harshness, the abrupt alliterations, and the syntax contorted almost to the extent of obliterating the meaning. No violence or contortion of language, it seems, can do justice to the feeling of outrage at the spectacle of the birth of a pauper child into this world.

With the last line in the fourth stanza, the poem reaches a climax of violence. Thereafter it recedes into a quieter, more gentle statement. The fifth and sixth stanzas, which conclude the poem, continue the harsh style, but they express tenderness and loving-kindness instead of outrage and desperation:

V

Fain would I, dear, find some shut plot
Of earth's wide wold for thee, where not
    One tear, one qualm,
    Should break the calm.
But I am weak as thou and bare;
No man can change the common lot to rare.

VI

Must come and bide. And such are we—
Unreasoning, sanguine, visionary—
    That I can hope
    Health, love, friends, scope
In full for thee; can dream thou'lt find
Joys seldom yet attained by humankind!

Here the jarring line of Latinate polysyllables characterizes human beings in a way that transcends the sense of a poetry atrophied. The words may not be poetic, and the effect may be ironic, but the meaning is benign. The final irony is that human beings in their flawed, defective world remain forever "Unreasoning, sanguine, visionary." Something prevents them from taking a rational view of reality; some spark of hope eternally enkindles their feelings; somehow the imagination constantly envisions better things. A man observing a poverty-stricken woman foresees accurately the kind of life her child is likely to have. He desperately desires to prevent the birth, and chides himself bitterly for the vanity of his unrealistic wish. And yet for the child he "hopes" and "dreams" a life of "Joys seldom yet attained by humankind," and in doing so, he confesses his own benign flaws. The heart of the child remains hidden, but the heart of the poet leaps out, ironically, in sympathetic love. To hope and dream unreasonably is to be fully human. It is true that hoping and dreaming seldom suffice; but they may be the best we can do.

Hardy's writings testify to his sense of the grimness of reality. His own life had been difficult in many ways. He was a poor boy who had largely to educate himself and struggle upward to find his place. He had feelings of desperate insecurity, resulting from his humble origins and from other causes at which one can only guess. He himself had suffered many disappointments—in love, in not having children of his own, and in the hostile reception of his work. His frequent, detailed, sympathetic treatment of guilt reflects the guilt in his own conscience, which he sometimes confessed directly. He had a strong impulse to withdraw from the world, to protect himself through noninvolvement, to conceal the workings of his own heart. Yet through his poetry Hardy fought back against all the thwartings of circumstance and feeling that he experienced in himself and saw in others, much as the speaker in "To an Unborn Pauper Child" rejects his desperate vision and expresses the inescapable impulse to hope and dream, to have benign visions of his own. Sometimes Hardy's poems are bitter exposées of reality. Sometimes he surrendered to the impulses to cry out in anguish, or to dramatize himself as a helpless victim. Yet a sense of quiet, steady, imaginative compassion emerges again and again, even in some of the most desperate poems. In the less grandiose moments of vision, Hardy reveals, with humility but without self-abnegation, the concealed powers of the sympathetic heart. The value in ordinary moments of life, the importance of little things that cause the "homeliest of heartstirrings," the community of all things, from the stars in the heaven to the stones and insects of the earth, the possibility of meaning in the smallest of events —Hardy's poems testify to all these realities. "He was a man who used to notice such things." To notice the world around him from moment to moment, and to arouse his readers to a similar alertness—this was the best Hardy could do. In doing so, he quietly triumphed over time, chance, and change.

NOTES
INDEX

NOTES

1. Wessex Poems

1. Page numbers throughout the text refer to Thomas Hardy, *The Collected Poems* (London: Macmillan, 1930), cited throughout as *CP*. Page numbers in the Macmillan, New York, edition are the same through *Late Lyrics and Earlier*. Pagination for *Human Shows* is slightly different in the two editions. The New York edition does not include *Winter Words*, Hardy's last collection of verse.

2. "Mr. Hardy's Poems," *Pall Mall Gazette*, 6 Jan. 1899; "Thomas Hardy As Poet," *The Saturday Review*, 87 (7 Jan. 1899), 19, reprinted in R. G. Cox, *Thomas Hardy: The Critical Heritage* (New York: Barnes and Noble, 1970), pp. 319–322. This last was one of the most unfavorable reviews of *Wessex Poems*. Hardy kept a scrapbook of reviews, which is now in the possession of the Dorset County Museum, Dorchester. Their many underlinings and marginal comments indicate that he read them carefully.

3. Coventry Patmore, for example, wrote to Hardy about *A Pair of Blue Eyes*, regretting "that such unequalled beauty and power should not have assured themselves the immortality which would have been impressed upon them by the form of verse." Florence Emily Hardy, *The Life of Thomas Hardy, 1840–1928* (London: Macmillan, 1962), pp. 104–105—referred to hereafter as *Life*. This is a combined reprinting of *The Early Life of Thomas Hardy, 1840–1891* (London: Macmillan, 1928) and *The Later Years of Thomas Hardy, 1892–1928* (London: Macmillan, 1930).

4. For the disparate critical reactions to Hardy's poetry, see Ken-

251

neth Marsden, *The Poems of Thomas Hardy: A Critical Introduction* (London: Athlone Press, 1969), pp. 1–11.

5. *Life*, p. 170.

6. Cf. J. Hillis Miller, *Thomas Hardy: Distance and Desire* (Cambridge: Harvard University Press, 1970). According to Miller, Hardy's characters are attempting to substitute lovers for God. Their attempts inevitably fail, and "Human existence for Hardy seems to end in the anguish of a futile desire for obliteration" (p. 237). Yet again and again, both indirectly and directly, Hardy honors the saving powers of compassion. The human heart is his alternative to a dead God.

7. See Samuel Hynes, *The Pattern of Hardy's Poetry* (Chapel Hill: University of North Carolina Press, 1961): "in his poetry [Hardy] could not be true to his pessimistic vision. Words like 'lovingkindness' and 'life-loyalties' creep in in spite of the philosophy" (p. 45). Hardy's positives seem rather to be an integral part of his vision.

8. *Wessex Poems* (London and New York, 1898), pp. 141–142.

9. *Life*, p. 302.

10. "Mr. Hardy As a Poet," *Daily Chronicle*, 21 Dec. 1898 (the author was identified as William Archer in Edmund Blunden, *Thomas Hardy* [London: Macmillan, 1942], p. 104); "Mr. Hardy's Poems," *Pall Mall Gazette*, 6 Jan. 1899; "Mr. Hardy As a Poet," *Westminster Gazette*, 11 Jan. 1899; "Mr. Hardy's 'Wessex Poems,' " *Speaker*, 24 Dec. 1898.

11. Carl J. Weber, *Hardy of Wessex*, 2nd ed. (New York: Columbia University Press, 1965), p. 231.

12. "Mr. Hardy As a Poet," *Daily Chronicle*, 21 Dec. 1898.

13. The manuscript of *Wessex Poems* is in the City Museum and Art Gallery of Birmingham, England.

14. "Literature," *Athenaeum*, 14 Jan. 1899, p. 42, reprinted in Cox, *Thomas Hardy*, pp. 325–328.

15. *Life*, pp. 300–301.

16. See Marsden, *The Poems of Thomas Hardy*, ch. 8, where in discussing Hardy's revisions of *Wessex Poems* in particular, he came to conclusions different from mine.

17. Weber, *Hardy*, pp. 44-47.

18. *Life*, pp. 301–302; *The Science of Fiction* (1891) and *Candour in English Fiction* (1890) in *Thomas Hardy's Personal Writings*, ed. Harold Orel (Lawrence: University of Kansas Press, 1966), pp. 136, 122—cited hereafter as *Personal Writings*.

2. On Poetic Art

1. *Life*, p. 384.

2. *Life*, pp. 443, 323. For Hardy as his own biographer, see Richard L. Purdy, *Thomas Hardy: A Bibliographical Study* (London: Oxford

University Press, 1954), pp. 265–267; *Thomas Hardy's Notebooks*, ed. Evelyn Hardy (London: Hogarth, 1955), pp. 118–119; Carl J. Weber, *Hardy of Wessex*, 2nd ed. (New York: Columbia University Press, 1965), pp. 284–286.

3. *The Profitable Reading of Fiction* (1888), in *Personal Writings*, p. 116; *Life*, pp. 182–183.

4. *Life*, pp. 384–385.

5. *Life*, pp. 146, 230.

6. *Life*, pp. 99–100.

7. Purdy, *Thomas Hardy*, pp. 337–338.

8. Weber, *Hardy*, p. 64.

9. *Personal Writings*, pp. 112–113, 120, 121, 116.

10. *Personal Writings*, pp. 114–115, 120; *Life*, p. 161.

11. *Personal Writings*, p. 118.

12. Preface to *Select Poems of William Barnes*, ed. Thomas Hardy (London: Henry Frowde, 1908); *Personal Writings*, p. 81.

13. *Life*, pp. 372–373.

14. *Life*, pp. 24–25, 124, 214–215.

15. *Life*, p. 174.

16. *Life*, p. 378.

17. *Life*, p. 403.

18. *Life*, pp. 148–149, 204, 16, 49, 53, 305, 384.

19. *Life*, pp. 209–210.

20. *Life*, p. 311.

21. *Life*, p. 246; *Personal Writings*, pp. 129, 131.

22. *Life*, pp. 284–285.

23. *Life*, pp. 386, 302.

24. J. Hillis Miller, *Thomas Hardy: Distance and Desire* (Cambridge: Harvard University Press, 1970), pp. 27, 32, 263.

25. *Personal Writings*, pp. 123–124.

26. *Life*, p. 291.

27. *Life*, pp. 182–185.

28. *Life*, pp. 202, 207.

29. *Life*, p. 230.

30. *Life*, p. 153; *Personal Writings*, p. 122; *Life*, p. 329.

31. *Life*, pp. 374–375, 377, 282; *CP*, p. 75.

32. *The Mayor of Casterbridge*, ed. Robert B. Heilman (Boston: Houghton Mifflin, 1962), p. xxvii; Bernard J. Paris, " 'A Confusion of Many Standards': Conflicting Value Systems in *Tess of the d'Urbervilles*," *Nineteenth-Century Fiction*, 24 (1969), 75, 79; *Personal Writings*, pp. 32–33.

33. *CP*, pp. 75, 175, 527.

34. *Life*, pp. 329, 225.

3. Poems of Irony

1. *CP*, p. 529.
2. For the affinity between these two poems, see also J. O. Bailey, *The Poetry of Thomas Hardy: A Handbook and Commentary* (Chapel Hill: University of North Carolina Press, 1970), pp. 288–289.
3. *Life*, p. 296.
4. *Life*, p. 302.
5. *Life*, p. 367.
6. *Personal Writings*, p. 181.
7. *Personal Writings*, pp. 170–171, 169, 172, 169.

4. Ballads and Narratives

1. *Personal Writings*, pp. 136, 134–135.
2. *Personal Writings*, p. 137.
3. *Life*, pp. 311–312.
4. Whatever information is available concerning the historical background for any of Hardy's poems is to be found in J. O. Bailey, *The Poetry of Thomas Hardy: A Handbook and Commentary* (Chapel Hill: University of North Carolina Press, 1970).
5. *Personal Writings*, pp. 229–230.
6. Bailey, *The Poetry of Thomas Hardy*, pp. 526–528.
7. *Life*, pp. 202, 230.

5. Philosophical Fantasies

1. *The Return of the Native* (New York: St. Martin's, 1964), p. 483.
2. *Life*, p. 149; *Far from the Madding Crowd* (New York: St. Martin's, 1965), p. 365.
3. *Jude the Obscure* (New York: St. Martin's, 1965), pp. 407, 422–423.
4. *CP*, p. 527.
5. *Life*, p. 163.
6. *Life*, pp. 171, 215.
7. *Life*, pp. 408–409.
8. *Selected Poems of Thomas Hardy*, ed. John Crowe Ransom (New York: Macmillan, 1961), pp. xii–xvi.

6. Poems of the Past

1. *Jude the Obscure* (New York: St. Martin's, 1965), p. 207.
2. G. M. Young, *Victorian Essays*, ed. W. D. Handcock (London: Oxford University Press, 1962), pp. 190–191, 200–201. This essay,

"Thomas Hardy," was first published as an introduction to *Selected Poems of Thomas Hardy*, ed. G. M. Young (London: Macmillan, 1940).

3. *CP*, pp. 75, 505.

4. J. Hillis Miller, *Thomas Hardy: Distance and Desire* (Cambridge: Harvard University Press, 1970), p. 242.

7. Love Poems

1. Emma Hardy, *Some Recollections*, ed. Evelyn Hardy and Robert Gittings (New York: Oxford University Press, 1961).

2. Carl J. Weber, *Hardy's Love Poems* (New York: St. Martin's, 1963). Weber's introduction includes a useful biographical summary of the romance and marriage.

3. There is a strong possibility that the girl left behind, referred to in poems like "The Wind's Prophecy" and "The Shiver," is Tryphena Sparks, who was allegedly engaged to Hardy before he met Emma. See Lois Deacon and Terry Coleman, *Providence and Mr. Hardy* (London: Hutchinson, 1966); see also Carl J. Weber, *Hardy of Wessex*, 2nd ed. (New York: Columbia University Press, 1965), pp. 75–77.

4. Emma Hardy, *Some Recollections*, p. 50; *Life*, p. 69.

5. *Life*, p. 73.

6. See J. O. Bailey, *The Poetry of Thomas Hardy: A Handbook and Commentary* (Chapel Hill: University of North Carolina Press, 1970), p. 447. Weber included this poem in his collection.

7. J. Hillis Miller, *Thomas Hardy: Distance and Desire* (Cambridge: Harvard University Press, 1970), ch. 6.

8. For this interpretation of Emma's character I am in part indebted to Weber, *Hardy's Love Poems*, pp. 28–32, 48–49, 62–66.

8. Moments of Vision

1. *Personal Writings*, p. 136.

INDEX

Wagner, Richard, 54
Weber, Carl J.: *Hardy of Wessex*, 27,
 33, 39n, 41-42, 195n; *Hardy's Love
 Poems*, 185, 215n
Wildeve, Damon (*The Return of the
 Native*), 126
Winterbourne, Giles (*The
 Woodlanders*), 125
Wordsworth, William, 81, 156

Yeobright, Clym (*The Return of the
 Native*), 125-126, 134
Yeobright, Mrs. (*The Return of the
 Native*), 125-126, 134
Young, G. M.: "Thomas Hardy,"
 168-169

Zola, Emile, 96